A HISTORICAL GUIDE TO
Langston Hughes

The Historical Guides to American Authors is an interdisciplinary, historically sensitive series that combines close attention to the United States' most widely read and studied authors with a strong sense of time, place, and history. Placing each writer in the context of the vibrant relationship between literature and society, volumes in this series contain historical essays written on subjects of contemporary social, political, and cultural relevance. Each volume also includes a capsule biography and illustrated chronology detailing important cultural events as they coincided with the author's life and works, while photographs and illustrations dating from the period capture the flavor of the author's time and social milieu. Equally accessible to students of literature and of life, the volumes offer a complete and rounded picture of each author in his or her America.

A Historical Guide to Ernest Hemingway
Edited by Linda Wagner-Martin

A Historical Guide to Walt Whitman
Edited by David S. Reynolds

A Historical Guide to Ralph Waldo Emerson
Edited by Joel Myerson

A Historical Guide to Nathaniel Hawthorne
Edited by Larry Reynolds

A Historical Guide to Edgar Allan Poe
Edited by J. Gerald Kennedy

A Historical Guide to Henry David Thoreau
Edited by William E. Cain

A Historical Guide to Mark Twain
Edited by Shelley Fisher Fishkin

A Historical Guide to Edith Wharton
Edited by Carol J. Singley

A Historical Guide to Langston Hughes
Edited by Steven C. Tracy

A
Historical Guide
to Langston Hughes

EDITED BY
STEVEN C. TRACY

OXFORD
UNIVERSITY PRESS

2004

OXFORD

UNIVERSITY PRESS

Oxford   New York

Auckland   Bangkok   Buenos Aires   Cape Town   Chennai
Dar es Salaam   Delhi   Hong Kong   Istanbul   Karachi   Kolkata
Kuala Lumpur   Madrid   Melbourne   Mexico City   Mumbai   Nairobi
São Paulo   Shanghai   Taipei   Tokyo   Toronto

Published by Oxford University Press, Inc.
198 Madison Avenue, New York, New York 10016

www.oup.com

Oxford is a registered trademark of Oxford University Press

Library of Congress Cataloging-in-Publication Data
A historical guide to Langston Hughes / edited by Steven C. Tracy.
p. cm.— (Historical guides to American authors)
Includes bibliographical references and index.
ISBN 0-19-514433-3; 0-19-514434-1 (pbk.)
1. Hughes, Langston, 1902–1967—Criticism and
interpretation—Handbooks, manuals, etc. 2. African Americans in
literature—Handbooks, manuals, etc.   I. Tracy, Steven C. (Steven Carl),
1954– II. Series.
PS3515.U274 Z663 2003
811'.52—dc21   2003002111

The following publishers have generously given permission to use quotations from copyrighted
works. From *Dictionary of Literary Biography v. 51: Afro-American Writers*, by R. Baxter Miller,
Vol. 51, Gale Group, © 1988 Gale Group. Reprinted by permission of the Gale Group.

Portions of "Langston Hughes and Afro-American Vernacular Music," subsequently revised,
appeared in the following: "Poetry, Blues, and Gospel" in C. James Trotman, editor, *Langston
Hughes: The Man, His Art, and His Continuing Influence*; and "William Carlos Williams and a
Magazine of New Rhythms," originally published in the *William Carlos Williams Review* 15, no. 2
(Fall 1989); reprinted with permission.

From *The Collected Poems of Langston Hughes* by Langston Hughes, copyright © 1994
by The Estate of Langston Hughes. Used by permission of Alfred A. Knopf,
a division of Random House, Inc.

1 3 5 7 9 8 6 4 2
Printed in the United States of America
on acid-free paper

For Cathy, Michelle, and Michael

Acknowledgments

The scholars who have undertaken to contribute to this volume are all committed to recognizing the seminal contributions of Langston Hughes to the American, Afro-American, and world literary traditions. Their work in this volume helps to keep the name and work of Langston Hughes alive and before the critics, students, and readers who will establish the literary canons of the future. To James de Jongh, Dolan Hubbard, Joyce A. Joyce, R. Baxter Miller, and James Smethurst I offer my sincerest thanks for their participation in this project.

No one who discusses the work of Langston Hughes can afford to do so without recourse to the important and inspiring work of Arnold Rampersad, whose scholarship laid and continues to lay the groundwork for what we as Hughes scholars produce. When I write of Hughes, it is generally with some work of Professor Rampersad's by my side for background, verification, consultation, and insight. It is also important to acknowledge the important work of the critics Donald Dickinson, James Emanuel, Onwuchekwa Jemie, Therman B. O'Daniel, and Jean Wagner, as well as the contributions of Patricia Willis, at the Beinecke Library, and Emery Wimbish, at Lincoln University.

Personally, my introduction to the serious study of Langston Hughes came at the instruction of Angelene Jamison-Hall,

Arlene A. Elder, and Wayne C. Miller, each of whom offered me important insights on how to approach the literature of Americans, and of Edgar Slotkin, whose courses in folklore and other subjects never failed to inspire. That instruction came to first-published fruition with a paper on Hughes generated for Robert D. Arner's "American Humor" graduate course, which found its way into the *CLA Journal*. I offer special thanks to these teachers for their passion, guidance, and support. Being in a wonderful Afro-American studies department at the University of Massachusetts, Amherst, offers the greatest opportunities to carry on scholarship in a community of top scholars committed to Du Boisian ideals of teaching, scholarship, and service, so every day in this environment is a loving and instructive interdisciplinary immersion that makes my job much easier and enjoyable. Special thanks to Ernest Allen for his invaluable assistance with consolidating various diskettes and programs into one manageable manuscript. And, of course, without my parents to start me off on this chosen course and my wife and children to sustain me, I wouldn't even be here. To all of these people, I owe my sincerest gratitude.

Special thanks also go to Elissa Morris, at Oxford University Press, for welcoming me to and guiding me through this project, and to Jeremy Lewis and all those at Oxford who have helped me with the production of this book. Linda Seidman, of Special Collections and Archives at the University of Massachusetts, Amherst, W. E. B. Du Bois Library, helped immeasurably with her assistance with the photo archives there.

And, finally, or course, we must acknowledge the genius of Langston Hughes, who avoided pretentiousness and snobbery and willful difficulty in the spirit and name of poetry, America, and freedom. May his books, recordings, and electronic media keep his words in the air about us.

Contents

Abbreviations

A HISTORICAL GUIDE TO
Langston Hughes

Introduction

Hughes in Our Time

Steven C. Tracy

O sancta simplicitas!
O holy simplicity!
—John Huss

I love to hear my baby call my name,
She calls so easy and so doggone plain.
—blues lyric

1

"So what are you going to do the other twelve weeks of the semester?" cracked one of my colleagues ten years ago with hearty laughs all around, in response to my announced intention to teach a fourteen-week course on the works of Langston Hughes. The remark and the response to it revealed not only an ignorance of the extent of Hughes's work—his output was voluminous—but also something more insidious and troublesome. There is the notion among some literary academics that Hughes is, well, too simple, too obvious, too shallow. What can one say about such plain and straightforward writing beyond, perhaps, paraphrases or expressions of sympathy? "We want befuddlement, prolixity, circumlocution, obscurity," they say. "We want not-Hughes."

Part of the problem is that the response to American literature in the twentieth century was largely conditioned by the aesthetics of the High Modernists. Emerging early in the twentieth century with their deep feelings of dislocation and discontinuity, they attempted to generate an aesthetic that reflected their feelings about their industrialized, materialistic, post–World War I world, employing the literary implications of late-nineteenth and early-twentieth-century scientific and technological advances. They felt that the only way to reflect and respond to the contemporary world of complexity, paradox, and bewilderment was to bewilder their readers with symbolic, linguistic, and typographical complexities and paradoxes that would force a simultaneous engagement with the energy, intellect, and emotion of literature and life. The best of this literature, by authors such as Gertrude Stein, T. S. Eliot, Ezra Pound, and e.e. cummings, is work of unquestionable power and value, admirably adapted to suit the artistic aims of its creators. Works such as *The Waste Land* (1922) continue to move, to inspire awe, among their readers. Through their complex and dazzling collages of the useful and valuable multilingual scraps of what the authors judged to be the best that human civilization has to offer, in novel and startling juxtapositions, they cause us to reconceive our internal and external worlds. The aim was to conceive a new kind of art that could reassemble and reintegrate the fragmented pieces of a universe made bewildering by violence, economic and social rapacity, and scientific challenges to the traditional conception of the nature of human beings and the universe.

Yet, in response to all of this we hear the words of Henry David Thoreau, channeling Emerson, "Simplify, simplify" (62), a prominent furrow in the American field of action. And, as Thoreau admonished in his earnestly whimsical mood, so the "loafing" Walt Whitman dwelt upon observing a spear of summer grass, an unvarnished marvel of the universe (yes, the grass; yes, Whitman). Cannot direct, straightforward, honest language teach and delight and move to action? Cannot that language, in fact, instruct and enlighten a broader audience than the ornamental and abstruse? And might not that language contain more, philosophically and artistically, behind its simple façade, behind its impression of artlessness? Can it not too reassemble and reintegrate the fragments of existence into a new and meaningful world that encompasses elements previously ignored or violently suppressed by a dominant culture bent on justifying its sociopolitical ascendancy? Plain style does not mean no style; plain style does not mean no substance.

Certainly, if one can trust the instincts and opinions of Ezra Pound, frequently one of the most obscure of the Modernists, the benefits of directness are self-evident. Early on an imagist, he advocated direct treatment of subject matter, elimination of unnecessary words, and composition that follows the musical phrase rather than an externally imposed metronomic pattern. Pound later developed a theory of Vorticism that helped him generate longer, more complex poems that have baffled readers and occupied literary critics for decades. Yet, here is Pound encountering a volume of Langston Hughes's poetry: "Thank God; at last I come across a poet I can understand" (Hentoff 27). And, during his infamous World War II radio speeches, he opined, "and Langston Hughes has a book in press; probably out by now, which is allus [*sic*] a good thing . . ." (Doob 16). Pound's rendering of the word "always" in the vernacular here as "allus" is perhaps unconsciously appropriate, given Hughes's use of the vernacular, and in another way. In Hughes's work, in style and subject matter and philosophy, we encounter the philosophy of the "all us" regularly. We need to understand and feel and act upon the idea that we are all "us," not "we" and "they." There is no not-us, and the concept of not-Hughes simply does not understand just where the Hughes aesthetic—the plain, the simple, the vernacular—fits in to both the contemporary and timeless aesthetic-at-large.

2

The idea of a plain style, of course, has frequently asserted its importance in American literature. Since at least the time of *The Bay Psalm Book* (1640), the plain style has been synonymous with guilelessness and directness, the converse of the style, for example, fashioned (and ridiculed) so brilliantly by John Lyly in

Euphues: The Anatomy of Wit (1578). In his introduction to the American book, Richard Mather references the directive of God to build not a silver or gold altar but an earthen one for sacrifices as evidence that "Gods Altar needs not our pollishings" [*sic*] (Miller and Johnson 672). For the Puritan, the baroque, vulgarly gaudy sentence was the scarlet Whore of Babylon, the Pope, the Catholic Church, the enemy, drawing our attention away from the eternal truth and to the trappings of language itself. To present God's truth, we must not thrust ourselves and our language between God and his people but rather facilitate the simple understanding of God's everlasting power and greatness. Clearly this is an oversimplification of the means by which writers choose language to express their ideas, since, practically speaking, any chosen words come from an individual and are not actually God's, divine inspiration notwithstanding. The Puritans themselves, while cultivating this image of plain stylists, were in fact much influenced by the translation of the Bible before them, and thus not as plain as they painted themselves to be. Yet, clearly, there are gradations of simplicity that shun the peacock for the sparrow in order to keep our eyes and minds where they need to be, be it on God or on some earthly manifestation of good and evil.

Of course, part of what animates the plain style in literature is its seeming lack of artifice and bookishness, its appearance of ease, and its easy accessibility, sometimes through the language of the "common" person. It was the American counterpart to the challenge Dante mounted against the ascendancy of Latin in *De Vulgari Eloquentia* (early 1300s), asserting the efficacy and legitimacy of the vernacular in literature. Plainly, such an idea is even more attractive in a country whose ideals are democratic and egalitarian and whose nascent national literature necessitates direct access to the diversity of heritage—including ethos, folkways, and language—encompassed within the expanding boundaries of the rich land to which they had been transplanted.

Hughes himself chose as one of his primary forebears the outsetting bard poised to sing the beauty of that diversity. In Walt Whitman, there was a poet who envisioned the possibilities of the American continent and spirit. He embraced America in his poetry, the prostitute and the president, the high and the low, and generated what he conceived of as a vast language experiment bursting with biblical, scientific, vernacular, and neologistic energy, with diction from the "scandalous" to the "sublime." Whitman boiled into being out of an Emersonian simmer to embody America in his work. In his published poetry, as early as 1925 Hughes acknowledged Whitman's work in the poem "I Too," which echoes Whitman's "I Hear America Singing." Later, Hughes's "Old Walt" acknowledges Whitman as, very importantly, a seeker and a finder. The younger poet championed Whitman by editing for a 1946 children's book a selection of Whitman's poetry—Hughes had a special interest in helping children appreciate great poetry and ideas—and writing three essays praising Whitman as an idealistic and inspiring poet. He also included Whitman poems in the anthology *The Poetry of the Negro, 1746–1949.* As Hughes acknowledged, in a notable defense of Whitman published in the *Chicago Defender* in 1953, it was Whitman's liberating poetic vision—a vision that pricked the bubble of the beaux-arts—that he most admired. He helped people see how worthy the breadth of human experience was to be embraced and expressed in art—not necessarily the prosaic, mundane realities of Whitman's life and actions but the highest ideals of America and the artistic aesthetic of the liberation artist. For Hughes, here at last were hierarchies challenged, modified, subverted, to include everyone, African Americans as well, in the American aesthetic dream.

Naturally, as Whitman was developing a poetic aesthetic that was more open and democratic than that which had preceded him, there were others who were making use of what they considered to be the specific "raw materials" of the lower classes, sometimes for ridicule, sometimes merely for comic purposes. But at times, significantly, they were used for the very serious business of re-forming American literature and society. Stories of Davy Crockett and Mike Fink, and the works of A. B. Longstreet and George Washington Harris, capture much of the vigor and color of the language of the Old Southwest. More important for Hughes was the work of Mark Twain, whose *Adventures of Huckleberry Finn* (1884) enthralled Hughes when he first read it as a

child. Years later, in 1959, Hughes was to write an admiring introduction to Twain's *The Tragedy of Pudd'nhead Wilson* (1894) that
praised Twain for novelistic treatments of African Americans superior to those of other southerners. And, as Whitman came to
see *Leaves of Grass* (1855) as a language experiment, so Twain was
experimenting with the social and linguistic resonance of dialects, as well.

Clearly, Twain's skill at employing the vernacular in a variety
of dialects was pivotal for American literature. Even more pivotal
was his decision to allow a young, uneducated, backwoods,
lower-class boy—four times marginalized—to speak for himself.
And to put into the mind and mouth of that boy a local and personal exemplification of the moral and ethical struggle over slavery that made the evils of slavery obvious and Huck's choice to
help steal Jim elementary. Now, Twain was not above using dialect to ridicule or merely entertain, and, indeed, we find some of
this in the novel. But his larger purpose was to show a postlapsar-
ian America how a young, unwashed innocent, something like itself some one hundred years before, could make a sound and
courageous moral and ethical choice based on a personalized
and individualized experience, rather than on the inherited
racism of his cultural heritage. Such recognition of the individual worth of each human being supposedly informed the
highest ideals of this country, and to show it in a language that
flouted the haughty artificiality of the Gilded Age ruling class
and language was a breakthrough of enormous importance to
American literature and culture. If Twain could do it for Huck,
couldn't someone do it for Jim?

Not that "Jim" hadn't been much discussed in the writing of
the day already. Cotton Mather, Samuel Sewall, Benjamin Frank-
lin, Phillis Wheatley, Olaudah Equiano, Royall Tyler, Washington
Irving, Thomas Jefferson, James Fenimore Cooper, George
Moses Horton, David Walker, Maria Stewart, William Lloyd
Garrison, Lydia Maria Child, James Monroe Whitfield, Martin
Delany, Herman Melville—the most important writers of
America had wrestled with the image and situation of African
Americans. For the most part, however, the slave was an object, a
problem, and the discussion was in the language of the educated

European, not the language of the field hand. Such an employment of language had its practical aspects. Nineteenth-century beaux-arts readers would neither have understood nor respected the language of the untutored, so any protest or plea needed to be made in a language that was accepted and admired, convincing the audience of the worthiness of the author to attain freedom and the full rights of citizenship.

3

Hughes, naturally, recognized the need for his art to take a sociopolitical stand, to make an art for life that affirmed the dignity and humanity of human beings. In this he followed in the polemical tracks of an American tradition that included the most famous of all protest novelists of the nineteenth century, Harriet Beecher Stowe. Again, as a child Hughes had read and admired Stowe's *Uncle Tom's Cabin* (1852), and he had the occasion, in 1952, to write an introduction for Stowe's novel, calling it "the most cussed and discussed book of its time" and "a moral battle cry" (Rampersad 1988, 203). In Stowe, Hughes recognized an artist of courage and principle who placed morality at the center of her art and attempted to use her writing to serve the broader interests of humankind. Whatever shortcomings we see in Stowe's work (indeed, in that of Whitman and Twain, as well) from the perspective of the present day, we must see that, in the context of her time, Stowe was a progressive social activist who used the contemporary conventions of the sentimental and gothic novels to fashion a sociopolitical affront to the slavery status quo. Certainly, we can see in this an early clarion call that Hughes was to continue to follow in his work in the Jim Crow and civil rights eras.

Obviously, these were not the only important influences on Hughes's stylistic choices and artistic ethos. The notion of a communal and functional art that is an integral part of daily existence rather than a separate and discreet entity unto itself was part of Hughes's African ancestral heritage, whether or not consciously remembered. Coupled with the clear necessity under slavery for a strong moral and creative voice to champion the sociopolitical and spiritual autonomy of the group, this view of art could easily influence an African American author to generate art of the character of Hughes's work. Hughes himself also recognized the profound influence of W. E. B. Du Bois, the author of one of the first books Hughes read on his own and whose journal, *The Crisis*, Hughes's grandmother read alongside the Bible in her home. The intellect, the education, the integrity, the commitment, the appreciation of what Du Bois termed "the sorrow songs"—these elements of Du Bois's character all inspired and propelled Hughes in his quest for personal, racial, and human fulfillment and dignity.

And, of course, one cannot underestimate the importance of folk culture to Hughes's artistic aesthetic: he drew from its wisdom, passion, directness, energy, and creativity a profoundly rooted art of consummate artistic and sociopolitical importance. If one examines the types of folktales, for example, included by Zora Neale Hurston in her classic *Mules and Men* (1935), one encounters tales that accomplish a variety of valuable functions in terms of ordering, disordering, and reordering the community and the world. There are tales that are used for entertainment, for venting frustrations and anxieties, for educating in practical matters, for educating philosophically, for examining social order and stability (to challenge or reinforce), for providing psychological and emotional support, and for promoting unity on the basis of race, gender, occupation, and general humanity.

One story has particular importance for the discussion of the uses of language in its acknowledgement of the ability of the "folk" to understand and see through the guises of the master's language to the practical and essential truth underneath. In this John and Ole Massa story, John is cast as the first African to come to this country. The master, in his own pseudo-Godlike way, presumes the ability to name the things of this world. So he goes around naming various objects for John, but giving the objects false names as a way of keeping John ignorant of the truth, glorifying his own image, and maintaining his power over his slave. The slave dutifully feeds back to the master all of the misinformation that has been given to him, presumably because it is all that he knows. Thus, the house is a "kingdom," the fireplace a "flame vaperator," the cat a "round head," the barn a "mound," and so on (79–80). However, as the climax of the story reveals, the slave knows far more than his master thinks he does, including the strategies of deception that will serve him well in a world in which he is enslaved. Attempting to use the master's language to inform him of a fire that threatens great damage to the master's property, John only confuses his master. Only when he drops the pretense of ignorance and reveals his knowledge of the true names of the objects does he inform the master clearly and directly of the imminent danger. The lesson—to learn the master's language but not become enslaved by it—is a very valuable one for the enslaved to learn, and a lesson revisited, for example, by Ralph Ellison in *Invisible Man* as part of his protagonist's re-education to his world. Further, John had only been playing ignorant for his master's benefit, but that "ignorance" in fact did not work out to be to the master's benefit at all, since if John truly had known only what the master had told him, the master would have lost his property. The master had clearly built his kingdom on the shakiest of grounds. Embedded in the folktales that Hurston and others collected is ample evidence that the "shit, grit, and mother-wit" of the folk community had much to offer the literary artist who recognized the motherlode of inspiration in his or her midst. Hughes was one artist who deeply cherished the value of that folk heritage.

Part of the point here is that Whitman, Twain, Stowe, and Du Bois sought to bring to bear upon their art a humanity and a sense of freedom and justice that Hughes recognized and with which he identified and that he sought to incorporate into his twentieth-century vision of art. Not coincidentally, this quality cost all of these authors in some way during their lifetimes in terms of their reputations. Whitman saw his first edition of *Leaves of Grass* vilified as a "gathering of muck . . . entirely destitute of wit" and himself compared to "a pig among the rotten garbage of licentious thoughts" (Zweig 266). Similarly, Hughes was called a "sewer dweller" (*New York Amsterdam News*) and the "poet low-rate" (*Chicago Whip*) of Harlem for the low-down folks poems of *Fine Clothes to the Jew* (1927). Twain saw his masterpiece both banned and relegated to the status of a children's book. Hughes too suffered censorship from right-wing anti-Communist fanatics and saw his work criticized as too simple for "serious" poetry. Stowe was scandalously insulted as a sullied woman and a gross propagandist for her antislavery efforts. One reviewer, George Frederick Holmes, called her "an erring woman" who practiced "criminal prostitution of the high functions of the imagination to the pernicious intrigues of sectional animosity" in a volume full of "poisonous vermin [and] putrescence" (McKitrick 110). Du Bois found himself at odds with his NAACP cohorts and under attack for his leftist activism, and he ultimately became an expatriate in order to find happiness and a place in the world. Hughes himself was shunned by his patron, Charlotte Osgood Mason, and others for the "agit-prop baseness" of his leftist literary efforts and then attacked by leftists for his insufficient radicality, in addition to the anti-Communist attacks that climaxed in his appearance before Senator Joseph McCarthy's Senate subcommittee in 1953. And yet, despite the efforts of the bastions of artistic and sociopolitical correctness, the artists also found support among a circle of friends and sympathizers, and in some cases among the "common" people who had not bought into the artificially elevated controls of the literary elite. Jessie Fauset, W. E. B. Du Bois, Carl Van Vechten, Amy Spingarn, and Noel Sullivan were among Hughes's influential supporters, and Hughes was frequently greeted with positive reviews of his work. However, it was, at times, difficult for Hughes to find acceptance and legitimacy in the avenues of attention frequently inaccessible to the African American artist: serious discussion in critical studies of American literature and inclusion in American literature anthologies that represented membership in the canon. To be treated as a "serious" writer, to become part of the American and world literary canon, was an achievement slow in coming, even as Hughes was recognized as the dean of African American writers.

But what about the "common people?" In the introduction to *Leaves of Grass*, Whitman applied Emerson's notion of the poet as representative man to assert that "The proof of a poet is that his country absorbs him as affectionately as he has absorbed it"

(731). Hughes learned with delight from Zora Neale Hurston, in a 1928 letter, that the African American "folk" were hearing with great excitement recited selections from *Fine Clothes to the Jew* (Hemenway 116). That same year, Hurston had advised Hughes, with reference to a "loafing bard" along the lines of Whitman, "to make a loafing tour of the South like the blind Homer, singing your songs. . . .You are a poet of the people and your subjects are crazy about you" (Rampersad 1988, 212–13). And, from 1944 on, Hughes made regular, extensive reading and speaking tours across the country and around the world to enthusiastic crowds, despite attempts to silence him in various quarters. He found popular success as a poet, fiction writer, dramatist, librettist, writer of Broadway musicals, children's author, lyricist, radio and television teleplay writer, newspaper columnist, editor, public speaker, and reviewer. He supported himself as a writer, attempting to prove, as Dizzy Gillespie attempted in starting his own Dee Gee record label, that "good art could be popular and make money" (370). Hughes made himself part of the American stew and began swapping juices brought to a boil by the African American folk, sociopolitical, and literary traditions with the other variegated elements of the American tradition.

4

All of which brings us back around to that charge of excessive simplicity. It was a charge that other American writers faced in their times as well, a charge that time and perspective have helped them face down. Ernest Hemingway, for example, was mercilessly parodied for his stripped-down, journalistic style and for creating characters that sought to distance themselves emotionally and intellectually from the overwhelming complexities of contemporary existence. Yet what style could more effectively present the stunned responses to the painful lessons of the world than the clipped, stripped, almost pathologically tight-lipped cadences of the famed Hemingway style? William Carlos Williams, too, wrote counter to the ascendant Eliotic poetic style and paid the outsider price for years until the tightly focused, concrete realities of such poems as "The Red Wheelbarrow," "This Is Just to Say," and other aesthetic-breaking poems emerged into an appreciative light after World War II.

In a famous (or infamous) review of Hughes's *Selected Poems* (1959), James Baldwin sounded more forcefully a note not alien to other reviews of the volume: "Every time I read Langston Hughes, I am amazed all over again by his genuine gifts—and depressed that he has done so little with them. . . . This book contains a great deal that a more disciplined poet would have thrown in the waste-basket." Baldwin continues, observing that some of Hughes's poems "take refuge in a fake simplicity in order to avoid the very difficult simplicity of the experience." Baldwin recognizes that Hughes employs elements of African American expressive culture in his work—he has little choice but to deal with them—but "he has not forced them into the realm of art where their meaning would become clear and overwhelming" (614–15). Coming in response not to a volume of contemporary writings but to a career-spanning collection, such a criticism is an even more forceful repudiation of Hughes and his aesthetic, backhanded compliment notwithstanding.

As Arnold Rampersad recognized, the clash between Hughes's and Baldwin's values was fueled by Hughes's feeling that "conspicuous intellectualism at the expense of human warmth was a kind of neurosis" (Rampersad 1988, 296). Obviously, all of Hughes's work is not of identical quality, but it is all ladled from the same pot and should be savored for its comprehensive vision and attitude. It can take a great deal of effort and discernment for a trained academic or devotee of haute culture to appreciate the full value of folk culture. A number of years ago, a Renaissance specialist colleague of mine conceived an interest in African American music and borrowed a number of recordings from me, among them the astounding recordings of the blues and ragtime performer Blind Blake. He returned the recordings to me impressed by Blake's recordings but mused about what an artist Blake might have been had he had some formal training in the classics. Now, Blake is an artist of great technical and emotional accomplishment, one of the most sophisticated of all performers among blues guitarists and a challenging model for any contemporary artist. Still, for this scholar, what he needed was a little infusion of the classics in order to gain entry to the Valhalla of the elite.

In this regard, several of Baldwin's word choices are particularly revealing. When he charges that Hughes has not "forced" his cultural resources into the realm of art, he calls attention to one of Hughes's particular strengths: the unforced nature of his work. Hughes is interested not in obfuscation and prolixity but in unobstructed communication. The force of Hughes's work arises from its unforced, natural speech and cadences, missives sent not from on high but from across the alley or through the fence, or slid, softly or harshly, into an unsuspecting hand. Baldwin's words also imply that African American music—blues, for example—is not "in the realm of art" in and of itself but rather must be forced there by the African American intellectual who uses them as a resource. This is not to say that Baldwin did not appreciate the blues, but his hierarchy of appreciation was different from Hughes's.

It was not the first time Hughes had encountered that attitude, that a "talented tenth" must lead the masses to their salvation, sometimes through cultural capitulation and outright rejection of the beauty of their own cultural aesthetic and productions, sometimes through a reinterpretation and "elevation" of those productions through Europeanization. But Hughes had made it clear as early as "The Negro Artist and the Racial Mountain" (1926) that he had an unflagging admiration for the creativity, energy, unpretentiousness, and unselfconscious pride of the "low-down folks." They could lead him in the path of righteous artistry if only he could encompass the soul of their blues. These folks "hold their individuality in the face of American standardization," and "[w]hereas the better-class Negro would tell the artist what to do, the people at least let him alone when he does appear. And they are not ashamed of him—if they know he exists at all. And they accept what beauty is their own without question" (692–94). Such feelings about "the folk" likely influenced Hughes to pursue his activities as a dramatist as well, where his work was meant to be spoken, performed as part of an oral tradition that involves the people immediately in his form and meaning. Additionally, his work with the Karamu Players, beginning in 1936, and his founding of the Harlem Suitcase Theater, in 1938, along with his many productions as a playwright, testify to this commitment to help himself and others use this medium to create a communal experience with the audience.

Exploring and affirming the pan-African component of the human experience, particularly the African American dimension of the American experiment: this was the aim of Hughes's entire artistic harvest. Implicit in that affirmation was a rejection of the social and literary pretentiousness that divided the African American lower and upper classes, emphasizing a commonality of colonialized experiences that united—or should have united— darker peoples in America and around the world. Hughes was aware of the criticism of his work as sometimes excessively simplistic, especially in the context of the Modernist vogue. So, in harmony with his artistic aesthetic, and perhaps as a satiric rebuff—sometimes Horatian, sometimes Juvenalian—to his critics, Hughes created a comic character whose very name confronts the disparagement of his critics: Jesse B. Semple. Semple— or Simple, as the name suggests in pronunciation—is Hughes's version of the old wise fool character so common in world, and American, literature. His outlook is simple, unpretentious, direct, launched from behind the armor of African American vernacular speech that prompted some to view him as uneducated and unintelligent, though he frequently revealed a propensity for deconstructing more "complicated" arguments with a well-turned vernacular phrase. If Simple represents the African American male told all his life in a variety of ways to "just be simple," he embraces his "simpleness"—he will just be Simple, himself—in response to the web of linguistic rationalizations that attempt to justify his enslavement. First appearing in 1943, as the United States was in the midst of a world war against Fascist enemies who claimed for themselves the label of a "master race," Hughes's Simple character was a retort to attitudes of racial superiority encountered by Africa Americans both at home and abroad. And in a century of exponentially increasing technological complexity, Hughes kept it simple—wisely, thankfully, frankly, heartwarmingly simple.

In the story "Jazz, Jive and Jam," Hughes emphasizes Simple's sense of himself and his own importance in the context of the middle-class pretensions of his fiancée, later his wife, Joyce. She is obviously impressed that the wise man, Solomon, found the Queen of Sheba to be "black and comely": "He was a king," Joyce throws in Simple's face, to which he replies, simply, "And I am Jesse B. Semple" (*SSC* 188). The episode, carried off in the plain language characteristic of Simple's speech, has complex implications. To Simple, Solomon's ranking as a king means nothing: it is an accident of birth that implies nothing about his worthiness or intelligence. Beginning his retort with the word "and," he implies a coordinate importance with this vaunted biblical king. The incident has further implications in the reputation of Solomon as a man noted for his great wisdom, since Simple, who is ridiculed by Joyce for his backwardness and simplemindedness, sees himself as Solomon's equal. It is difficult not to think of Jim's famous discussion of Solomon in Twain's *Huckleberry Finn* in this regard, since Jim, too, challenges Solomon's reputation with reasonable alternatives and a strong moral argument regarding the value of human life. Furthermore, since Sheba is, in the Kebar Negast, a ruler who converts from the sun worshipping of her people to worship of the Hebrew God through Solomon's influence, she could well be perceived as a cultural traitor, not the vaunted model Joyce makes her out to be. Surely Joyce should have at least emphasized her ruling abilities rather than her beauty, though it seems perfectly in keeping with Joyce's superficiality that she would fixate on her outward beauty. Whereas Jesse B. Semple is just being Simple, Joyce "Simple" is just simple, duped by the Dr. Conboys of the world into uninformed pretentious elitism. "I will not deny Ma Rainey," Simple says of the famous blues singer in the "Shadow of the Blues" story, "even to hide my age. Yes, I heard her! I am proud of hearing her. To tell the truth, if I stop and listen, I can still hear her . . . " (*TBOS* 178). She is in the air Simple breathes, in the universe of sounds Simple habitually hears. Simple's formula for solving race relations—jazz, the medium; jive, the language; and jam, the collective action—is a marvelous social and cultural affirmation, beautiful in its naturalness and directness. And

Hughes accomplishes all of this and more in a story that is humorous and entertaining even while it is subtly instructive, even revolutionary in its plan for re-forming American society through African American cultural channels.

A current in those channels, the words of the African American blues singer rise up again to instruct us here at the climax of our discussion. "I love to hear my baby call my name," he sings, indicating not only a love of the summons but a joy in speech, in pronunciation, in inflection, and a delight in being named, recognized, and affirmed. "She calls so easy and so doggone plain." The singer indicates an intense response, both spiritual and sexual, effected by the easy, plain style, which elicits passion through the simple act of address. We should further note that the woman does not just call "easy" and "doggone plain," but *so* easy and *so* doggone plain, indicating that this kind of *super* easiness and plainness magnifies the effectiveness of her address. No complex mating ritual, no woven gossamer snare of language, no mythic allusions. Just her voice and his name rolling naturally off her tongue. One of life's simplest and deepest pleasures.

Like Langston Hughes.

5

The essays included in this volume place Langston Hughes and his art in the context of his historical times with regard to his sense of place, his appreciation and use of music, his understanding of gender and racial concepts, and the changing political climate to which he responded. In each essay, we encounter a sense of Hughes passionately engaged with important political, social, and artistic issues through his actions and his work. Hughes's revisions of his nineteenth-century ancestors and his commonalities with and divergences from his twentieth-century contemporaries reveal to us a man very conscious of the trajectory of his historical occurrence and importance.

James de Jongh's "The Poet Speaks of Places: A Close Reading of Langston Hughes's Literary Use of Place" tracks Hughes's developing sense of the position of the African American in

America with regard to "literal spaces" that are transformed into "topical spaces for rhetorical and figurative purposes." Rooting the discussion in Hughes's literary portrayals of the meaning of the African Diaspora to African Americans, de Jongh goes on to explore how Hughes's attitude toward Africa and Africans and their descendants and relatives in America evolves in his art as time progresses. De Jongh's detailed and specific discussions of Hughes's use of the setting of Harlem as a symbol of not only a variety of African American responses to the historical abuses of America but also the elements of the community that are not merely responding but are proactive demonstrate clearly Hughes's poetic reply to the physical, social, and psychological conditions produced by slavery, Reconstruction, and Jim Crow and the struggles to deal with the problems they produced. In this context, Hughes generates a new and empowering image of the places and place of African Americans in the twentieth century.

Steven C. Tracy's essay "Langston Hughes and Afro-American Vernacular Music" documents how Hughes's sense of the history of the varieties of African American music—their origin, form, and function—informed his sociopolitical and aesthetic sensibility and profoundly affected his art in poetry, prose, and drama. By exploring the emergence of spirituals, jubilees, minstrel songs, ragtime, blues, ballads, gospel, and jazz and relating Hughes's own artistic portrayals and uses of these musical genres, Tracy demonstrates how Hughes championed the widespread appreciation of music that has increasingly come to be mainstreamed and venerated in American and world culture. Through the efforts of Hughes and others to foster the appreciation of this music, American music and literature, and American and world culture in general, have been transformed into places where the masters of African American music are recognized and appreciated for their essential contributions to art and culture.

Joyce A. Joyce confronts issues of gender and race in her essay on Hughes, from his treatment of women to reflections on the nature of Hughes's own sexuality. In "Hughes and Twentieth-Century Genderracial Issues," Joyce roots her discussion of these issues in George Kent's concept of the folk-derived "isness" of Hughes's literature, as well as in the work of feminist and womanist critics and artists such as Deborah McDowell, Sherley Anne Williams, Annette Kolodny, Delores P. Aldridge, and Maria Stewart and in documents such as the Combahee River Collective's Black feminist statement. For Joyce, Hughes is well attuned to the issues and problems that confront African American women, and in fact Hughes's portrayal of female figures in his work is marked by an awareness of how the historical and contemporary conditions of African American women produced the variety of contemporary women Hughes seeks to understand, portray, and honor in his work. Examining Hughes's life, poetry, and prose from the standpoint of the historical times as they related to women's lives, Joyce makes a strong case for Hughes as a feminist writer for his many frequently sensitive and discerning portrayals of the struggles and dreams of women throughout his work. In Hughes's work, women frequently speak for themselves, in distinct and powerful tones, about themselves and the ways that life treats them, and Joyce's article documents Hughes's positive contributions to the literary exploration of women's lives.

Much of the discussion of Hughes's career has been of his justly celebrated work related to the Harlem Renaissance of the 1920s. James Smethurst's "The Adventures of a Social Poet" refocuses attention on the bulk of Langston Hughes's career, from the Popular Front to the Black Power eras. Hughes's artistic output during these times has been unfairly ignored or maligned as a result of a refusal or inability of critics to consider fairly the function and quality of this work. Smethurst identifies a constant "core" to Hughes's work of the 1930s and beyond; yet he also demonstrates how Hughes continued to develop as an artist by engaging forms and ideas brought to his attention by his sociopolitical consciousness as it evolved in the historical march of time. As a result, Smethurst deepens our understanding of Hughes's post-Renaissance work and suggests a direction for studies yet to be done on his unjustly neglected periods and works.

As the Hughes biography by R. Baxter Miller and the bibliographical essay by Dolan Hubbard readily demonstrate, Langston Hughes was an artist acutely aware of history and his place in it, as well as a figure who garnered an increasing amount of attention over the course of the twentieth century. Miller and Hubbard track Hughes's career and critical reputation with a careful eye toward historical times and trends, revealing a Hughes very much a part of his times who nonetheless generated work that very much not only reflects but transcends it. During the centennial year of Hughes's birth, there were no fewer than four major conferences dedicated to his life and work, including conferences at the University of Kansas, Yale, and Lincoln University. The papers at the conferences demonstrated a continuing and deepening interest in Hughes's work, now made available nearly in its entirety through the University of Missouri Press's *Collected Works of Langston Hughes*. As the Press acknowledged, one of its aims was to put Hughes's work in the hands of "the people," as many as possible. Of course, this is the aim of most, if not all, presses. But Hughes is in particular a people poet, a popular poet. A visit to the centennial conferences found nonacademics there in significant numbers, numbers not frequently put up by literary artists at academic conferences. In his work, Hughes has been able to attract academics and nonacademics alike through his deceptively simple style—an issue explored here in this introduction. His life's work was about bringing people together, socially, politically, and artistically.

He is still doing it.

WORKS CITED

Baldwin, James. "Sermons and Blues." *James Baldwin: Collected Essays*, ed. Toni Morrison. New York: Library of America, 1998. 614–15.

Doob, Leonard, ed. *"Ezra Pound Speaking": Radio Speeches of World War II*. Westport, Conn.: Greenwood, 1978.

Gillespie, Dizzy. *To Be or Not . . . to BOP: Memoirs*. New York: Doubleday, 1979.

Hemenway, Robert. *Zora Neale Hurston: A Literary Biography*. Urbana: University of Illinois Press, 1977.

Hentoff, Nat. "Langston Hughes: He Found Poetry in the Blues." *Mayfair* (August 1958): 26, 27, 43, 45–47, 49.

Hughes, Langston. "Introduction." *Uncle Tom's Cabin*, by Harriet Beecher Stowe. New York: Dodd, Mead, 1952.

————. "The Negro Artist and the Racial Mountain." *The Nation* 122 (1926): 692–94.

Hurston, Zora Neale. *Mules and Men*. New York: Harper Perennial, 1990.

McKitrick, Eric L., ed. *Slavery Defended: The Views of the Old South*. Englewood Cliffs, N.J.: Prentice Hall, 1963.

Miller, Perry, and Thomas H. Johnson, eds. *The Puritans: A Sourcebook of Their Writings, Volume 2*. 1938. Rpt. New York: Harper, 1963.

Rampersad, Arnold. *The Life of Langston Hughes, Volume 1: 1902–1941, I, Too, Sing America*. New York: Oxford University Press, 1986.

————. *The Life of Langston Hughes, Volume 2: 1941–1967, I Dream a World*. New York: Oxford University Press, 1988.

Review of *Fine Clothes to the Jew. New York Amsterdam News*, February 5, 1927.

Review of *Fine Clothes to the Jew. Chicago Whip*, February 26, 1927.

Thoreau, Henry David. *Walden and Civil Disobedience*. Ed. Owen Thomas. New York: Norton, 1966.

Whitman, Walt. *Leaves of Grass*. Ed. Sculley Bradley and Harold Blodgett. New York: Norton, 1973.

Zweig, Paul. *Walt Whitman: The Making of the Poet*. New York: Basic, 1994.

Langston Hughes, 1902–1967

A Brief Biography

R. Baxter Miller

As a now somewhat legendary name for so many readers of varying persuasions (he was more popular and less revered in his own century), Langston Hughes was perhaps the most wide-ranging and persistent black American writer in the twentieth century. From the Harlem Renaissance of the early twenties, to the Black Arts reorientations of the sixties, his short stories, novels, dramas, translations, and seminal anthologies of the works of others at home and abroad helped unify peoples in the African Diaspora. He helped nurture, in other words, so profoundly the generations after him. His early writing was an innovative complement to the talent of his contemporaries, including the Keatsian verse of Countee Cullen, the avant-garde and even prophetic painting of Aaron Douglas, and the musical flamboyance of Josephine Baker. In his late twenties and early thirties, he helped inspire the writers Margaret Walker and Gwendolyn Brooks. Later, he encouraged writers of a third generation, including Mari Evans and Alice Walker. All the while, he helped indirectly open the doors of publishing to them and to others of various races; he helped charm the American audience to the future of ethnic equality and pluralism. In many ways, he crafted, better perhaps than any poet since Walt Whitman, whom he celebrated and eventually became skeptical of, the noblest visions of what America could be.

Between 1921 and 1967, Hughes became both famous and beloved. Even before he had helped young blacks gain entry to the major periodicals and presses of the day, his innovations in literary blues and jazz were acclaimed. As he worked to free American literature from the plantation tradition (Wright 600–601), he introduced new forms that reflected confidence and racial pride. He displayed social awareness in his fictional characters and technical mastery in his works.

Hughes, a product of the African American and American 1920s, helped produce four subsequent decades of literary history. In addition to the decade of the twenties—one into which his innovative poetry of blues and jazz emerged—the thirties provided him with a lasting insight into the class inequities of the United States. By the forties, some of his finest lyrics appeared as artistic relief to the racial lynching at the time. Such ritualistic atrocities came nearly to an end during the fifties after an incredible run of nearly half a century.

Especially during these fifties—perhaps the most popular era of his own short stories in more than two decades—Hughes advocated a policy of racial desegregation. Equality was an idea whose time had come. So, when the times were right, Hughes voiced the most telling issues of his life with great moral authority; and, when they were wrong, he pointed to better times that would surely come. By the sixties, he witnessed the desegregation of public accommodations in the country and the advance of the Black Arts Movement. Despite the nearly overwhelming circumstances of history, he lived to see the desegregation of the U.S. Supreme Court. In his final decade—one that marked the collapse of an interracial alliance on the liberal Left—he projected a timeless voice of what pragmatic idealists had stood for and one day would stand for again. What made him special was his talent for laughing at history without any underestimation of either history or the compulsion to struggle against it. He voiced the historicity of events, yet the human will to defy such determinism. He wrote for and beyond his time.

Langston Hughes wrote about a need to balance politics and

beauty. He is very much an author for the African American masses and of democrats throughout the world. His stories encapsulate our struggle to remain human during the past sixteen centuries. Everything that precedes the last sentence here, except for the finest points, can easily be reduced to its simple truth. A fine reward for writing about Langston Hughes is recognizing that we can express an appreciation of his stories in different words to diverse people. All of his audiences are worth writing for.

James Langston Hughes was born to Carrie Langston Hughes and James Nathaniel Hughes on 1 February 1902 in Joplin, Missouri. Carrie's father, Charles Howard Langston, moved to Kansas in search of greater racial and financial freedom. His penchant for the literary and his desire to transcend the farm and the grocery store in Lawrence, Kansas, were passed on to Hughes. Charles's brother, John Mercer Langston, the poet's great-uncle, contributed to the family's literary efforts by penning an autobiography, *From the Virginia Plantation to the National Capital* (1894). The financially secure John Mercer Langston willed to his descendants a big house, as well as stocks and bonds.

Hughes's mother, Carrie Langston, briefly attended college, and she demonstrated a dramatic imagination through writing poetry and delivering monologues in costume. James Nathaniel Hughes, the poet's father, studied law by correspondence course, but, when he was denied permission by the all-white examining board to take the Oklahoma Territory bar examination, he moved, in 1899, to Joplin with his wife. There, after four years of marriage and the death of his first child (in 1900), angered by unremitting poverty and faced with supporting an eighteen-month-old child, James Hughes left the United States in October 1903 for Mexico, where he eventually prospered and thus was able to contribute to the support of his son. Carrie Hughes refused to accompany him, and, unable to get even menial jobs in Joplin, she moved constantly from city to city looking for work, occasionally taking the young Langston with her. For most of the next nine years, however, the poet lived in Lawrence with his maternal grandmother, Mary Leary Langston, although he visited his mother briefly in Topeka, stayed with her in Colorado, and traveled with her to Mexico in 1908 to see his father.

As a youngster, Hughes was acutely aware of the luxury in which his cousins lived in Washington, D.C., in contrast to the poverty in which he and his grandmother lived, but she never wrote to them for help. He learned early that bills do not always get paid but that resourcefulness was essential to survival. Unlike most other black women in Lawrence, Kansas, his grandmother did not earn money by domestic service. She rented rooms to college students from the University of Kansas, and sometimes she would even live with a friend and rent out her entire house for ten or twelve dollars a month.

In 1907, Langston's mother took him with her to a library in Topeka, where he fell in love with books, in part because he was impressed that the library did not have to pay rent. Through the double perspective of boy and man, he recalled: "even before I was six books began to happen to me, so that after a while there came a time when I believed in books more than in people which, of course, was wrong" (Hughes, *TBS* 26).

Hughes's grandmother influenced his life and imagination deeply. She was a gentle and proud woman of Indian and black blood. He remembered that she once took him to Osawatomie. There, she shared the platform as an honored guest of Teddy Roosevelt because she was the last surviving widow of the 1859 John Brown raid. Following her death, in April 1915, Hughes lived briefly with his mother, who had by then (possibly in the previous year) married Homer Clark. When Clark left town to seek a job elsewhere, Carrie Hughes left Langston with his grandmother's friend Auntie Reed and her husband, who owned a house a block from the river near the railroad station. Devout Christians, they constantly urged Hughes to join the church. In a revival meeting, Hughes saw his friend bow to adult pressure and claim to having seen Jesus. The boy was immediately saved, or at least his elders thought so. Feeling guilty for keeping the elders up late, Hughes feigned a religious conversion, but that night he could not stop crying alone in bed. The Reeds thought he was pleased with the change in his life, but Hughes marked the incident as the beginning of his disbelief because Jesus had not intervened to save him.

In the seventh grade, Hughes secured his first regular job—

cleaning the lobby and toilets in an old hotel near school—which would later inspire "Brass Spittoons," a poem he published in *Fine Clothes to the Jew* (1927). Late in the summer of 1915, Hughes rejoined his mother, stepfather, and Clark's son Gwyn. They lived in Lincoln, Illinois, for a year, and in 1916 Homer Clark moved the family to Cleveland. Hughes entered Central High School that autumn and had a successful four years there. He wrote poems for the *Belfry Owl*, the student magazine, helped win the city championships in track, was on the monthly honor roll, and edited the school yearbook. Among the teachers, many of whom he found inspirational, was Helen Chesnutt, a Latin instructor and the daughter of the well-known novelist Charles W. Chesnutt.

From 1916 to 1920, Hughes had many Jewish friends, because he found the children of foreign-born parents to be more democratic than those of other white Americans. He escorted a Jewish girl when he first attended a symphony orchestra concert. Fellow students introduced Hughes to socialist ideas; they lent him Ethel Boole Voynich's *The Gadfly* (1891) and copies of the *Liberator* and the *Socialist Call* and took him to hear Eugene Debs, a socialist leader. Though Hughes never became an extreme leftist, his early years shaped his commitment to the poor and led him to read Arthur Schopenhauer, Friedrich Nietzsche, Edna Ferber, and Guy de Maupassant, whom he found especially fascinating.

Hughes spent the summer of 1919 with his father in Mexico. Unfortunately, the son found that he disliked his father's materialistic outlook. Depressed most of the time, Langston contemplated but rejected the idea of committing suicide. Back in the United States, Hughes dated a seventeen-year-old black woman who was newly arrived from the South. They had met at a dance in a school gym, and she inspired the lyric "When Sue Wears Red," the first of many poems in which the writer would celebrate the beauty of black women.

In July 1920, on the train to visit his father in Mexico, crossing the Mississippi River to St. Louis, Hughes wrote the short lyric "The Negro Speaks of Rivers" (*CP* 23). Through the images of water and pyramid, the verse suggests the endurance of human spirituality from the time of ancient Egypt to the nineteenth and twentieth centuries. The muddy Mississippi made Hughes think of the roles in human history played by the Congo, the Niger, and the Nile, down whose water the early slaves once were sold. And he thought of Abraham Lincoln, who was moved to end slavery after he took a raft trip down the Mississippi. The draft he first wrote on the back of an envelope in fifteen minutes has become Hughes's most anthologized poem.

Hughes lived with his father in Mexico until September 1921, agonizing over his father's desire for him to attend a European university and his own preference for attending Columbia University in New York. As an escape, he went to bullfights in Mexico City almost every weekend. He was unsuccessful in writing about them, but he did write articles about Toluca and the Virgin of Guadalupé. *The Brownies' Book*, a magazine just begun by W. E. B. Du Bois's staff at *The Crisis*, published two poems by Hughes in the January 1921 issue and *The Gold Piece*, his one-act play for children, in the July 1921 issue. Jessie Fauset, the literary editor, also accepted one of his articles and the poem "The Negro Speaks of Rivers" for the June 1921 issue of *The Crisis*.

In the fall of 1921, with his father's permission, Hughes enrolled at Columbia University. His dream quickly turned into grim reality: the cold weather was depressing, the buildings were like factories, and the program and students were not to his liking. He abandoned school in favor of attending Broadway shows and lectures at the Rand School; he read what he wanted. In the spring, he missed an important exam to attend the funeral for the black performer Bert Williams, and each night he went to see *Shuffle Along*, where he sat in the gallery and adored Florence Mills. After finals, Hughes dropped out of Columbia and worked at various odd jobs while he gave his undivided attention to the milieu and the people who would shape the Harlem Renaissance.

During the winter of 1923, Hughes wrote the poem that would give the title to his first volume of poetry. "The Weary Blues," about a piano player in Harlem, captures the flavor of the night life, people, and folk forms that would become characteristic of the experimental writing of the renaissance (see Barksdale). The piano player uses his instrument to create the "call and response" pattern essential to the blues. He is alone and lonely, but his piano "talks" back to him. Through the process of playing the piano and singing about his troubles, the man is able to exorcise his feelings and arrive at a state of peace. In structure and subject matter, the poem varies from traditional forms. Although there are rhymes and onomatopoeic effects ("Thump, thump, thump, went his foot on the floor"), there are also unusual lines, such as

> Sweet Blues!
> Coming from a black man's soul.
>   O Blues!

Such lines serve to move the poem beyond its traditional components to locate the ethos in Afro-American culture. A frequently anthologized poem, "The Weary Blues" treats blues as theme and structure and was a fitting choice as the title of a volume designed to focus on the masses of black people rather than the elite.

Alain Locke, a philosophy professor at Howard University, wrote to commend Hughes on the poems that had appeared in *The Crisis*. But when Locke, a former Rhodes Scholar, asked to visit Hughes, the young poet declined fearfully because he did not think he was prepared for such distinguished company. In the spring of 1923, Hughes left Harlem for sea travel; he secured work as a cabin boy on the *West Hesseltine*, a freighter, to Africa (see Rampersad, 1, 72–81). Off the point of Sandy Hook, New Jersey, he threw into the sea a box of books that reminded him of the hardships of his past: attics and basements in Cleveland, lonely nights in Toluca, dormitories at Columbia, and furnished rooms in Harlem. He wrote, in *The Big Sea* (1940), of his first reaction to seeing Africa: "My Africa," he says, "Motherland of the Negro" (10).

Hughes returned to the United States late in 1923 but was in Paris by the spring of 1924. Locke visited him there to solicit poems for a special issue of the *Survey Graphic*, an issue that was the basis for the book *The New Negro* (1925). Locke, who invited Hughes to Venice and gave him a personally guided tour, knew who the architects of the stately old buildings were and where Wilhelm Wagner, the nineteenth-century German composer, had died. Hughes was not impressed; in less than a week, he was bored with palaces, churches, and paintings, as well as English tourists. He confirmed that Venice, too, had back alleys and poor people. He left for New York, where he took a few poems to Countee Cullen, whom he had already met and whose work he admired. With Cullen, he attended an NAACP benefit party, where he met Carl Van Vechten.

In 1924, Hughes met Arna Bontemps, a crossing of paths that would have happy consequences for the two writers throughout their lives. They formed a mutual fan club, with Hughes greatly admiring Bontemps's ability to create in the midst of a demanding domestic life and Bontemps probably admiring Hughes's freedom and ability to write in spite of constant movement. The two writers complemented each other and worked well on a number of projects that extended for decades, including collaboration on children's books and a plethora of anthologies. Hughes, the faster writer of the two, sometimes had to wait for the slower Bontemps to complete his share of a promised work, but the delays did not harm their friendship or the quality of the work. When Bontemps became librarian at Fisk, he kept in touch with Hughes while the latter traveled to various parts of the world; indeed, perhaps Bontemps formed one of the centers around which Hughes would revolve for the remainder of his life.

The winter of 1925 found Hughes working in Washington, D.C., with Carter G. Woodson, at the Association of Negro Life and History. This employment turned out to be brief because the paperwork hurt his eyes. He quit the "position" to take a "job" as a busboy at the Wardman Park Hotel, where he met the poet Vachel Lindsay. One afternoon, Hughes put copies of his poems "Jazzonia," "Negro Dancer," and "The Weary Blues" beside Lindsay's dinner plate and went away. On his way to work the next day, Hughes read in the headlines that Lindsay had discovered a Negro busboy poet. Lindsay advised Hughes to continue writing and to seek publication for his poems.

In 1925, Hughes won his first poetry prize, in a contest sponsored by *Opportunity*, the official magazine of the Urban League, and by Casper Holstein, a wealthy West Indian numbers banker. At the gathering at which prizes were awarded, Hughes met Mary White Ovington and James Weldon Johnson and renewed his acquaintance with Carl Van Vechten, who asked Hughes whether he had sufficient poems for a book. Hughes sent a manuscript to him, and Van Vechten liked the verses well enough to forward the volume to Alfred A. Knopf, his publisher. Blanche Knopf informed Hughes of her intention to publish the book.

Through Van Vechten, Hughes met Arthur Spingarn, a prominent lawyer. Earlier that day he had accepted a long-standing invitation to tea from Spingarn's sister-in-law, Amy Spingarn. In Faith Berry's words, "emotional ties were formed between Hughes and the Spingarn family that lasted for the rest of their lives" (Berry 67–68). As Hughes's attorney and personal friend for more than forty years, Arthur Spingarn made the poet's personal concerns his own and was unstinting in his public praise and admiration for Hughes. Amy Spingarn became a secret benefactor of the poet and provided him continual encouragement. She even offered to finance his education.

Hughes's poetry during this period is youthfully romantic. In the elevated lyric "Fantasy in Purple," the African drum of tragedy and death becomes a metaphor for humanism and survival. "As I Grew Older" (*CP* 93) blends reflection and nostalgia as the speaker, framed by light and shadow, seeks to rediscover his dream. In "Mexican Market Woman" (*CP* 25), Hughes's narrator uses simile to create a dark mood of weariness and pain. And through the persona in "Troubled Woman" (*CP* 42), the narrator portrays humanity similarly bowed but unbroken. With blues irony, the voice modifies implicitly the pessimistic side of the spirituals ("nobody knows de trouble I seen") into the more optimistic side ("I know trouble don't last always"). "Mother to Son" (*CP* 30), a dramatic monologue, shows how dialect can be used with dignity. The image of the stair as a beacon of success inspires hope in both the son and the reader. All of the poems appeared in *The Weary Blues*, which was published in January 1926.

Critical response to *The Weary Blues* was mixed. Reviews in the *New York Times, Washington Post, Boston Transcript, New Or-*

leans Times-Picayune, *New Republic*, and elsewhere were lauda-
tory; the only derogatory review in a white publication was in
the *Times Literary Supplement*, which called Hughes a "cabaret
poet" (see Miller, *Guide* 7–10). Reviewing the book in the February 1926 issue of *Opportunity*, however, Cullen found some of the
poems "scornful in subject matter . . . and rhythmical treatment of whatever obstructions time and tradition . . . placed
before him" and called Hughes one of those "racial artists instead of artists pure and simple." In *The Crisis*, Fauset praised
Hughes's liberation from established literary forms. No other
poet, she said, would ever write "as tenderly, understandingly,
and humorously about life in Harlem." Admiring the book for its
cleanness and simplicity, Locke viewed Hughes, in *Palms*, as the
spokesman for the black masses.

After a brief visit to Lincoln, Illinois, in February 1926, Hughes
enrolled at Lincoln University, in Pennsylvania. When classes
were over for the summer, he moved to New York and into a
rooming house on 137th Street, where the novelist Wallace Thurman also lived. Thurman, managing editor of the *Messenger*,
joined with Hughes, John P. Davis, Bruce Nugent, Zora Neale
Hurston, Aaron Douglas, and Gwendolyn Bennett to sponsor
Fire!!, a progressive and innovative periodical. Its first and only
issue earned indignation from Du Bois and dismissal from Rean
Graves, a critic for the *Baltimore Afro-American*: "I have just tossed
the first issue of *Fire* into the fire. . . . Langston Hughes displays his usual ability to say nothing in many words" (*TBS* 237).

Hughes attended lively parties sponsored by the heiress
A'Lelia Walker and by Van Vechten. Many of the same people
usually attended the gatherings of the two sponsors, though
more writers typically attended Van Vechten's. There Hughes
met Somerset Maugham, Hugh Walpole, and Zora Neale
Hurston's one-time employer Fannie Hurst, as well as William
Seabrook and Louis Untermeyer.

In New York that summer, Hughes wrote and rewrote the
poem "Mulatto" (*CP* 100), which would appear in the *Saturday
Review of Literature* and in the collection *Fine Clothes to the Jew*
(1927). When Hughes read the poem one evening at James Weldon Johnson's, Clarence Darrow called it the most moving poem

he had heard. While Hughes himself said the verse was about "white fathers and Negro mothers in the South," the craft transcends the autobiographical paraphrase. Through the view of one son, a victim of miscegenation, the speaker judges the father's contemptuous indifference and illustrates the callousness of white America in particular and humanity in general. Finally, he shows the hatred of the legitimate son for the bastard speaker, for the former signifies the inner collapse of the human family through racism.

"Mulatto" reinforces the techniques used in the ballad "Cross," published earlier but also collected in *Fine Clothes to the Jew*. In the poems, Hughes enlarged the basic inequality among blacks into social and symbolic meaning, the "problem of mixed blood . . . one parent in the pale of the black ghetto and the other able to take advantage of all the opportunities of American democracy." He also emphasized the peculiar plight of the mulatto, who wonders where he is going to die, "[b]eing neither white nor black" (*CP* 59).

Critics in the black middle class objected to *Fine Clothes to the Jew* on ideological grounds. Their philosophical differences with Hughes went back to 1922 because he had decided then to serve the black masses and to avoid middle-class affectation. Black academicians had insisted, on the contrary, on a social image that would still promote racial integration. When it became apparent that Hughes had not complied, a headline in the *Pittsburgh Courier* read "Langston Hughes's Book of Trash," and another appeared in the *New York Amsterdam News*: "Langston Hughes, the Sewer Dweller" (see *TBS* 266–68).

Of all the early stories, "The Childhood of Jimmy" (May 1927) provides many narrative traces that help so much with our interpreting the importance of the writer's literary world. Hughes makes it fun to be a kind of popular detective snooping out the nice clues to his life and stories. When a man washes overalls in a backyard, as in *The Big Sea*, one envisions Toy and Emerson Harper, those reliable two family friends of Langston's mother Carrie during the writer's childhood days in Kansas. Regarding the six impressions of the writer' life, Jimmy's town represents a secular place in which he learns about racial difference while seeking a personal balance of body and spirit. The poise makes for the artistry of his enduring stories—a suspension of human death. Once, Jimmy and the American virgin emerge from the same innocence:

> Before the village boy this young sailor from Newark seemed a model of all the manly virtues. And Mike had lived a life which the Virgin envied and wished to emulate. He, like the Virgin, had left home without *telling* anybody and in his three years away from the paternal roof *had visited half the ports of the world.* Furthermore, to hear Mike talk, there had been many *thrilling and dangerous adventures in the strange places he had known.* The Little Virgin would sit for hours, with the greatest credulity, *listening to the Newark's boy's stories. Then he would dream of the things that would happen to himself someday and how he would go back home and tell the fellows in his little village about them while they stood open-mouthed and amazed around this wanderer returned.* [Editor's italics.] (Hughes, Harper, ed. 27)

Hughes draws a picture that would become his personal signature, from story to story, for nearly thirty years. The wanderer, who listens to a mentor's tale, revises an already embellished story to the amazement of new initiates. Every public hearer is a new initiate for the civic writer. Like the wedding guest in Coleridge's *Rime of the Ancient Mariner*, the hearer surely must listen to the African American folk tale. In his advance from listener to teller, the everyday storyteller accepts the practical survival and the wondrously sublime responsibility of speaking and therefore writing the wisdom of the epic journey by an African American everyman. The everyday wanderer, or homeless person, turns up later in "Berry" and "Home," while the mate Chips, along with his "falsetto" in "The Little Virgin" (1927), looks forward to Delmar in "Blessed Assurance" (1963). Taken together, the tales may make for the overarching story told overall by Langston Hughes.

During his ensuing years of study at Lincoln, Hughes met Charlotte Mason (who liked to be known as "Godmother") on a weekend trip to New York in 1927. A friend had introduced him to the elderly white lady, who delighted Hughes immediately and who, despite her age, was modern in her ideas about books, Harlem theater, and current events. She became his literary patron, a title both disliked. With her support, Hughes began work on his first novel, *Not Without Laughter* (1930), which he envisioned as a portrait of a typical black family in Kansas. His personal background could not serve as a resource since his grandmother had never worked in domestic service and rarely attended church; his mother had been a newspaperwoman and stenographer. Hughes began writing furiously, tacking short biographical sketches of characters to the walls in his room. At first, he wrote a chapter or two a day and revised them, but the revisions were so unsatisfactory that he decided to write the book straight through. After completing the first draft in about six weeks, he went to Provincetown for a vacation before classes started. In the summer and fall of 1929, his senior year at Lincoln, Hughes revised the novel, continuing the process after graduation and through the summer. What had seemed acceptable to him before he went to Canada seemed to have diminished in quality upon his return. Yet the novel was accepted for publication and appeared in 1930.

In *Not Without Laughter*, Hughes chose fidelity to the folk spirit instead of abandoning it for the middle-class trappings of his Lincoln education. The novel relates the growth of Sandy Rogers, who lives with and is greatly influenced by Hager, his religious grandmother. Sandy's mother, Annjee, spends most of her time working as a domestic and waiting restlessly for Jimboy, her guitar-playing, rambling husband, to make one of his trips home. Hager's oldest daughter, Tempy, has separated herself from the family by assimilating middle-class culture and adopting values alien to her upbringing; Harriett, the youngest daughter, is the vibrant lover of life who defies her mother by attending parties and aspiring to become a blues singer. After Hager's death, it is the unlikely Harriett who carries on her values and encourages Sandy to continue his education.

Family and home unify the novel, with Hughes's combining fiction and history in his depiction of social setting and character. The writer, in his portrayal of the Williams family's disintegration and reunification, draws upon his familiarity with the barbershop in Kansas City and his experience with a wandering stepfather. He includes songs from childhood and has Sandy go to Chicago as he once did. The book is successful in capturing the folk flavor so vital to Hughes.

In the early winter of 1930, Hughes broke irreparably with Mason. He had loved her kindness and generosity, including her sincere support for black advancement and liberal causes. He had admired her awareness of then-budding stars Duke Ellington and Marian Anderson, and he had appreciated the humility that had made her remain his anonymous patron. In providing excellent supplies for his creative work, she had broadened his cultural life through visits to the Metropolitan Museum of Art, to concerts at Carnegie Hall, and to the musicals of the day. Yet the two of them had disagreed on political philosophy and race. Mason believed that blacks linked American whites to the primitive life and should concern themselves only with building on their cultural foundations. Hughes rejected such a simplistic view of the role of blacks in the modern world. Although he did not openly criticize Mason, he became psychosomatically ill following his final meeting with her.

Hughes also severed his ties with Hurston that winter. After one of her many trips to the Deep South, she and Hughes had begun to work on the folk comedy "Mule Bone," a play based on an amusing tale she had collected, one that portrayed a quarrel between two church factions. Apparently, Hughes outlined the plot, while Hurston embellished the dialogue and strengthened the humor. Before Hurston returned south, the two were supposed to complete a first draft from which Hughes was to write the final revision. Hughes, back in Cleveland to live with his mother, attended a performance by the Gilpin Players, after which he learned that Rowena Jelliffe, the director, had just received an excellent Negro folk comedy from Hurston. Though a group in New York had turned down the play, an agent had given Jelliffe permission to try it out in Cleveland. Unable to reach Hurston by phone, Hughes wired her unsuccessfully, and, after three unanswered letters, she replied finally from New York. She admitted sending the play to her agent and speculated angrily that Hughes would only have spent his half of the royalties on some girl she disliked. She went to Cleveland later to close the deal but then recanted. The incident led to a rift that was never mended and has become one of the classic breakups in Afro-American literary history.

Now almost thirty, Hughes was determined to make a living from writing. He set out with Zell Ingram, a student at the Cleveland School of Art, to tour the South by car. In Daytona Beach, he met Mary McLeod Bethune, who suggested that Hughes do readings throughout the region, since his achievements could be inspiring in the prevailing climate of racial restriction. Hughes considered the advice but did not act upon it until his trip was over. He and Ingram spent the summer in Haiti. Although he did not use the letters of introduction by Walter White, William Seabrook, Arthur Spingarn, and James Weldon Johnson to meet upper-class Haitians, Hughes did meet Jacques Roumain, a cultured Haitian who appreciated indigenous folklore. Later, Hughes and Ingram, with approximately four dollars between them, arrived back in Miami. When they returned to Daytona Beach, Bethune cashed a thirty-dollar check for them and asked to share the ride back to New York. About then, Hughes received a grant for one thousand dollars from the Rosenwald Fund to tour black colleges in the South. He purchased a Ford and, having no license, struck a deal with Lucas Radcliffe, a fellow alumnus of Lincoln, who would drive and manage accounts while Hughes read poetry. Both men would share the profits.

The trip, starting in the fall of 1931, deepened Hughes's commitments to racial justice and literary expression. When the nine Scottsboro boys were accused unjustly of raping two white prostitutes, he observed unhappily that black colleges were silent. "Christ in Alabama" (*CP* 143), a poem comparing the silence of the black colleges to that of the bystanders at the Crucifixion, caused a sensation in Chapel Hill, North Carolina, where the playwright Paul Green and the sociologist Guy B. Johnson had invited Hughes to read, in November. About a week before his scheduled arrival, Hughes received a note from a white student, Anthony Buttitta, who invited him to share a room. Buttitta and

Milton Abernethy, his roommate, had printed two of Hughes's publications, including "Christ in Alabama," in *Contempo*, an unofficial student magazine. The poem had included lines such as:

> Most holy bastard
> Of the bleeding mouth,
> Nigger Christ
> On the cross
> Of the South. (*CP* 143)

The subsequent appearance by Hughes nearly caused a riot, but his rescue from the angry crowd that attended the reading did not deter his challenge to racial segregation. He ate with the editors in a southern restaurant and thereby helped to set a new tone for race relations in Chapel Hill. At various stops in other towns, the poet's audiences overflowed. Blacks admired the young poet who had "walked into a lion's den" and come out, like Daniel, unscathed (*IWW* 47; see Berry 131). Bethune praised the same heroism in Hughes's poetry. For her and others, he read "The Negro Mother," which projects spiritual inspiration and endurance through images of fertility. In the remembrance of suffering, the speaker urges her children to transform the dark past into a lighted future. When Hughes completed the reading, Bethune embraced and consoled him: "My son, my son." Communal love and history informed the poet's life and work. Following a program in New Orleans, he took an hour to encourage the then-adolescent poet Margaret Walker. In preparing for a reading at Tuskegee Institute, in February, he thought about the educator Booker T. Washington, who had founded the institution in 1881. Often at odds with the more militant Du Bois, a Hughes mentor during the Renaissance, Washington had won at least partial approval from Sandy in *Not Without Laughter*. As a youngster in Lawrence, Hughes had been taken to hear Washington speak at Topeka. Later, Hughes had read *Up From Slavery* (1901), Washington's well-known autobiography. At Tuskegee, Hughes met the president at the time, Robert Moten, as well as the famous scientist George Washington Carver. The writer's talks with many English classes continued to be a source for his literary imagination, as did his whole trip.

The 1932 trip, which ended in San Francisco (at the home of Noel Sullivan, who would later be helpful to Hughes) after stops in Arkansas and other places, encouraged the literary relationships that shaped Hughes's imaginative life and made him speculate on both the nature and the obligation of art. This heightened awareness framed his journey to Russia that year as part of a film company. When Hughes met the Hungarian-born British writer Arthur Koestler, in Ashkhabad, the two explored Soviet Asia together, the latter providing Hughes with the opportunity to reflect on emotion and creativity: "There are many emotional hypochondriacs on earth, unhappy when not happy, sad when not expounding on their sadness. Yet I have always been drawn to such personalities because I often feel sad inside myself, too, though not inclined to show it. Koestler wore his sadness on his sleeve" (see *IWW* 101–43). Schooled in Western individualism, Hughes defended the artist's autonomy against the political directives of bureaucrats. Koestler retorted that the simultaneous expression of politics and individuality were difficult, especially when politicians lacked appreciation for creativity. At certain moments, Koestler argued, social aims transcended personal desires, though the Russian writer had begun to see Stalinist repression and to turn against communism. Hughes, grateful for the discussions with Koestler, probably thought his own ideas unchanged, but the encounter had renewed his leftist inclinations.

His first volume of stories, *The Ways of White Folks* (1934), appeared in the United States of the Great Depression of the 1930s. In a study of thirty cities, the demographic data of the era were grim. In the North, 52.2 percent of African Americans were on government relief, in contrast with 13.3 percent of European Americans; in the border states, the figures were 51.8 percent and 10.4 percent; and in the South, 33.7 percent and 11.4 percent (Bergman 464–66). In the three cities of Charlotte, North Carolina; Norfolk, Virginia; and Washington, D.C., nearly three-fourths of all African American households were on relief. The National Association for the Advancement of Colored People (NAACP) initiated a systematic challenge in the courts to racial discrimination in the public schools. Of the 24,536 members claimed by the Communist Party, only approximately 2,500 were black. Though Hughes's volume was likely the most prominent one by an African American during the decade, Zora Neale Hurston's *Jonah's Gourd Vine* (1934), an expression of the folk sermon, appeared in the same year, as did *Legal Murder*, a Broadway drama by the white playwright Denis Donague about the Scottsboro trials in 1931. The run turned out to last only seven nights (Bergman 420–28).

Hughes's meeting with Marie Seton furthered his leftist leanings. When he moved into a Moscow hotel, she lent him a copy of D. H. Lawrence's short-story collection *The Lovely Lady* (1933). He liked "The Rocking Horse Winner" particularly because the possessive, terrifying, and elderly woman reminded him of Charlotte Mason. In attempting futilely to write an article about Tashkent, he began to remember a story told once by Loren Miller, a young lawyer in California. In a small Kansas town, a very pretty black woman attracted the attention of the only black doctor, undertaker, and minister. While all three enjoyed her favors, she became pregnant but wasn't sure who was the father. When the doctor performed an abortion, the girl died. The undertaker took charge of her body, and the minister preached at her funeral. Hughes reworked the tale into an interracial story that appeared in *The Ways of White Folks* (1934). The black "girl" became a white middle-class youngster, Jessie Studevant, whose parents do not want her to have a relationship with a Greek boy, Willie Matsoulos, an immigrant whose father runs an ice-cream stand. When the girl's mother forces her to have an abortion, Jessie dies. Hughes revised his source satirically in order to picture the deep pathos and hypocrisy in American society.

Yet, the craft of the story transcended any social message. Through the setting of Melton, a small town in Iowa, the shrewd narrator clarifies misplaced values. He sets Cora's daughter, the black Josephine, against Mrs. Art's white Jessie. Whereas the first dies from unavoidable neglect, the second dies through willful decisions. Indeed, even the name "Art" allegorizes coldness in Western creativity. Through the omniscient, ironic narrator, Hughes reflects on aborted life while he implies the need for human sympathy.

In 1933, the stories "Home" (*Esquire*, 1934) and "The Blues I'm Playing" (*Scribner's Magazine*, May 1934) were accepted for publication. "Home" juxtaposes the artist's quest for beauty and truth and the lyncher's self-indulgent animalism. Roy Williams, a violinist by day and a jazz player by night, returns from Europe to Hopkinsville, Missouri, where he provokes envy in the local whites. When he bows to Mrs. Reese, a benevolent white music teacher, he is killed by the whites, who are jealous of his talent, clothing, and education. The story shows that music can neither transform such mobs nor protect the artist from vicious attack. Despite the apparent defeat, the humane greeting of the two musicians survives spiritually.

In "The Blues I'm Playing" (see Tracy), Hughes reworks the disturbing break with Mason into a plot involving a black pianist, Oceola Jones, who abandons the Western classics. Though her patron, Dora Ellsworth, a childless widow, believes in art alone, Jones believes in both art and life (Mason actually preferred "primitive folk art" to the classics), but a more complex psychology informs the story. To accept the innovative ideas of Oceola would mean to admit the misdirection of Ellsworth's own life and to transcend Western dualism. When Ellsworth refuses to do so, the two women represent a theoretical and ideological struggle over aesthetics. In the story, Oceola's wildly syncopated jazz is contrasted with both the classical music and the slow-singing blues. In the onomatopoeic climax of Oceola's final song, music becomes both a personal and a cultural liberation. Oceola has the last word, as through her the writer transmutes the personal life into the symbolic quest for self.

"The Blues I'm Playing" (*Scribner's Magazine*, 1934), one of Hughes's most carefully developed fictions, expresses a natural tension between classical and innovative art. The pianist plays her bluesy sound in folk time, but the Persian vases exist in the patron's drawing room within elegantly modern space. An interface between history and fiction occurred on October 29, 1929, the day the New York Stock exchange crashed, ending so many opportunities for publication and artistic performance during the New Negro Movement. From a posture in 1930, the storyteller refers obliquely to the year that preceded and produced the story.

Situated at a carefully crafted intersection—the Great Depression and the spiritual resistance of African American blues to it—the narrator shows a complexity of power dynamics. When social class and race divide people on the basis of interests and of conflicts of power, the potential force of humanity diminishes in capacity to change the world. A state of "Depression" is consequently a metaphor of history and of the human mind. Once a voyeur such as Ellsworth becomes jaded, she views creativity as a polished sublimation for living. Her cold vases set into relief the warm black velvet the pianist wears. Without children of her own, Ellsworth, who indulges her elitism to "share her richness with beauty," fails to distinguish between the product and the process—"youngsters . . . what they made . . . the creators or the creation." Even her objects of art must give way to time and, hence, to decay.

During spring excursions into the mountains of New York State, the patron and the player entertain guests in a lodge. Often, the subtle narrator switches the point of view between the two in alternate paragraphs, balancing the counterpoint of classicism and modernism. Siding finally with the pianist, the teller gains the moral authority necessary to advance to the closure of the tale. The pianist has lived at the patron's expense for two years in the Village. Well situated, with a small apartment in the Latin quarter of Paris, she has studied with an internationally acclaimed painter. She has learned about the African background of Claude Debussy (1862–1918), whose harmonic innovations inspired controversy about the function of music in the twentieth century. In meeting with many Algerians and French of African ancestry, she has delighted in an almost inexplicable intensity of exchange, thereby seeking out the hidden purpose of great writing, one that seems to have eluded even the musicians. Here are the famous controversies, ranging from those about the Jamaican black nationalist Marcus Garvey (1887–1940), through those around the renowned painter and sculptor Pablo Picasso (1881–1973) and the German philosopher Oswald Spengler (1880–1936), to, finally, those about the Frenchman Jean

Cocteau (1889–1963), who experimented with many diverse creative forms.

> Why did they [the students] or anybody argue so much about life or art? Oceola merely lived—and loved it. Only the Marxian students seemed sound to her for they, at least, wanted people to have enough to eat. That was important, Oceola, thought, remembering as she did, her own sometimes hungry years. But the rest of the controversies, as far as she could fathom, were based on air. (*TWW* 109)

Skeptical about the redemptive possibilities of art in the modern world—especially since the decline of the New Negro Movement in 1929—she speaks for the creator who scripts the words. "And as for the cultured Negroes who were always saying art would break down color lines, art could save the race and prevent lynchings! Bunk! Said Oceola. 'Ma ma and pa were both artists when it came to making music, and the white folks ran them out of town for being dressed up in Alabama. And look at the Jews! Every other artist in the world's a Jew, and still folks hate them." She favors an African American folk over a more refined middle class. Despite the allure of art for art's sake, she voices the memory of her inventor: "I was there [the Harlem Renaissance of the 1920s]. I had a swell time while it lasted. But I thought it wouldn't last long. . . . For how could a large and enthusiastic number of people be crazy about Negroes forever?" (*TBS* 228).

Whatever the disinclination of Hughes to theorize about fiction, his assumptions are clear. Fiction must subvert the status quo of bigotry. If fiction seems only to sublimate a real release from world hunger—to substitute, in other words, for the dead lecturer who has been erased from the modern story—it reminds us to make a real difference in the historical world. Fiction and life are imperfectly exclusive of each other, an inseparability that vindicates storytelling.

In visiting the patron at night for the last time, the pianist sees a room full of long-stemmed lilies. Dressed in a black velvet gown, the patron flashes a collar of white pearls about her white neck. How she may have "whitened" or wanted to "whiten" the pianist's playing implies her most unconscious design for the world. Though she proposes to have loved the player, her arrogant tone confirms the inequity of power ("to a child who has done a great wrong") (*TWW* 118). Despite the "technique" of playing—one for which the patron has paid—the blues vibrate the [white] lilies in her vases. Hughes remembers his benefactor, Charlotte Osgood Mason, for the year 1930:

> I cannot write here about the last half-hour in the big bright drawing-room high above Park Avenue one morning, because when I think about it, even now, something happens in the pit of my stomach that makes me ill. That beautiful room, that had been so full of light and help and understanding for me, suddenly became like a trap closing in, faster and faster, the room darker and darker, until the light went out with a sudden crash in the dark. (*TBS* 325)

By recasting himself as writer into the mask of innovative musician, he achieves his most compelling story of artistic freedom.

In Russia, Hughes had learned well the relationship between writing and myth making. The representative of a leading American newspaper had intentionally printed a story in New York claiming that the film company with which Hughes was traveling was stranded and starving in Moscow. When the film-makers showed the reporter the clippings, he merely grinned. But Hughes, to provide a clearer picture, praised the many positive changes in revolutionized Russia that Americans were ignoring, particularly the open housing and the reduced persecution of Jews. Yet Hughes turned away from Russia eventually because he refused to live without jazz, which the Communists banned, for they limited artistic freedom generally.

Determined to confront worldwide fascism and racism, Hughes returned to San Francisco by way of Asia in 1933. His trip home demonstrates his headstrong personality. Though Westerners in Shanghai had warned him that the watermelons were tainted and potentially fatal there, he ate well, enjoyed the fruit, and lived to write the story. Warned to avoid the Chinese districts, he visited those areas and found the danger illusory. In Tokyo, the police interrogated, detained, and finally expelled him. In the Japanese press's inflated stories of Korean crimes, he read the pattern of racism so familiar in the States. Aware that victims become victimizers in turn, he understood the Japanese debasement of the Chinese, and, on the way back to the United States, he warned that Japan was a fascist country.

Between 1933 and 1934, Hughes retired temporarily from world politics. In Carmel, at Sullivan's home "Ennesfree," he completed a series of short stories that were later included in *The Ways of White Folks*. He also wrote articles, including one on the liberation of women from the harems of Soviet Asia. Grateful to Noel Sullivan for the time to write, Hughes worked from ten to twelve hours a day, producing at least one story or article every week and earning more money than he ever had. He sent most of his earnings to his mother, who was ill at the time. Having broken with his father in 1922, Hughes learned, too late to attend the funeral, that his father had died in Mexico on 22 October 1934. Hughes traveled to Mexico and remained there from January to April 1935, during which time he read Cervantes's *Don Quixote*. From Cervantes he derived a masterful blend of tragedy and comedy to complement the appreciation of natural beauty he had learned from Maupassant and the complexity of literary psychology he had learned from Lawrence.

"The Blues I'm Playing" excels as the most refined of his "art" stories, but "Father and Son" ranks a little coarsely as his foremost "history." Preoccupied with the theme of miscegenation during most of his forty-six-year career in publication, Hughes included the forty-eight-page novella in the *Ways of White Folks* (1935), his first collection, and in *Something in Common and Other Stories* (1963), his final one. The long story, reappearing twenty-eight years after its first publication, unifies consequently the pattern of his life's work in short fiction. During the early period of the twenties, Hughes had written the short ballad "Cross," about the son of a mixed parentage. His eventual rewrite of "Father and Son," as the play *Mulatto,* opened at the Vanderbilt Theater on 24 October 1935 and ran on Broadway for more than a year. A libretto of the same plot was performed at the Broadhurst Theater on 2 November 1950.

Returned into the real time of an immediately occurring action, by the fourth section of the tale "Father and Son" Bert comes again to Norwood's Crossroads (the first section foretells the coming) after a six-year absence. Even now he remembers that his father beat him long ago "beneath the feet of horses" as the father himself remembers the event early on and Cora recalls it at the end. Hence, the recurrence of the deed in all of their memories serves as a unifying device within the fiction. The storyteller, relating the interwoven destinies, narrates three of the finest pages Hughes would ever write. After what seems to be service in the Civil War rather than World War I, the apparently antebellum colonel has lived into the dawn of the twentieth century. Meanwhile, the Ford (probably a Model T) driven by Bert resembles the driver, the one image of a revolutionary man and the other of a revolutionary machine. Bert is to humanity as the Ford is to modern technology.

A claim of primacy for the story depends initially on the figurative arrival of the Revolutionary Dreamer, then the specified time for African American storytelling within American history, and, finally, the explosive chemistry of social change in Georgia. Bert enters what seems to be an antebellum landscape, one set within the very early days of the twentieth century. Driving his new Ford, he looks out on the sprawling streets of the Junction while African Americans lounge at the storefronts. Of the poor whites, he glimpses the daily workers and disheveled women. In hearing the train exit the station, he advances into the Deep South, beset set on all sides by a line of sharecrop cabins against a cotton landscape. "Then he sees the gradual rise of the Norwood plantation, the famous Big House, surrounded by its live oaks and magnolias and maples, and its many acres of cotton. And he knew he was nearing home" (*TWW* 212). Though the narrative takes place in the third-person point of view, the consciousness is his. For six years he has been away; the story hardly clarifies either the reason or place, for Bert never really completes college during his long term of study that might have taken only four years. Now that his sister Sallie has followed him to the university, from whence he has returned during summer, the small county school at Norwood's Crossroads has closed. If, the public choice (Crossroads) between African American desire and social limitation has been temporarily decided, the figurative Cross-

roads still exists. As the coming of Bert, the Prodigal Son, signifies, his personal decision of one moment—facing the Father—at
the Crossroads does not exist as a desired manner for all martyrs
in all times, for different leaders direct the flow of history vari-
ously. Once the variety is accounted for, the story suggests that
the African American Dream is only deferred.

By a sleight-of-hand, Bert exists outside history while oppos-
ing the racist prejudice within it. He encapsulates the timeless
imagination that functions *through* and *beyond* the shackles of
time. "There are people," the narrator intrudes, "(you've probably noted it also) who have the unconscious faculty of making
the world spin around themselves, throb and expand, contract
and go dizzy. Then, when they are gone away, you feel sick and
lonesome and meaningless" (*TWW* 220). Elegiac conventions set
the tone for a poetic visionary, transforming a mental state, one
in which the absent chorus mourns the heroic dead, into an
epiphany in which the storyteller mourns the historical survivor.
So it is that the narrator, as stand-in or surrogate chorus, reaf-
firms the grandeur of the heroic dead, one vindicated by lyrical
power's defying a burning sky. While many inorganic com-
pounds have a potential for life, they lack a catalyst to incite
them. To be a medium means to deliver life, a continuance of
creativity.

> The tube is suddenly full of action and movement and life.
> Well, there are people like those certain liquids or powders; at
> a give moment they come into a room, or into a town, even
> into a country—and the place is never the same again. Things
> bubble, boil, change. Sometimes the whole world is changed.
> Alexander came. Christ. Marconi. A Russian named Lenin.
> (*TWW* 220)

As I wrote earlier,

> Taken together the references are sometimes ironic and even
> contradictory. Alexander, the doctor and charismatic leader,
> was a conquering soldier; Christ proposed that the meek were
> blessed, so they would inherit the earth; Marconi abused the

genius of his talent by helping his native homeland, guided by the fascist Benito Mussolini during World War II; Lenin was certainly a fashionable name to the proletarian Left in the America of the thirties, though his dream brought about the murder of thousands. Even Bert makes the mistake of thinking that he deserves his rights because he is Norwood's bastard son, but the real reason is that he is a human being. So it is that Bert's presence disrupts the revival that Norwood arranges in order to restore the status quo on the plantation. Hence, blacks are " not *quite* the same as they had been in the morning. And never to be the same again." (Miller, "Physics" 136; *A& I*, 104–9)

Clearly, the story benefits from an overarching sense of Time and lifts the text beyond a record of history. Herein Time becomes conflated. Through a work written into the world of the Great Depression of the thirties, Hughes writes an innovative spirit of the twenties back into the nadir—the lowest spiritual point of African American life—at the turn of the twentieth century. Consequently, his story, written from within a miserable era, recovers the spiritual reaffirmations of an inspiring time (the New Negro Renaissance). As in his autobiography, *The Big Sea,* Hughes envisions at least two complementary narratives, a presumed line of history but also a cycle of the Redeemer; a story of things as people have seen them, a tale of what the writer imagines humans to become.

The storyteller negotiates a discrepancy between history and Time, between 1900, when the story might well take place, and 2003 and beyond. The storyteller, expressing "The day that ends our story," looks forward to the death of Bert. Meanwhile, we project a reasonable time to the closure of the tale, but the resolution of civil rights in the nation has no expected date. A reference to *documented events* (the story) marks the era of the Depression, while an unfulfilled goal of African American freedom points to a limitless *process in time*. The story for Bert Lewis Norwood will end soon, but that of African American freedom will proceed indefinitely. The work achieves a tragic resolution through deaths in the closure, but the story of freedom concludes only at the finishing of Time.

The tension in the post office of the Junction results from the conscious and subconscious meaning of the word "change." A young white female clerk, who is used to having her superior way with African Americans, gives Bert sixty-four cents in change after he has purchased eight three-cent steps with a dollar. Having looked at the "incorrect change," he demands an additional twelve cents. Subsequently "counting the change," she urges him to move along in line so that impatient whites can go on to make their purchases. Then, looking at the "change," she realizes the error of her figures, thereafter expressing racist thoughts ("A light near-white n . . . You gotta be harder on those kind"). Still unwilling to correct the "change," she screams, "her head falling forward to a window" (*TWW* 227; Miller, "Physics," 136–37).

By the time of "Little Old Spy" (*Esquire*, September 1934), Hughes had become more realistic. Nevertheless, he kept his original promise:

> I was reading Schopenhauer and Nietzsche and Edna Ferber and Dreiser, and de Maupassant in French. I never will forget the thrill of first understanding the French of de Maupassant. The soft snow was falling through one of his stories in the little book we used in school, and that I had worked over so long, before I really felt the snow falling there. Then all of a sudden one night the beauty and the meaning of the words in which he made the snow fall, came to me. I think it was de Maupassant who made me really want to be a writer and write stories about Negroes, so true that people in far-away lands would read them—even after I was dead. (*TBS* 34)

Perhaps because of submissions to *Esquire* and to the *New Yorker*, Hughes began to write in a more modern style of expression His experimentations with narrative technique directed him away from the lyrical modernism of Jean Toomer's *Cane* (1923) toward the more condensed style of Ernest Hemingway's *In Our Time* (1924).

Hughes's story about a Cuban spy in Havana, during the rule of the Liberal Party leader Gerardo Machado y Morales, especially from November 1924 until August 1933, provides a personal signature for a lifelong voice: "A mile away on the Malecon—for I [narrator] had continued to *walk along the sea wall*—I *looked* at my *watch* and saw *the hour* approaching *seven*, when I was to meet some friends at the *Florida Café* [editor's italics]. I *turned* to *retrace* my steps. In *turning*, whom should I *face* on the sidewalk but the little old man! Then I became *suspicious*. He *said nothing* and *strolled on* as though he had not *seen* me. But when I *looked back after walking* perhaps a quarter mile toward the center, there he was a *respectable distance behind*" (*LKC* 154).

Particularly during the journey or *walk* down the seashore, the traveler *looks* into the meaning of the *hour*. Meanwhile, the spy who follows him lacks his gift for words. Hughes responds to the artistry through which we engage history. Beyond the human moment of comfort and fraternity (café), we *turn* to *face* history. And it is our conscientious *turning* that makes the writer and us so perceptively *suspicious* about political reality. The newspaper editor Carlos sits in the café with a cousin, Jorge the poet, a dancer named Mata (reminiscent of Sylvia Chen in Hughes's own life), and an African American writer.

Of the religious comedies, "On the Road" ("Two on the Road," *Esquire*, January 1935) depicts the Great Depression of the thirties through the ironic portrait of a fake holy man, "The Reverend Mr. Dorset," set against the cold snow.

> Sergeant blinked. When he looked up the snow fell into his eyes. For the first time that night he *saw* the snow. He shook his head. He shook the *snow* from his coat sleeves, *felt hungry, felt lost, felt not lost, felt cold,* He *walked* up the *steps* of the *church*. He *knocked* at the *door*. No answer. He tried the *handle*. Locked. He put his *shoulder against the door* and his long black body slanted like a ramrod. He *pushed*. With loud rhythmic grunts, like the grunts in a chain-gang song, he *pushed* against the door. [Editor's italics.] (Harper, *Short Stories*, 91)

Though the historical plot appears on the landscape of the thirties, the parable exists on a dream canvas of righteous Time (see Emanuel). It is all part of a shared cultural experience with

African Americans and others with a similar fine command of biblical stories. In other instances, the reading may seem to be esoteric or distant, but these are the public stories we know from childhood. The code is not difficult because we learned to read it so easily long ago. The narrator presents the fable of Sargeant (Sergeant), a homeless man and a deliverer of judgment for a divine court. So much of the meaning derives from the very name. In implying a biblical story, moreover, the narrator recounts the tale of Samson, a Hebrew judge who by *journeying* to Gaza falls into sin. Once the locals seize the figure at midnight, he *uplifts the doors* and posts of the city gates, thereby carrying them to the *top of a hill* before Hebron. Later, Samson looks forward to Christ at Calvary, in other words, at Golgotha, the place of skulls. Exhibited as a public spectacle at Gaza, Samson asks a boy attendant to place him at the two middle pillars of the great temple full of people, three thousand of whom are on the roof. Ever hopeful that God will grant him a final manifestation of strength, he shakes the pillars from their foundations, thus collapsing the roof and perishing with his enemies. The ancient story underlies the contemporary hardships of the modern African American *wanderer*—the homeless person today on our urban streets—who has so unsuccessfully sought sanctuary in the American Christian church, the walls crumbling like those of an ancient temple, "covering the cops and the people with bricks and stones and debris." When the homeless man—the African American Dreamer in 1935 and beyond 2003—awakens, the police are whacking his knuckles in a real jail. Hence, history means the very impoverished world of the thirties, the one in which the hero really exists, but history means also the world that we as modern readers must eventually reenter. Comedy means being funny, but most of all comedy means the chance to achieve a happy end one day. Hughes writes about simple decencies, but his rich voice is certainly far from simple. This is the deceptive greatness of his legacy.

He needed the humor for the Broadway production of *Mulatto*, the dramatic rewrite of the short story "Father and Son" (see Trotman). Hughes was amazed at the changes proposed. The character Sallie Lewis, sister of the protagonist Bert, should have gone away to school; instead, she remained at home to provoke sexual sensationalism by getting raped. The play was banned in Philadelphia and nearly prohibited from playing in Chicago. But on Broadway it had a long run. *Mulatto* played there for a year, from 1935 to 1936, and it was on the road for two more seasons.

As a correspondent in 1937 for the *Baltimore Afro-American*, during the Spanish Civil War, Hughes was deeply impressed by Pastora Pavón, the famous flamenco singer known as "La Niña de los Peines," whose bluesy art resisted both war and death. When Hughes heard that she had refused to leave besieged Madrid, he traveled there to see her. Her midmorning appearance among hand-clapping, heel-tapping guitarists was striking. She sat in a chair and dominated the performance as she half-spoke and half-sang a solea. To Hughes her voice was wild, hard, harsh, lonely, and bittersweet, reminding him of black Southern blues because, despite the heartbreak implied, it signified the triumph of a people. Hughes stayed on the top floor of the Alianza de Intelectuales in 1937; his room faced the fascist guns directly. Yet he stayed and met with the white American writers visiting Spain, including Ernest Hemingway, Martha Gellhorn, Lillian Hellman, and with the critic Malcolm Cowley. Nancy Cunard and Stephen Spender turned up, as well, as did non-English-speaking writers such as the French novelist André Malraux and Pablo Neruda, the leftist poet from Chile. Of these writers, Hemingway influenced Hughes most deeply. Hemingway had won a fight with an Englishman over some misunderstanding concerning the man's wife. When the squabble resurfaced as a short story, Hemingway described the incident so pointedly that few people in Madrid at the time could mistake the source, though he had exaggerated the other man's slightness and the woman's stockiness. He portrayed the man as hiding under a table as shots rang out, thereby leaving his wife unprotected. Actual witnesses, however, claimed that the Englishman took cover only after assurances that his wife was safe. Hughes appreciated the writer's imaginative revision of the event but hoped to disguise better the autobiographical sources for his own fiction. Still, Hemingway had melded history and autobiography successfully into imaginative writing.

In December 1937, Hughes went to Paris for the holidays, where he saw Nancy Cunard, Ada "Bricktop" Smith, and the Roumains. Louis Aragon introduced him to George Adam, who translated short stories into French, and to Pierre Seghers, who would become Hughes's publisher. Hughes had heard from Russian intellectuals that Spain was to be considered only a training ground for Hitler's and Mussolini's armies. It was a country for bombing practice by fascist pilots, and the impending World War II would take place everywhere.

When Jacques Roumain claimed the world would end, Hughes quipped, "I doubt it . . . and if it does, I intend to live to see what happens." Hughes's work continued to earn public recognition from 1938 to 1967, the year of his death. The poems in *A New Song* (1938) are politically sensitive and direct, yet replete with social irony and personal determination. "Let America Be America Again" shows the loss of an ideal, yet invokes the reappearance of it. Through the images of eye sores, the satirical poem "Justice" emphasizes social blindness.

After founding the New Negro Theater in Los Angeles during 1939, Hughes wrote a script for the Hollywood film *Way Down South*. From May through September he completed *The Big Sea*, the first segment of his autobiography, and when the book came out the next year (1940), he received a Rosenwald fellowship to write historical plays. In 1941, he founded the Skyloft Players, which produced his musical *The Sun Do Move*, in Chicago, in 1942. Whatever his claims for poetry, his imprint on Afro-American drama was certain.

Shakespeare in Harlem (1942), his next book of poems, was well crafted. In the blues monologue "Southern Mammy Sings," a poor black narrator opposes a white socialite. In a speech with biblical overtones, the speaker criticizes present and past wars, as well as the failure of interracial democracy. "Ballad of the Fortune Teller" presents, humorously and colloquially, the situational irony of a woman who allegedly foretells the future of others but fails to prophesy her lover's desertion of her. In the deceptively simple "Black Maria," an enthusiastic urbanite focuses, almost allegorically, upon the music playing in a tenement upstairs instead of on a hearse passing in the street below.

Such meanings escaped most of the critics. Saying that *Shake-speare in Harlem* was a "careless surface job" and that Hughes was "backing into the future looking at the past," Owen Dodson was unduly harsh. Alfred Kreymborg, however, was reminded of such "master singers of Vaudeville as Bert Williams and Eddie Leonard . . . a subtle blending of tragedy and comedy, which is a rare, difficult, and exquisite art." Eda Lou Walton, overlooking the poet's new growth in complexity and symbolic depth, wrote: "Hughes only writes as he always has. His poems, close to folk songs, indicate no awareness of the changed war world. . . . Easily listened to, they do not invoke sufficient thought" (Miller, *Guide* 19–20).

When *Shakespeare in Harlem* had been published, Hughes returned to New York. for a gathering with friends, and he wrote verses and slogans to help sell U.S. Defense Bonds. In a weekly column for the *Chicago Defender*, a black newspaper, he began to publish the tales of Jesse B. Semple, later called Jesse B. Simple— a folk philosopher who would capture the hearts of thousands of readers. In 1946, Hughes won a medal and a prize of one thousand dollars from the American Academy of Arts and Letters. In the early months of 1947, he served as visiting professor of creative writing at Atlanta University. For a few weeks in 1949, he was poet in residence at the Laboratory School of the University of Chicago.

His *Fields of Wonder* (1947) appeared in a United States still full of racial strife but with a promise of social and artistic progress. Over the next fifteen years, twelve African Americans would be lynched, and the twenty-seven-year-old John H. Johnson, of Chicago, would found *Ebony* magazine. Hughes, with the lyrics for Kurt Weill's score, would help produce what some observers called the first Broadway opera. Theodore Ward's *Our Lan'* would also be performed on stage. When Dizzy Gillespie hired Chano Pozo, an African Cuban drummer, to play in a town hall concert, the Pan-American impact of jazz would be complete. Jackie Robinson, who would become a fleeting image in one of Hughes's final volumes of poetry, would become the first black to compete on a major league baseball team, the Brooklyn Dodgers.

In *One-Way Ticket* (1949), Hughes infused humorous realism with satire and biblical irony. His well-known persona, Alberta K. Johnson, became the hilarious folk counterpart in poetry to his comic character, Jesse B. Simple, in prose. In one poem, Madam asserts her independence from the phone company, as well as from a lover. Madam blames society for her misfortunes in life and love while she directs the criticism inward to her own character. Her self-image is sometimes overblown and superstitious. Possibly happiness has eluded her because she doubts her worthiness to be loved.

The critical reception to *One-Way Ticket* was mixed. G. Lewis Chandler observed the humor, irony, and tragedy, as well as the folksiness, subtlety, puckishness, and hope. The communal "I" reminded him of Walt Whitman, and he praised the poet's ability to deepen racial material into universal experience. Rolfe Humphries, who acknowledged Hughes's forbearance, praised the basic restraint of vocabulary, the simple rhymes, the short lines, the absent violence, and the missing hyperbole. Hughes needed, he thought, to be more elaborate, involved, and complex, to exploit more fully education, travel, reading, and music other than the blues (Miller, *Guide* 23–24).

However modern he was, Langston Hughes would never abandon black folk life for Western imagism. In *Montage of a Dream Deferred* (1951), his first book-length poem, dramatic and colloquial effects challenge his lyricism. Numerous projects in the writing of history and short fiction, such as *The First Book of Negroes* (1952) and *Simple Takes a Wife* (1953), drained his poetic energies. His style became more sophisticated. Through monologue and free verse, he stressed dramatic situations and mastered the apostrophe. In blending content with form, he fused narrative with sound effects.

By the publication of *Laughing to Keep from Crying* in 1952, the color line of the twentieth century had faded. For the first time in seventy-one years, no racial lynching was recorded. Despite political differences, all of the major political parties came out in the favor of racial equity. Only 21 percent of African Americans voted for Dwight D. Eisenhower for president, because the General's testimony had undermined President Truman's efforts to desegregate the army. Ralph Ellison's classic novel, *Invisible Man*, came out. Hughes's world was certainly changing.

The critics of the fifties overlooked Hughes's skill. Rolfe Humphries commented that the poems in *Montage of a Dream Deferred* confused him, as work by Hughes often did. The statement, he said, was oversimplified and theatrical. Babette Deutsch believed that the verses, which invited approval, "lapsed into a sentimentality that stifles real feeling." Conscious of the limitations of folk art, she asserted that Hughes should resemble more his French contemporaries. Saunders Redding said Hughes offered nothing new; he called his idiom constant and his rhythms more bebop than jazz. Despite a sophisticated ear, according to Redding, Hughes was too concerned with personal reputation and innovation (Miller, *Guide* 25–26).

For several years after he testified, in 1953, before the Senate subcommittee chaired by Joseph McCarthy as part of its investigation into the purchase of books by subversive writers for American libraries abroad, Hughes received fewer offers to read his poems. But he still enhanced the craft of his fiction. When *The Best of Simple* (1961) appeared, it presented a comic veneer and lightness that artfully concealed its complex symbolism. Through urban dialect, Hughes juxtaposed the seriousness of the Great Migration in Simple's past with the humorous tone of the moment. Simple's folk imagination struck a balance with the polished reason of Boyd, his bar buddy.

In "Feet Live Their Own Life," Simple's comic discourse suggests an awareness of the present and the past. Through the caricatured figure of the former Virginian, Hughes helps the reader to laugh at himself and at American society. In "There Ought to Be a Law," Simple calls for a game preserve for "Negroes." Another tale, "They Come and They Go," is a narration about Simple's eighteen-year-old second cousin, Franklin D. Roosevelt Brown, coming North. The youngster's stepfather has whipped him, and the mother has predicted the same failure for the youth as that which beset his "no-good" father. But Hughes's narrator manages a sympathetic tone for all involved.

In 1960, Hughes visited Paris for the first time in twenty-two years, and he would subsequently make many trips on cultural

The Poet Speaks of Places

A Close Reading of Langston Hughes's Literary Use of Place

James de Jongh

I

It has been the longstanding practice of African American verbal culture to transform literal spaces into topical spaces for rhetorical and figurative purposes. Like the broader culture of black Americans, our literature tempered the historic experience of dislocation, slavery, and discrimination by seeking terms with which to root itself in the African Diaspora. Over time, this discourse of spatial signing has evolved into a literary strategy of allusion to a diversity of symbolic and spiritual spaces in the figurative practice of black writers.[1] Allusions to the Old Testament iconography of place by which enslaved blacks identified themselves with the enslaved Israelites in Egypt and Babylon in the geography of their song reverberate distinctively in "The Negro Speaks of Rivers," the debut poem young Langston Hughes scribbled on an envelope as the train taking him to another summer in Mexico with his father crossed the Mississippi. In "Rivers," Hughes claimed this legacy-vocabulary of place—encompassing "downriver," the term for all the dreaded places in the lower South to which slaves were sold off, "the riverside," one of the relative safe havens and sites of resistance within the domain of the plantation itself, and "over Jordan," the beckoning frontier of freedom visible from inside the bounds of enslavement and exile—as it was elaborated and interpreted in the nineteenth century in the traditional Negro spirituals and in such classic fugitive slave narratives as Frederick Douglass's and Harriet Jacobs's as sites of meditation, rebellion, and recuperation. By placing that inherited vocabulary of place within a wider geographic perspective, however, Hughes proposed a reconstituted imagery of place for the twentieth century, one associated with a progression across continents in a historic and prophetic language of belonging and entitlement, beyond enslavement. This usage of spiritual geography, rooted in the characteristic idiom of the oral traditions of enslaved Americans of African descent and in the narrative texts of former slaves, and present even in Hughes's earliest published work, would remain a lifelong figurative strategy.

This legacy language of place bequeathed by the oral tradition and claimed so authoritatively in "The Negro Speaks of Rivers" is always at hand for Langston Hughes. It is consistently voiced throughout his career in the terms of the tradition, but it is also turned to unusual and innovative uses. The encompassing places of the spirit that cohere and give order to Langston Hughes's literary vocabulary are three: the unremembered place of origin in Africa, the unrealized yet perfectible social space of America, and the unprecedented enclave of black Harlem. This essay focuses on the poetry for practical as well as philosophical (theoretical if you prefer) reasons. First of all, the practical instrument for such a critical overview of his poetry is now available in *The Collected Poems of Langston Hughes,* edited by Arnold Rampersad and David Roessel. More to the point is my view of Langston Hughes as fundamentally a poet, a prolific writer who turned his talents with greater or lesser success to a multiplicity of other genres over time but one whose vocation (his calling as an artist) was poetry. In his usage of the legacy language of place in his poetry, one perceives the clarity and coherence of Langston Hughes's vision of himself as an African American citizen-poet: "A poet is a human being. Each human being must live within his time, with and for his people, and within the boundaries of his country. Hang yourself, poet, in your own words. Otherwise you are dead" (*CP* 5).

grants from the state department, an irony indeed, since until 1959 he had been on the "security index" of the FBI's New York office. He would visit Africa again and revisit Europe, also. The year 1961 saw the publication of Hughes's crowning achievement. *Ask Your Mama* is as much Juvenalian as Horatian in its satiric response to the rising anger of the 1960s. Hughes, fusing poetry with jazz innovations, interweaves myth and history. He moves now into the child's mind and then into the man's; he reverses himself and begins afresh. Through allusion, fantasy, travesty, and irony, he depicts actors, musicians, politicians, and writers. He draws upon the rich themes of his entire career, such as humanism, free speech, transitoriness, and assimilation; nationalism, racism, integration, and poverty. With a deepened imagination, he speculates about Pan-Africanism and personal integrity.

With the publication of *Ask Your Mama*, in 1961, Hughes had lived from one great movement of African American culture in the twentieth century—the Harlem Renaissance—to the second great one, the Black Arts Movement of the sixties and seventies. He encountered a curious blend of struggle for civil rights and opportunity for the creative arts. Martin Luther King, Jr., was arrested along with seven hundred demonstrators in Albany, Georgia, and Adam Clayton Powell, Jr., a congressional representative for Harlem, won the chairmanship of the Education and Labor Committee in the House of Representatives. Diana Sands starred in the film version of Lorraine Hansberry's 1959 play, *A Raisin in the Sun*, the title drawn from a phrase in Hughes's poem "Harlem." James Baldwin's second collection of essays, (Baldwin and Hughes were different feathers of very different Harlem generations) *Nobody Knows My Name*, won national attention. Edmund Wilson proclaimed the younger writer "the best Negro writer ever produced in the United States." LeRoi Jones, the leader of a new vanguard, was already bringing out *Preface to a Twenty Volume Suicide Note*. Langston Hughes was one of the few writers capable of bridging the generation gap.

Rudi Blesh, praising Hughes's commitment to universal freedom, called *Ask Your Mama* "a half angry and half derisive retort to the bigoted, smug, stupid, selfish, and blind." Dudley Fitts, who compared it to Vachel Lindsay's *Congo* (1914), drew parallels between Hughes and the Cuban poet Guillén, as well as between Hughes and the Puerto Rican Luis Matos. Though many white Americans believed blacks had moved too fast, Hughes complained about slowness and regression. The last poem he is said to have submitted for publication before his death in New York City's Polyclinic Hospital on 22 May 1967 was "The Backlash Blues."

Yet other poems are more optimistic. In "Frederick Douglass," his narrator anticipates the return of good, despite a period of regression, like that which began in 1895, the year of Douglass's death, with the Atlanta Compromise speech in which Booker T. Washington spoke of the races as being "separate as the five fingers." Douglass is one of the many complex figures whom Hughes had portrayed in his work—along with fictional ones such as Roy Williams, Oceola Jones, and Bert Norwood (all in *The Ways of White Folks*). Creative and good people reinforce one another in human history, and they come again.

His *Something in Common and Other Stories* (1963) came out during one of the most turbulent years in American history, one that marked a crucial advance in civil rights. By May 10, Martin Luther King, Jr., had negotiated with the Senior Citizens committee of Birmingham, Alabama, a document outlining the desegregation of public facilities in the city and calling for greater equity in public hiring. While only 21 percent of whites believed that demonstrations helped African Americans, 72 percent of African Americans themselves thought so. With the publication of *Blues People*, LeRoi Jones (later Amiri Baraka) became even more of a leader for a new vanguard of black aestheticians, while *Walk in Darkness*, a play by the African American playwright William Hairston, and *Tambourines to Glory*, by Hughes, opened off-Broadway. Sidney Poitier earned an Oscar that year as best actor for his depiction, in *Lilies of the Field*, of a helpful African American among an order of nuns.

In August of that year, a quarter of a million Americans, led by the public activists A. Philip Randolph and Bayard Rustin, gathered to protest the state of civil rights in the United States, thereby laying the foundation for the Civil Rights Bill of 1964. The "I have a dream" speech, delivered during this massive protest by King, came during a era that saw ten thousand racial demonstrations that led to the arrests of more than five thousand African Americans. Governor George Wallace of Alabama nearly shouted during his inaugural, "I draw a line in the dust and toss the gauntlet before the feet of tyranny and I say segregation now, segregation tomorrow, segregation forever." John F. Kennedy, who directed the country down a nobler course, became the first American president to say that segregation was morally wrong.

Hughes's *Something in Common,* so out of tone with the times, avoids the often biting sarcasm of his last poetry and final Simple columns. Of all his artistic forms, his stories may well show the least historicity after 1935. Of the thirty-seven stories in the final volume (ten new ones), only "Blessed Assurance" ranks among his most original works. His simple truth is that two bar comrades of different race are equally Americans.

Until forty-eight months before his death, Langston Hughes had for nearly forty years steadfastly avoided any controversy over what today would be called gay rights. In "Blessed Assurance," by exploring the complexity of sexual orientation, he exposes the sacredness of God-given talent. Despite the audience's discomfort with a boy singer, especially the troubled father's, the uniqueness of the boy's voice compels the female audience to suspend the rules of sexuality.

In Hughes's final year, the national energy for civil rights declined. Martin Luther King, Jr., had determined to oppose the Vietnam War, which he thought drained resources from a Great Society promised by President Lyndon Johnson, Kennedy's successor. President Johnson named Thurgood Marshall to be the first African American to sit on the Supreme Court. The civil rights movement began to collapse in the South due to lack of funds and the transfer of other funds to the North. In truth, the decline dated back to the end of the march that King had led from Montgomery to Selma in 1965 and the consequent rise in black nationalism, which had fragmented the fragile alliances of the intraracial Left, especially within the Student Nonviolent Coordinating Committee (SNCC) and the Congress of Racial Equality (CORE).

On the night of May 6, 1967, Hughes sought emergency care

at the Polyclinic Hospital, in New York City, for an undisclosed ailment that was diagnosed later as both an infection of the prostrate gland and a heart condition. Having taken a cab from the local Wellington Hotel, he registered as "James Hughes," receiving the same quality of care as any other perceived indigent. The irony was so appropriate for the life. The African American folk poet died by the theory he had lived by. When a black orderly informed hospital authorities that Langston Hughes was suffering for lack of emergency care, it was already too late. On May 22, the poet passed. In intensive care at another hospital, Toy Harper, a family friend of Hughes's mother, Carrie, since the early Kansas days, awoke to tell the nurse a disturbing dream: "Langston Hughes had climbed atop a pole to reach toward a tower and had fallen" (Berry 328–29).

Following his death, critical commentary was respectful. Bill Katz, reviewing *The Panther & The Lash* (1967), praised the writer's commitment to diverge from both liberal and reactionary views of race. Lamine Diakhaté called Hughes a "pilgrim who affirmed the identity of man in the face of the absurd . . . showed the problems of blacks in a democratic society, restored the rhythmical language of Africa introduced by jazz in America, and demonstrated inextinguishable hope." François Dodat observed Hughes's humanistic faith. Most celebrators mentioned the writer's great generosity (Miller, *Guide* 45–50).

The 1980s marked a timely renaissance in Hughes's reputation. A Langston Hughes study conference, in March 1981, at Joplin, Missouri, helped inspire the founding of the Langston Hughes Society, in Baltimore, Maryland, on 26 June of the same year. After a joint meeting with the College Language Society, in April 1982, the Society became, in 1984, the first group focused on a black author ever to become an affiliate of the Modern Language Association. In the fall of 1988, Raymond R. Patterson directed, at the City College of the City University of New York, "Langston Hughes: An International Interdisciplinary Conference," one of the most satisfactory tributes ever paid to the author. There, shortly after a public television release, so similarly titled, had reaffirmed the high place of Hughes among the most celebrated national poets, more than a dozen renowned scholars and artists reassessed the contributions of Hughes to the reshaping of American voices and visions.

Hughes's impact on American history is clear. He introduced some of the most experimental forms of African American music into our poetics of the twentieth century. During the despair of the Great Depression, he presented many deceptively simple stories that would endure within and beyond his time. He proved, during the late forties, that lyricism would prosper, despite the despondency of history. Neither the pessimism of the cold war of the 1950s nor the mainstream backlash to the civil rights movement of the sixties disillusioned him completely. He discerned a disturbing cycle of inhumanity within history, but not without laughter. A man for all seasons, he was especially a voice of the mid-twentieth century. His was a measured declaration on behalf of a most optimistic future. Thus, his words outlived his own century. He read the vicissitudes of history, often revealing the implications of it to fellows who lived with him within it. His historical imagination was for all time.

WORKS CITED

Barksdale, Richard. *Langston Hughes: The Poet and His Critics*. Chicago: American Library Association, 1977.

Bergman, Peter M. *The Chronological History of the Negro in America*. New York: Harper and Row, 1969.

Berry, Faith. *Langston Hughes, before and beyond Harlem*. Westport, Conn.: Hill, 1983.

De Santis, Christopher C., ed. *Langston Hughes and the* Chicago Defender *Essays on Race, Politics, and Culture, 1942–62*. Urbana: University of Illinois Press, 1995.

Dickinson, Donald C. *A Bio-Bibliography of Langston Hughes*. Hamden, Conn.: Shoe String, 1967.

Emanuel, James A. *Langston Hughes*. New York: Twayne, 1967.

Harper, Akiba Sullivan, ed. *Short Stories of Langston Hughes*. New York: Hill and Wang, 1996.

Mikolyzk, Thomas A. *Langston Hughes: A Bio-Bibliography*. New York: Greenwood, 1990.

Miller, R. Baxter. *The Art and Imagination of Langston Hughes*. Lexington: University Press of Kentucky, 1989.

———. *Langston Hughes and Gwendolyn Brooks: A Reference Guide.* Boston: Hall, 1978.

———. "The Physics of Change in 'Father and Son.'" In *Langston Hughes: The Man, His Art, and His Continuing Influence.* Ed. C. James Trotman. New York: Garland, 1995.

Nichols, Charles H. *Arna Bontemps–Langston Hughes Letters, 1925–1967.* New York: Dodd, Mead, 1980.

Rampersad, Arnold. *The Life of Langston Hughes.* 2 vols. New York: Oxford University Press, 1986–1988.

Tracy, Steven C. "Blues to Live By: Langston Hughes's 'The Blues I'm Playing.'" *Langston Hughes Review* 12, no. 1 (1993): 12–18.

———. *Langston Hughes & the Blues.* Urbana: University of Illinois Press, 1988.

Trotman, C. James, ed. *Langston Hughes: The Man, His Art, and His Continuing Influence.* New York: Garland, 1995.

Wright, Richard. "Forerunner and Ambassador." *New Republic*, July/December 1940, pp. 600–601.

HUGHES IN
HIS TIME

2

In the first decades of the twentieth century, as black intellectuals sought what Alain Locke called "full initiation into American democracy" and "a spiritual Coming of Age" in "The New Negro,"[2] the journey of identity back to Southern roots among New Negro artists also required an African counterpart. For most of the nineteenth century, Africa had been inscribed in the discourse of black Americans as a receding memory, an alien and inaccessible ancestral landscape obscured by time, distance, and deliberate distortion. With the prohibition of the international slave trade in 1808, interest in literary treatments of Africa and the Atlantic middle passage, such as *The Interesting Narrative of the Life of Olaudah Equiano, or Gustavus Vassa, the African* (1789), gave way to a fascination with the antebellum fugitive slave narratives published as part of the antislavery campaign to discredit and eliminate the internal slave trade of the United States. The impulse among black Americans to colonize and/or evangelize the African homeland persisted in fits and starts among such varied figures as John B. Russwurm, Alexander Crummell, Martin Delany, and Edward Wilmot Blyden, however, and as the nineteenth century waned, a fresh interest in the ancestral setting began to develop among some black intellectuals, notably Frederick Douglass and W. E. B. Du Bois.

Alain Locke chose to make the point editorially in the collection *The New Negro* by juxtaposing Arturo Schomburg's essay "The Negro Digs up His Past" with Countee Cullen's provocative interrogative "What Is Africa to Me?" in "Heritage," and, in the Harlem issue of *Survey Graphic Magazine* (March 1925), at least, Locke used images of African artifacts to offer a visual counterpoint to Cullen's long poem rather than to the shorter pieces of Langston Hughes in the same volume. But it was Hughes, rather than Cullen, who would focus lifelong attention on the literary topos of Africa in his poetry.

Africa was already a presence in "The Negro Speaks of Rivers," Hughes's first contribution to *The Crisis* (July 1921), for two of the four rivers named are on the continent of Africa. The terms of the theme of Africa were proclaimed, in "Negro," Hughes's next ap-

pearance in the pages of *The Crisis* (January 1922), early the next
year, to be continuity of a common African culture and identification with a shared African experience of racist oppression associated both with the blackness of the night and the blackness of his
skin: "I am a Negro: / Black as the night is black, / Black like the
depths of my Africa" (*CP* 24). The expressive medium for both
continuity and identity for Hughes is revealed in "Danse
Africaine," another offering to *The Crisis* (August 1922), to be "the
low beating of the tom-toms / [that] Stirs your blood" (*CP* 28).
The value of these figurative terms for Africa is crystallized with
perfect economy in "Afraid," published in *The Crisis* (November
1924), two years later, where the isolation, fear, and sadness of the
African ancestors amid the palm trees at night are paralleled to the
sadness of contemporary African Americans amid the skyscrapers
of the urban setting. All four poems were reprinted in Hughes's
first published collection, *The Weary Blues* (1926), and the terms
they established of continuity of shared culture and identity of
shared suffering, voiced above all in the cry of the drums and associated both with dark skin and the night, were repeated throughout the decade of the twenties in other poems that invoked the
African homeland explicitly and in allusions that assumed these
terms without explicit reference, such as in "Lament for Dark Peoples," *The Crisis* (June 1924), when the speaker, who has been both
a black man and a red man in his time, deplores being "Caged in
the circus of civilization" (*CP* 39).

In "I, Too," first published in *Survey Graphic* (March 1925) and
reprinted in *The New Negro* (1925), Hughes claimed the role and
the voice of a poet of America, as well as of Africa, by identifying
himself with the most American of poets, Walt Whitman: "I,
too, sing America" (*CP* 46). Like the topos of Africa, which was
reprised in the pages of *The Crisis* in the year of its first appearance, the theme of America was immediately restated and developed a few months later with "America" in the pages of *Opportunity* (June 1925), where it took third prize in the literary
competition sponsored by the magazine. The poem is an apostrophe to two excluded infants, one black and one Jewish. The
speaker is the Black American Every[wo]man, explicitly Crispus
Attucks, Jimmy Jones, Sojourner Truth, "Today's black mother,"

"the dark baby," and "the ghetto child," each of whom would take center stage at one moment or another in Hughes's later work. The speaker's America is immanent like the infants', not yet realized but in a struggle for realization. America, like the speaker imparting his faith to the two infants, is "seeking the stars" (*CP* 52).

In his earliest poems, Hughes's imagery of place was employed also to articulate the faith that, at least in some places, the promise of America was available to blacks. In increasing numbers, black migrants were fleeing poverty, peonage, segregation, and socially sanctioned violence in the South in hope of a better life of opportunity and self-realization in the urban centers of the North in the period when Langston Hughes was finding his poetic voice, and Hughes's development of a literary language of place reflected that expansive psychology of possibility, as well as the desperation and fear that motivated the Great Migration.

In the early 1930s, Hughes linked the literary topoi of Africa and America to each other and constituted the themes formally as interpenetrating figurative terms in his literary language of place. In "Negro," Langston Hughes had underlined the historic progression from Africa to America that was merely implied in "The Negro Speaks of Rivers": "All the way from Africa to Georgia / I carried my sorrow songs" (*CP* 24). In "Afro-American Fragment," published in *The Crisis* (July 1930), the title fragment is a scrap of "song of atavistic land / Of bitter yearnings lost / Without a place" in which Africa and America are somehow inescapably different and yet the same, simultaneously converging and diverging, reciprocal though alienated, both paradoxically parallel and interconnected (*CP* 129).

In poems written in 1932–1933, in the early days of his sojourn in the Soviet Union during the period of the Great Depression and published in avowedly Marxist journals in the United States, Hughes's speakers rail against inequality, exploitation, and injustice in America and call unambiguously for revolution in a proletarian register. "Good Morning Revolution," published in *New Masses* (September 1932) after being rejected by the *Saturday Evening Post,* greets the allegorical figure of Revolution, routinely castigated as a "troublemaker, a alien-enemy, / In other words a son-of-a-bitch" (*CP* 162), as a best friend and buddy (with an ironic turn on Carl Sandburg's "Good Morning America"), and "Always the Same," published in *Negro Worker* (September–October 1932), extends the indictment of American capitalism and the embrace of revolution to Africa, as well as America. "One More 'S' in the USA," published in the *Daily Worker* (April 2, 1934), a year later, persisted in this vein after Hughes returned to the United States. However, he continued to inflect the usage of the images and diction he had established for Africa in the early 1920s. In the "night-dark face" of "Call of Ethiopia" (*CP* 184), *Opportunity* (September 1935), Hughes compressed the association of black night and black skin established in "Negro" into a single image and restored something of the earlier hopeful tone to his treatment of the figure of America. In "Let America Be America Again," in *Esquire* (July 1936), he conceived of America as "the dream it used to be" (*CP* 189), returning to the earlier vision of the flawed but potentially perfectible society of "I, Too" and "America" without abandoning the indictment of increasing inequality and social injustice.

Langston Hughes traveled to Europe in the summer of 1937 to cover the Spanish Civil War for the *Baltimore Afro-American* and other black newspapers. Traveling in Spain with Nicolás Guillén as a war correspondent for African American newspapers, Hughes complicated the interplay between black Africa and black America and the simple dichotomy between fascism and freedom. "Postcard from Spain," in *Volunteer for Liberty* (April 9, 1938), takes the form of a letter addressed to blacks in the United States from an African American volunteer named Johnny who is fighting in the Abraham Lincoln Battalion on the side of the Spanish loyalists against the Fascists in the Spanish Civil War. Johnny's letter expresses the comfort he takes as an African American from his place in the international struggle for freedom. In "Letter from Spain," published earlier in *Volunteer for Liberty* (November 15, 1937), however, Hughes employed the same conceit to dramatize an emerging sense of perplexing new perspectives in the struggle for freedom when Johnny writes a letter home about a dying Moorish prisoner he comes across among some captured Fascist soldiers. The presence of black Africans among the enemy provokes confused and conflicted feelings. Despite the barrier of language, Johnny is able to recognize and identify with a common experience of abduction, bondage, and exile in the situation of the prisoner, which only makes their places on opposite sides of the battle more disturbing. Finally, Johnny takes the hand of his African opponent in a simple gesture of brotherhood, but the captured Moor is imprisoned by death throes and does not understand.

In the final moments before the outbreak of war in Europe, Hughes clung to the theme of "America seeking the stars" in remarkably optimistic terms, even in the belly of the racist beast, in "Daybreak in Alabama," in *Unquote* [Yellow Springs, Ohio] (June 1940). And, during the war years, he continued to refine the literary terms of his Africa. In a few lines from "Me and My Song," in *Jim Crow's Last Stand* (1943), he distilled the practice and diction of his Africa poems from the 1920s in a single phrase—"My song / From the Dark Lips / Of Africa / Deep / As the rich Earth / Beautiful / as the black night" (*CP* 296)—and associated those Africa poems with "The Negro Speaks of Rivers" with the resonance of a single word: "Deep."

3

The specific dictionary entries of Langston Hughes's vocabulary of place for America would encompass too many archetypal black settings to catalog in any kind of detail in this essay, except to suggest their variety and range. Hughes's allusions to New Orleans, Memphis, Cairo, and St. Louis, the consummate river towns of the Mighty Mississippi, gave voice to a ripe and vigorous America of migrants constantly in motion. The states of the Deep South, a.k.a. Dixie, particularly Mississippi, Alabama, and Georgia, were still Egypt and Babylon, places of exile, bondage, and terror, recalling the iconography of the Africans enslaved in America, though blacks were no longer legal chattel there. The cities of the North were less oppressive, but Hughes's frequent evocations of the communal spaces where African Americans lived their lives in public, such as the road, the riverbank, the bridge, the park bench, the street corner, the lonesome corner, the late corner, the back porch, the waterfront, the river town, the Jim Crow car, the gin mill, and the juice joint, located the co-ordinates of fear, injustice, and hope on both sides of the Mason-Dixon line. The place names of Jamestown, Tuskegee, Scotts-boro, Birmingham, and Selma were stations of the cross on the winding road of an American history that was not yet what it could potentially become, and the places named for Abraham Lincoln—the Lincoln Monument, the various Lincoln theaters, Lincoln University—resonated with different degrees of irony, as well as reverence. Religious settings, such as the Bible Belt, over Jordan, at the feet o' Jesus, in the amen corner, or on the cross of the South, were evoked repeatedly, especially in early poems. At the same time, references to places like the Dennison Hotel, in Jersey, and the Club Harlem, in Atlantic City, conveyed the texture of Hughes's own wanderings on the unredeemed wild side of the black world. Quite a number of poems, set typically at sunset or early evening, with titles like "Georgia Dusk," "Caribbean Sunset," "Sunset: Coney Island," "Sunset in Dixie," "Summer Evening (Calumet Avenue)," "Suburban Evening," and "Moonlight Night: Carmel," struck a contemplative, almost ele-giac note, at so many moments in Hughes's American wander-ings. Nonetheless, the predominant cultural movement from Africa to Georgia trended northerly and toward Harlem over the course of a long career until almost the moment of his death in a period of civil rights victories and violent ghetto uprisings.

In the first decades of the twentieth century, black New York-ers had created a black city that seemed to offer both the promise of America and a coming of age of the displaced Africans in America in the years following World War I. By 1910, the great migration had tripled New York City's black population in less than two decades. This dislocated demographic group had to go somewhere in New York City, and circumstances, chance, and the canny moves of some black realtors opened up Harlem to the migrants. New legendary addresses (409 Edgecombe Ave-nue), districts ("Strivers' Row," "Sugar Hill," and "Bucket o' Blood"), avenues (Lenox, Edgecombe, and St. Nicholas), old churches in new locations (Abyssinian Baptist and St. Philips

Protestant Episcopal), bars, dance halls, and cabarets (the Cotton Club, Small's Paradise, the Renaissance Casino, and the Savoy Ballroom), and cultural sites (the Tree of Hope, Dark Tower, Lafayette Theater, and the Harlem YMCA) absorbed the energy of the former areas of Little Africa, Chelsea, Hell's Kitchen, and San Juan Hill. Newer, younger writers appropriated the bohemian lifestyle of the Tenderloin District depicted in Paul Laurence Dunbar's *Sport of the Gods* (1902) and Johnson's *Autobiography of an Ex-Colored Man* (1912) as a subject for literature. Virtually every African American author of note of the 1920s— Claude McKay, Countee Cullen, Zora Neale Hurston, Helene Johnson, Walter White, Jessie Redmon Fauset, Nella Larsen, Wallace Thurman, Sterling Brown, and Rudolph Fisher— produced one or more poems, novels, short stories, and/or plays for which Harlem provided a literal or figurative setting. Over the decades, the unprecedented figure of black Harlem became a familiar part of the lexicon of place for literary artists, as many black writers born outside the United States, including Jacques Roumain, Nicolás Guillén, Léopold Senghor, among many others, along with many authors, such as Carl Van Vechten and Federico García Lorca, who were not black, celebrated black Harlem in their works.[3] And the black and racially mixed social constellations of Old New York were consigned virtually to oblivion with the African Burial Ground to await rediscovery at the turn of another new century.

Like the other poets of his generation, Langston Hughes celebrated Harlem in the 1920s as a mythic landscape imbued with intimations of cultural possibility, but, unlike them, Langston Hughes identified the daily life of Harlem with the sounds from the regional centers of jazz and blues, such as the Mississippi Delta, New Orleans, Memphis, St. Louis, and Kansas City, being heard on "race records" cut in Harlem, as well as with African drums. Harlem first appears as a theme in the poetry of Langston Hughes in "Jazzonia," published originally in *The Crisis* (August 1923). "Jazzonia," the only Harlem poem by Langston Hughes reprinted in *The New Negro*, speaks, if cryptically and indirectly, to the relevance of blues and its free-form derivative, jazz, in the riddling complexity of Harlem. The physical scene of a Harlem cabaret is juxtaposed to its contrasting landscape of the spirit: "Oh, shining tree! / Oh, silver rivers of the soul!" (*CP* 34), and the resonating opposites are amplified in unanswered riddles.

No writer addressed the spiritual setting of black Harlem as often as did Langston Hughes in the 1920s. In *The Weary Blues* (1926), Hughes synthesized the urban setting of Harlem with the popular forms of jazz and blues the folk had brought with them to the city. Hughes's first poetry collection, named for the poem that had won him first prize in the *Opportunity* magazine prize competition, contained more Harlem poems, including "Jazzonia," than the entire corpus of all the other New Negro Movement poets combined. The collection's first section, also entitled "The Weary Blues," consisted of fifteen individual poems, which, like blues, flowed together to form a unified continuum for which a mostly nocturnal Harlem is the stated or implied setting. The title poem, "The Weary Blues," paired at the beginning of the sequence with "Jazzonia," captures the blues experience in process with a classic blues. A similar pairing concludes "The Weary Blues" sequence on a similar note. "Blues Fantasy" emphasizes the aesthetic experience of the blues, which transforms trouble and pain into a kind of paradoxical laughter. The intervening poems are Harlem vignettes, cabaret voices validating the truth of the two pairs of poems framing the other eleven. In the Harlem of the blues, Langston Hughes found a term to specify the struggle for human possibility of the America poems, but one perceived through the culturally significant medium of the blues, which retained the expressive character of the drums and the black night of the Africa poems.

With these poems, Langston Hughes initiated a commitment to Harlem as a literary place, the landscape and dreamscape of the blues, which over half a century would be a principal force shaping the development of the Harlem motif among the several generations of black poets since the 1920s. Hughes returned repeatedly to the motif of Harlem as the landscape and dreamscape of blues and jazz over four decades with a maturing and evolving vision. Except for Langston Hughes and Melvin B. Tolson, whose Harlem poems were mostly unpublished in his lifetime, the emerging ghetto Harlem was abandoned as a theme for poetry in the 1940s and 1950s, though several brilliant novels, notably Ann Petry's *The Street* (1946), Ralph Ellison's *Invisible Man* (1952), and James Baldwin's *Go Tell It on the Mountain* (1953), found significance in the deteriorating enclave that had been once associated with optimism, success, and racial amplitude. Hughes's synthesis of the urban setting of Harlem with the popular forms of jazz and blues in *The Weary Blues* (1926) and *Fine Clothes to the Jew* (1927) carried with it the possibility of aesthetic as well as thematic adaptation as Harlem changed for the worse. Langston Hughes's reformulation of the motif was able to respond to disheartening alterations in Harlem's circumstances just as his original usage had reflected the enclave's initial promise, and his evolving practice pointed the way for Harlem's continued elaboration in the poetry of others.

Shakespeare in Harlem (1942), Langston Hughes's first major poetry volume in the forties, continued to see Harlem as a landscape of jazz and blues, but the texture and flavor were very different. The nurturing and liberating Harlem night of *The Weary Blues* was now often dangerous, oppressive, and violent. Three poems were about a dying lover, a hearse, and a suicide, respectively. Others were about loneliness and abandonment. Love, "the little spark" of John Henry's hammer "dying in the dark" in "Love" (*CP* 263), is intertwined with violence and, in "In a Troubled Key," is on the verge of turning "into a knife / Instead of a song" (*CP* 249). The title of the collection specified Harlem, but the Harlem that had seemed unique in the 1920s was now typical, often just a stand-in for Beale Street, West Dallas, or Chicago's South Side. Even the character of the blues had changed. In "Reverie on the Harlem River," a contemplation of suicide, the blues singer's answer-response is oddly defeatist, lacking the traditional resilience of the blues.

Shakespeare in Harlem captured Harlem's existential change but was not Hughes's final word. In *Fields of Wonder* (1947) and *One-Way Ticket* (1949), the bitterness was balanced with irony and transformed in expression. The Harlem poems in *Fields of Wonder* resist the note of despair and bitterness at Harlem's decline. "Dim Out in Harlem" expresses the death of silence, the opposite of transformation through desire and the instrumentality of blues and African drums, but "Stars," first published in *Lincoln University News* (November 1926), was reprinted in the "Stars Over Harlem" section to confront the oblivion of silence with the admonition to dream.

In *One-Way Ticket,* the speaker of "Puzzled," later entitled "Harlem," confronts himself bluntly with the challenge of "What we're gonna do / In the face of / What we remember" (*CP* 263). "The Ballad of Margie Polite," which celebrates the historic anger of the woman who belied her name in the lobby of the Braddock Hotel and provoked the Harlem riot of 1943, gives one kind of answer, but "Negro Servant," first published in *Opportunity* (December 1930), identifies Harlem with the former sense of liberation and release for the black worker on the job: "O, sweet relief from faces that are white!" (*CP* 131).

Montage of a Dream Deferred (1951), though, offered Langston Hughes's new formulation of Harlem in the vocabulary of place for a coming literary generation. The title alludes to the cinematic technique of cutting rapidly from one shot to another, juxtaposing disparate images, and superimposing one frame of film over another without transition. The poems are voices of America's ghettos, edited by Hughes in a montage of more than eighty individual poems, some as brief as a couple of lines, as an evocation of the dream deferred. The vast majority of the individual pieces are unspecified as to setting, and the thematic issue of deferred dreams is defined as broader than either race or place, but it is underscored repeatedly, as by the speaker in "Comment on Curb," that *"I'm talking about / Harlem to you!"* (*CP* 428).

In *Montage of a Dream Deferred,* the theme of Harlem was explored once again in musical terms but now in the contemporary jazz modes of boogie-woogie, bop, and bebop. Many of the poems alluded specifically to the Harlem poems of *The Weary Blues.* "Dream Boogie" (388) introduces the theme of the dream deferred with insinuating rhetorical questions, which recall the riddles about Eve and Cleopatra of "Jazzonia": "Ain't you heard / The boogie-woogie rumble / Of a dream deferred?" The answer, which reoccurs in several inflections throughout, is usually another question ("You think it's a happy beat?"), which restates the question of "Cabaret": Does a jazz band ever sob?" (*CP* 35). And "Juke Box Love Song" echoes the invitation of "Harlem Night Song" as the speaker makes more contemporary sweet talk with common elements of Harlem boogie-woogie neon nightlife.

The volume's most explicit protests against racial injustice are framed by several poems that specify Harlem. "Movies" and "Not a Movie" introduce these poems. In "Movies," Harlem personifies the black community's ironic laughter "in all the wrong places" at the "crocodile art" and "crocodile tears" of Hollywood's falsification of authentic black images in the medium that articulated America's dreams (*CP* 395). "Not a Movie," by way of contrast, presents Harlem's historic role as a city of refuge, even on the street whose reputation for violence earned it the sobriquet "bucket o' blood": "there ain't no Ku Klux / on 133rd" (*CP* 396). And "Projection," whose title and startling animation of Harlem buildings puns on "Movie" and "Not a Movie," imagines the cultural interplay of disparate Harlem social spaces—the Savoy and the Renaissance; Abyssinian Baptist and St. James Episcopalian; 409 Edgecombe and 12 West 33rd—with an improbability that suggests the technique of montage.

"125th Street" and "Dive," two brief poems placed at the midpoint of *Montage of a Dream Deferred,* intersect geographically at Harlem's social center. "125th Street" sketches the elusive face of Harlem with three provocative images—a chocolate bar, a jack-o'-lantern, and a slice of melon— suggesting the black community's resources and inner properties, as well as its often bizarre and misleading exterior, and "Dive" identifies the precipitous quality of Harlem nightlife with Lenox Avenue as it plunges across the map-face of Harlem like a river emptying into the sea of Central Park.

Middle-class Harlemites whose aspirations were more attuned to Bach than to bop but whose dreams were also deferred are a subject too for *Montage of a Dream Deferred.* "College Formal: Renaissance Casino" reprises the diction and romanticism of "Juke Box Love Song" in a different social context. "Deferred" sketches the material, middle-class dreams of some blacks—to graduate, study French, buy two suits at once, see the furniture paid for, pass the civil service examination, and take up Bach. "High to

Low" contrasts St. Philip's, 409 Edgecombe Avenue's, and Sugar
Hill's strivings with the casual down-low ways of the brothers in
the Harlem valley in "Low to High," but "Shame on You" cautions all strivers to consider that there is only a movie house
named after Lincoln in Harlem and nothing at all after John
Brown: "Black people don't remember / Any better than white"
(*CP* 415). "Theme for English B," one of the principal achievements of this section, concerns an essay offered by a student to
his instructor in fulfillment of the assignment to write: "a page
tonight / And let that page come out of you—." The truth that
issues from this young, black CCNY student is the voice of
Harlem. But the youth takes the opportunity to remind the
white teacher that he, too, sings America: "As I learn from you, /
I guess you learn from me— / although you're older—and
white— / and somewhat more free" (*CP* 409–10). "Passing" plays
a particularly ironic riff on the dream deferred. Harlem of the
dream deferred includes even those who have realized their
dreams by fleeing their blackness, for on sunny Sunday after-
noons the ones who have crossed the color line miss "Harlem of
the bitter dream, / since their dream has / come true" (*CP* 417).
"Night Funeral in Harlem" almost turns the theme of deferred
dreams on its head, when everything that is required for the funeral of a destitute Harlemite materializes out of the generosity
of Harlem's common humanity and when even the mechanical
objects of the cityscape contrive to give the poor man a dignified
departure: "the street light / At his corner / Shined just like a
tear" (*CP* 419).

With "Dream Boogie: Variation," which returns to where the
volume began, *Montage of a Dream Deferred* prepares for its thematic finale. This last section, given the subheading "Lenox Avenue Mural," is the most thematically direct. The opening poem,
"Harlem," perhaps the most familiar in the volume because it became the source of the title of Lorraine Hansberry's *A Raisin in
the Sun*, identifies the dream deferred explicitly with Harlem.
"What happens to a dream deferred?" (*CP* 426) the poem asks but
answers in the form of other questions. Here the technique of
posing rhetorical riddles, which Hughes employed in "Jazzonia"
in *The Weary Blues* and in "Good Morning Daddy" in *Montage of a*

Dream Deferred, has now become a complete and self-contained discourse. The poem, constituted entirely of answer-questions, becomes a kind of climactic moment in *Montage of a Dream Deferred*, for the ominous kinetic potential of "the something underneath" is finally revealed as potentially explosive. In "Good Morning," whose title recalls the opening poem of *Montage of a Dream Deferred*, a reverie by a native Harlemite about the growth of his community with neighbors who came "dark / wondering / wide-eyed / dreaming" (CP 427) from all over the Americas concludes with the same question that begins "Harlem" ("What happens / to a dream deferred?") and answers it with the mocking rhetorical retort of "Dream Boogie" ("Daddy, ain't you heard?"). And "Comment on Curb," cited earlier, erases any lingering doubt that Harlem and the dream deferred are illustrations of each other in Langston Hughes's lyric vocabulary.

The final implication of Harlem's physical and spiritual geography as the site of the dream deferred is revealed with a new formulation about rivers. In "Island," the poet of "The Negro Speaks of Rivers" triangulates the site of the dream deferred in Harlem in the narrow stretch of Manhattan between the Hudson River and the Harlem River. The Harlem-dream deferred identification is, then, perfected with a restatement of its three principal riffs. Harlem, the great black metropolis, within New York City, the great white metropolis, symbolizes the dreams of black America deferred within the American dream, in terms that still echo the Africa poems of the 1920s. Finally, Langston Hughes's *Montage of a Dream Deferred* ends with the same jazzy interrogative with which the volume began: "Good morning, daddy! / Ain't you heard?"

After *Montage of a Dream Deferred*, a new generation of African American poets began to turn to Harlem for inspiration, for among Langston Hughes's achievements was the volume's successful rehabilitation of Harlem as an Africana motif offering some promise in spite of the ghetto's decline, just as he had established Harlem's emblematic relevance and potential more profoundly than any other New Negro poet a generation earlier. By characterizing Harlem as a montage of the dream deferred, Hughes not only presented a valid new concept of Harlem, one consistent with the discourse of rivers, but also issued an implicit challenge: "Ain't you heard?" Younger poets in the literary constellations of the Umbra Workshop, in New York City, and of *Dasein: Quarterly Journal of the Arts*, at Howard University, in Washington, D.C., turned, slowly at first and then with increasing frequency and intensity, to Harlem as the civil rights movement took hold in the black American consciousness and as the dream deferred threatened to explode. Their Harlem poems, anthologized in such groundbreaking collections as *Beyond the Blues: New Poetry by American Negroes* (1962), *Sixes and Sevens: An Anthology of New Poetry* (1963), and *Burning Spear: An Anthology of Afro-Saxon Poetry* (1963), were often landscapes of clashing imagery that conveyed the Harlem ghetto's oblique beauty while depicting its desperation. Their perceptions of Harlem, published on the eve of the Harlem uprising of 1964, prepared the way for a vision of racial possibility within the landscapes of the inner city, which would be sifted from the ashes of the Harlem riot of 1964.

4

In the early 1950s, the push and the pull of Africa's and America's promise and frustration had shifted again. In a pithy stanza, published in *Phylon* (3rd quarter 1951), a voice like the speaker's in "Negro" declares his Negro self to be the "American Heartbreak" in a tone of mild exasperation. In "Prelude to Our Age: A Negro History Poem" [379–84], a kind of verse tableaux vivant published in *The Crisis* (February 1951), and in "Ballad of Negro History," a kind of verse chronicle published a year later in *Negro History Bulletin* (February 1952), Langston Hughes opened up the movement from Africa to America, which he had implied in powerful but economic strokes in "The Negro Speaks of Rivers" and in "Negro," with a considerably more detailed picture of the historic progression that had preceded Jamestown. In both poems, Hughes places the American relationship with persons of African descent that began in Jamestown in the context of a longer, more glorious past, which could be traced back even to the most ancient pages of history. In "Prelude to Our Age," the emphasis is on "the chapters / Of recorded time / [where] Shadows of so many hands / Have fallen, / Among them mine. / *Negro*" (*CP* 379). In "A Ballad of Negro History" the emphasis is on how "[o]n each page of history / Glows a dusky face" (*CP* 434). The epic catalog of black heroes / heroines is similar in both poems. Though "Prelude to Our Age" gives pride of place to writers, intellectuals, and other cultural workers of African origins (from Homer's "blameless Ethiopians," Aesop, Antar, Terence, and Juan Latino to T. Thomas Fortune, Franklin Frazier, William Hastie, and Charles R. Drew), whereas "A Ballad of Negro History" gives more attention to political and military heroes (pharaohs, generals, and leaders of slave uprisings), the celebration of African America's roots in an ancient and glorious Negro past is central to both.

In poems published in the decade before his death, during the period of the civil rights movement in the South and of National Liberation Movements in Africa, Hughes's well-established literary terms for Africa continued to inflect his sense of America's possibility, now tinged with hints of a momentous arousal in America anticipated and precipitated by events in his ancestral homeland. "Africa," in *The Crisis* (March 1953), announces the awakening of a "Sleepy giant" with images of "the thunder / and the lightning / in your smile" (*CP* 441). "We, Too," in the *New Orlando Anthology* (1963), pairs the civil rights movement in the South with the emergence of new nations from colonialism in Africa: "from ageless darks / . . . We, too, / Congo Brother, / Rise with you" (*CP* 538). And "Junior Addict," in *Liberator* (April 1963), expresses the faith that a "Sunrise out of Africa" will offer prospects even to the despairing youth with "ears that close to Harlem screams" (*CP* 539), who stick needles in their arms in America's black ghettos. Characteristically, Hughes had refined his literary language for Africa and America in the early poems— continuity of shared culture and identity of shared suffering, voiced above all in the cry of the drums and associated with both dark skin and the dark night—to such a degree of transparency and simplicity that it has been easy to miss the fact that, in some poems in which the context is specifically American, Hughes was still working within the imagery and diction established in the Africa poems, and vice versa. Juxtapose "Dinner Guest: Me," published in *Negro Digest* (September 1965), with "I, Too," Hughes's initial statement of his sense of American perfectibility, for example, or "Suburban Evening," published in *The Crisis* (April 1967) not long before his death, with "Afraid," one of the four basic Africa poems of the 1920s discussed earlier. It is as much because of the many achievements of the African liberation movements, as the civil rights movement, that the speaker in "Dinner Guest: Me" now sits at a dinner table on Park Avenue with white diners, instead of waiting in their kitchen like the speaker of "I, Too," but the largely unchanged question of America under discussion at the dinner table is expressed in the shorthand of Hughes's literary terms for Africa: "The why and wherewithal / Of darkness U.S.A." (*CP* 547). Similarly, only if those terms are recalled on some level will the reader understand how the emotional tranquility of "Suburban Evening" can be transformed for the speaker for no apparent reason when a dog howls in a peaceful desegregated suburb. Langston Hughes's carefully and consistently cultivated diction of place "[m]ay play host / To quiet / Unreasonable / Ghosts" (*CP* 553).

5

Each year, when I attend the choral reading program of the City College Langston Hughes festival and see one elementary school student after another reciting Hughes's poetry—especially the Harlem poems of blues and jazz—as part of a familiar and reassuring exercise of our African American cultural legacy, I have to remind myself of what I have learned as a literary historian about Langston Hughes. Hughes's celebration of the culture of the migrants was neither familiar nor reassuring to important elements of his readership in the 1920s. The migrants' down-home culture of southern ways was just what needed to be changed and refined in the name of uplift, according to the programs of some of the same organizations that provided institutional encouragement for the young black artists of the Harlem Renaissance. Over time, the spirituals had come to be accepted as dignified and ennobling folk forms, but blues and jazz were still embarrassing reminders of a low-down status and a too-flexible sexual morality that the Negro elite was striving to live down. It required daring, impudence, and genius for Hughes to choose the music the black migrants had brought with them to the North as the aesthetic for his American song. It was provocative and controversial to do so. Reviews of Hughes's poetry were often discouraging, and few of the major African American poets of his generation followed his lead. Nonetheless, Langston Hughes was the primary figure of his generation in this respect. In the literary usage of his American places, Hughes subsumed the two-ness and the double self, which W. E. B. Du Bois had defined in *The Souls of Black Folk* (1903) as the striving to be both a Negro and an American and which Alain Locke reinterpreted as the mission of a new generation in "The New Negro." Hughes responded to Du Bois's call to the new century, and, like his contemporaries, he shared Locke's faith that a coming of age for the New Negro in Harlem would correspond to the emergence of a new but still developing America. But, unlike his literary counterparts, Langston Hughes placed his Harlem squarely in an African American cultural and philosophical frame of reference in which medium as well as message could be embodied in culturally received forms by associating the Harlem setting with jazz and blues and, later, bebop, musical folk forms recognized to be black and even African in origin and values. By connecting the black urban experience of the first half of the twentieth century with the very forms the folk had chosen to bring with them to the city, as their enslaved ancestors had carried their sorrow songs "from Africa to Georgia," Hughes played the role of both receiver of a popular cultural legacy and shaper of this tradition into literary form. He rooted his literary language of place in music, the singular cultural form in which blacks had always managed to find self-expression and plenitude in America. In the terms of his own literary language, his faith in America resided in his understanding of the expressive character and the power of the music that the Negro had created across time and carried across continents as his soul grew deep with the rivers. And, because he conjoined the struggles and hopes of blacks in motifs of place reflecting the cultural terms of their subjectivity, in the crucible that was transforming them from a rural to an urban people, his poetry continued to respond and develop in the face of historic adversity and change, and his literary voice retained its resonance and timbre while most of his celebrated literary contemporaries in the New Negro Movement lapsed into relative silence.

A brief poem by Langston Hughes puts his literary usage of place in perspective. In "Aesthete in Harlem" [128], the only Harlem poem in *Dear Lovely Death* (1931), the dramatized speaker seems to speak for Langston Hughes and his literary use of place as he ponders the ironies and paradoxes of universality and literary transcendence: "Strange, / That in this nigger place, / I should meet Life face to face" (*CP* 128).

NOTES

1. See my article "Places" in *The Oxford Companion to African American Literature* (New York: Oxford University Press, 1997): 575–79.

2. Alain Locke, "The New Negro," in *The New Negro*, ed. Locke (1925; rpt. New York: Touchstone, 1997), 16.

3. See James de Jongh, *Vicious Modernism: Black Harlem and the Literary Imagination* (New York: Cambridge University Press, 1990).

Langston Hughes and Afro-American Vernacular Music

Steven C. Tracy

> Like the waves of the sea coming one
> after another, always one after another,
> like the earth moving around the sun,
> night, day—night, day—night, day—
> forever, so is the undertow of black
> music with its rhythm that never be-
> trays you, its strength like the beat of
> the human heart, its humor, and its
> rooted power.
>
> —Langston Hughes, *The Big Sea*

It was the year that the opera star Enrico Caruso made his first recordings; that the Dinwiddie Colored Quartet made the first phonograph recordings by Afro-Americans; that Ma Rainey initiated her singing career in a traveling show and first heard the blues in a small Missouri town; that the blues performers Son House, Skip James, Barbecue Bob, Viola "Miss Rhapsody" Wells, and Peetie Wheatstraw were born. And 1902 was the year that the Missouri-born Langston Hughes first drew breath in a new and exciting century bursting with technological and artistic energy and poised to revolutionize pop culture and transform the gulf between so-called high and low art to a steppe gladly and easily traversed. It was a small steppe for man, but a giant leap for humankind. These occurrences were all events of importance to Hughes, and though their significance may not be immediately apparent to us, we can see in Hughes's life their synthesis. Caruso's name became synonymous with the opera. The sacred and secular music of Afro-Americans began to emerge in twentieth-century incarnations on phonograph records. The music known as the blues was expanded and exercised to a remarkable breadth of diversity for its humble form, as evidenced by the dissimilar styles of the fellow Mississippi blues performers House and James and by the stylistic differences between their music and that of Atlanta's Barbecue Bob, the cabaret singer Viola Wells, and Peetie Wheatstraw, of St. Louis. In comparison, Langston Hughes's name became synonymous with Afro-American literature, with the recognition and honoring of Afro-American folk music, and the expansion of the boundaries of American high art to include the remarkable variety of blues culture. His work is a profound and courageous embrace of American cultural ideals in the face of shameful sociopolitical actualities.

Poet, short story writer, novelist, playwright, essayist, autobiographer, children's writer, translator, librettist, Hughes envisioned Afro-American vernacular music on the printed page, on the Broadway stage, and in the opera house. Then he helped put them there, and without ever losing sight or sound of the fact that they didn't need to be there to be important. But for some people, he knew, those were the only places they would encounter them, and encounter them they must. If art could indeed advance social causes, could help overcome the prejudices that separated Afro-Americans into an inferior social and political position—if it could ameliorate the problem of the twentieth century, as W. E. B. Du Bois called it, the problem of the color line—then it would have to be an art with the vigor, energy, passion, wisdom, and perseverance of the so-called folk, served up in the bubbling pot of Afro-American vernacular music. That pot would be like the one Huck Finn described at the outset of "his" novel novel, one in which the elements swapped juices in a marvelous stew because, gustatorially, nutritionally, and democratically speaking, things just go better that way.

The source is speech: the language and thoughts and impulses of the people, ushered into print in the rip-roaring tall tales of the frontier, the stories of the literary humorists, the regional sketches of the local colorists, the colloquialism of the dialect poets, the isochronic bardic lines of Walt Whitman, all of which was relegated in the nineteenth century to a substratum of American literature, buried beneath literature sometimes worthy of its Minnehahas. American society and literature, rooted in a European world based on aristocratic privilege, even as it tried to rise above it, desperately needed to get acclimated to the idea and the actuality of democracy in order to be able to make it work.

Nineteenth-century American Romantics, declaring their literary independence by championing native themes, styles, and/ or genius, sought to express their nationalism in a variety of ways. One prominent way was to reflect upon New World Nature and its rustic inhabitants, through idyllic nature poetry, myth making out of the lives of frontier folks, or creating a raucous strain of American humor out of the language and actions of rural "primitives." Such eighteenth-century writers as William Byrd II, Ebenezer Cook, and Sarah Kemble Knight, coming from similar socioeconomic levels, had looked down their collective proboscis at their social inferiors as they explored the language and lifestyles of the lower classes with a disinterested or bemused attitude, for derisively comic purposes, or with outright mockery or contempt. However, American Romantics attempted to take a more sympathetic, if still sometimes condescending, look at vernacular culture and, following Robert Burns's nationalistic use of dialect, vernacular dialect began to find its way into the Romantic literature of America. Later, the Realists, with their quest for absolute fidelity to external realities and details, and the local colorists, with their post–Civil War imperative to capture and portray the life of regional communities feared to be fading with the advance of industrialization, began to employ dialect to reflect both the national identity and regional distinctiveness and individualism. Dialect poets, those writing both within and against the southern "Plantation school" of apologists, frequently relied upon superficial spelling and punctuation grotesqueries and contorted syntax to portray their subjects, though the best and most successful, such as the poets James Whitcomb Riley, Paul Laurence Dunbar, Daniel Webster Davis, and James Edwin Campbell, at times transcended those limitations. Clearly, American literature was wrestling with the problem of accurately depicting the vernacular socially, stylistically, and politically.

What we have in Hughes is the New Negro Modernist, heir to the varied strands of Romanticism, Realism, American humor, local color regionalism, and dialect poetry that converged in his work to provide a staff on which Hughes could compose his syncopated musical score. Significantly, the source of the word for this prominent element of Afro-American music is "syncope," which means a skipped heartbeat. Hughes regularly made the connection between Afro-American music and the beating of the human heart, which keeps the stream of life pumping in our veins. In this case, a missed heartbeat is that which makes us aware of life through its exciting, offbeat, unexpected, and sudden, rollicking refocusing of our beating and breathing on the unjustly ignored territories of sound and art. That is, we are redirected to a fuller consideration of the possibilities of our lives from the domination of the accented increment—into the vernacular space, the democratic space, the inspiration and expiration space. Hughes knew that if you take the breath away from poetry, then it will surely die. The breath is the inspiration, the giver of life and voice to be neither trifled with nor judged to be trifling. And this black man's inspiration is the exclusive white world's expiration, reflex actions at odds with each other that must be synchronized in order to stimulate and support life. A truly American literature must breathe with all of its people, breed with all its people, or descend to a slavishness most unbecoming to American ideals. Nearly a millennium before Hughes lived, Horace wrote, in *Ars Poetica*, that "It is hard to be original in treating well-worn subjects" (83). This was the challenge Hughes faced as an Afro-American writer: to utter the actual thoughts and concerns of his people, expressed in a style appropriate to its sources, in a way that allowed him to establish a valued identity in relation to both the folk and literary traditions. For Hughes, the folk and literary traditions were not mutually exclusive, nor were the vernacular tradition and the polemical tradition. He was assuredly the heir to his politically committed Afro-American forebears as well, from Phillis Wheatley to Gustavus Vassa, David Walker, Martin Delany, Frederick Douglass, Frances E. W. Harper, Booker T. Washington, W. E. B. Du Bois, and so many others. Significantly, Hughes described hearing the blues as a child on Independence Avenue ("Jazz as Communication" 493), and when you're hearing something on Independence Avenue, you sho nuff know you *got* to listen to the full swing of freedom. And if you're a black child in the South in the early twentieth century—well! You know the euphonious sound of freedom when you hear it.

I

That sound, of course, had been making its intermittent, halting clangs heard politically, socially, and literarily for more than a century before Hughes's birth. Ringing most ominously and promisingly for Afro-Americans at the epoch of the second American revolution, the Civil War, the battleground had been forced to the forefront decisively, in part by John Brown's raid on Harpers Ferry, in which Hughes's maternal grandfather took part. As America emerged from its trial by firearms into an era of Reconstruction, it found itself poised to usher in a century of American ascendancy, one necessarily focusing on the rights and privileges of the masses of Americans whose lives were not always touched by the beneficence of democracy.

Indeed, American popular music was being transformed in the nineteenth century by the interest in plantation melodies and dances that began to find its way slowly into the popular arena on the emerging minstrel stage. The spirituals and jubilee songs, as well as the work songs, reels, game songs, and, later, ballads, were much remarked and praised for what was often described by white commentators as their weird but affecting beauty. Publication of the collection *Slave Songs of the United States* (1867) and the tours of the Fisk Jubilee Singers (1871) and the Hampton Jubilee Singers (1872) helped solidify the popularity of these religious songs in this country and in Europe. Hughes himself, following the lead of such New Negro forefathers as W. E. B. Du Bois, James Weldon Johnson, and Alain Locke, would pay tribute to spirituals as one of the "two great Negro gifts to American music" ("Songs Called the Blues" 143), calling them, following Du Bois's nomenclature, "the sorrow songs" in both "Aunt Sue's Stories" and "Negro" (*CP* 23–24). "All the way from Africa to Georgia," Hughes writes in the latter, "I carried my sorrow songs," equating their source and strength with the powerful blackness of the African spirit. Although the spirituals don't occur in Hughes's poems and plays as frequently as the blues, he does reference spirituals such as "Swing Low Sweet Chariot," "Go Down Moses," "Nobody Knows the Trouble I've Seen," and "Oh, Freedom" in a variety of poems, such as "Ballad of Seven Songs," from 1949, and in the folk protest play *Don't You Want to be Free?* In the poem "Spirituals," Hughes associates the genre with the sources of great things—rocks, roots, and black mothers that produce mountains, trees and branches, and black children. "Song," he pronounces about not only spirituals but all song, "is a strong thing" (*CP* 102). Significantly, it is the "dicty" Tempy and her husband, who scorn "Swing Low" and other spirituals as being beneath "respectability," who are the middle-class "villains" of Hughes's novel *Not Without Laughter*, foils to the blues-singing heroine Harrietta, who reconciles the religious and secular in her life and art. They could not recognize, as did the composer Antonin Dvořák, the beauty of the spirituals as he employed their strains in his *Symphony No. 9* (1893). Hughes clearly found the spirituals as affecting as the heroine of his short story "The Blues I'm Playing," Oceola, who loves to teach spirituals to choirs in her churches because of the way the songs make them move, promote action. Reginald Wilson associated Hughes's work with both Africa and the sacred tradition in America: "In Africa, one would call Langston, 'Nommo,' the carrier of the Word, and his word is 'Do, Jesus!'" The spirituals were not just melodies and lyrics but imperatives, exhortations, calls to movement.

As early as the late 1700s, white performers had begun blacking up to perform "Negro" comic and sentimental songs based on strains from the religious and secular songs of southern plantation Afro-Americans. But it was not until 1828, when Thomas D. Rice learned "Jump Jim Crow" from a crippled Afro-American stablehand and took his act on the road in the early 1830s, that minstrelsy began to emerge in earnest. By February 1843, when the Virginia Minstrels, Dan Emmett, and others performed a full evening of minstrel entertainment that marked the official emergence of the minstrel show in New York City, and 1855, when the first recorded Afro-American minstrel troupe, The Mocking Bird Minstrels, was formed, it was clear that a major, influential form of entertainment was about to take center stage in American popular culture.

Minstrel show performances served a variety of purposes for both white and black audiences and performers. The negative stereotypes employed in minstrel shows are apparent in the "coon" songs that were quite prominent in nineteenth-century American popular music. The chicken and watermelon stealing, grotesque appetites and violent actions, naïveté and simplemindedness, and occasional egotism attributed to the characters, and the sentimental condescension toward slaves inherent in the shows, were all couched in grammatical and syntactical contortions that rivaled the grotesqueries of the burnt-cork mask and lazy physical displays on the stage. But, even as they exaggerated and demeaned this alien culture, the songs and performances provided white audiences with a much-needed glimpse into a culture foreign to theirs. There was, in a sense, a cultural informing that was taking place, though the stereotypes undercut the cultural transmission and acceptance by reinforcing the feelings of superiority and the legitimacy of superior social status in the white audience.

Although we imagine black participation in such shows to be quite demeaning, minstrel shows in fact also provided opportunities for gainful employment and artistic expression for Afro-Americans, even as the stereotypes frequently reinforced the ceiling on their level of advancement. Will Marion Cook's "Clorindy, The Origin of the Cakewalk," for example, opened on Broadway in 1896, just six years before Hughes was born. "A Trip to Coontown" (1898–1899) provided Afro-Americans with their first full-length musical comedy with a continuous plot to act out on the stage. Irving Jones ("The Ragtime Millionaire" and "All Birds Look Like Chickens to Me") and James Bland ("Carry Me Back to Old Virginia" and "Dem Golden Slippers") were both popular composers in the minstrel tradition, as was Ernest Hogan, author of the infamous "All Coons Look Alike to Me" (originally titled the more offensive [!] "All Pimps Look Alike to Me"). And Ike Simond's *Old Slack's Reminiscence and Pocket History of the Colored Profession from 1865 to 1891* (1892) provides a brief but specific look at the performers involved in the minstrel shows on the stage, attesting to its popularity among audiences and to its value as an employer of Afro-American performers.

It would be impossible to believe, however, that black and white performers and audiences responded in the same ways to the depictions of Afro-Americans in minstrel shows. Surely black audiences perceived stereotypical portrayals of themselves with a jaundiced and ironic eye, even as naïve white audiences might swallow the chicken- and watermelon-stealing whole. It was possible, even likely, that black and white audiences walked away from such productions with entirely different perceptions of what had taken place on stage. A number of years ago, an older Afro-American musician informed me that he had been in minstrel shows when he was in elementary school in the South. When I asked him how it felt to be portraying the stereotypical chicken and watermelon thievery, fully expecting his embarrassment, he responded, "It was true." He recalled having to steal to survive as a child, a social reality of his racial childhood that, although not explicitly portrayed in the performances themselves, was implicit in his understanding of the stereotypes as he acted them out. Psychologically, the minstrel shows could also allow white performers to flirt with "race mixing" by offering them a black persona in which they could act out fantasies, desires, and stereotypes with impunity. Meanwhile, they offered black performers a chance to mock the stereotypes, and the white audience, from behind a "white" black mask—and to collect money (albeit frequently an insufficient amount) at the end of the performance. Behind these songs and performances, behind the songs of the composer Stephen Foster, who sold "Camptown Races" to the Christy Minstrels in 1850 and went on to write other famous songs in the tradition, lay crouching the gothic horror story of American chattel slavery and race relations, restrained by a thin layer of burnt-cork mask.

Hughes confronted the minstrel tradition briefly in several instances in his creative work, opting to challenge the stereotypes of the minstrel persona. In the poem "Song for a Banjo Dance," a poem in the Dunbar dialect tradition complete with "honey," "chile," and plunking banjo, these stereotypically carefree elements form a backdrop to a serious carpe diem message—that the sun is going down and might never rise again (*CP* 29). One needs to look beneath the surface of the situation in order to perceive the serious possibilities inherent in the experience. "Minstrel Man" again reminds of Dunbar, this time of his classic statement, in "We Wear the Mask," of the need for African American subterfuge to promote safety. Hughes cautions the reader that the superficial elements of the minstrel mask and pose are illusory, that the minstrel is, as the blues tradition would have it, "laughin to keep from cryin." The supposedly comic minstrel in fact reaches a tragic end with the final words of the poem, "I die" (*CP* 61). However, as Hughes makes clear in "The Blues I'm Playing," the minstrel is not in and of himself a negative figure but is a figuration of the tragedy of African American life. In that story, Oceola recalls fondly the days when her stepfather traveled with Billy Kersands's minstrels, and how he entertained the small child by allowing her to put both of her hands inside his mouth simultaneously. This was a sign not only of the comic largeness of his mouth, but evidence as well of his sensitivity and thoughtfulness in entertaining the little girl traveling on the road with the troupe. By looking at and dealing with the minstrel as man, innocently, without preconception, the child laughs not at him but with him, one of Hughes's primary humanistic goals. In the poem "Laughers," Hughes characterizes the heirs of the minstrel shows, the black vaudevillians, as being among "his" people, "loud-mouthed laughers in the hands / Of Fate," whose defiance, perseverance, strength, and joie de vivre exemplify the E Pluribus Unum of the Afro-American spirit (*CP* 27).

One other type of Afro-American music was capturing the imagination of Americans in the popular culture of the time. It was music with a rough and rollicking quality that spirits its listeners into the social, spiritual, and musical vernacular space so valued by Hughes. Ragtime music likely had been developing for some time by the 1870s, when there are suggestions that it was being performed by various now-anonymous pianists. Certainly it had been around for at least a decade by the time it began to gain a following in Sedalia, St. Louis, and Louisville and at the Chicago World's Fair in 1893, three years before the first songs labeled "ragtime" were published and four years before the banjoist Vess Ossman recorded the first ragtime songs. Ragtime's major piano composers and practitioners—Scott Joplin, James Scott, Joseph Lamb, and James P. Johnson among them—were Afro-American pianists with great skill at this highly syncopated, Afro-European hybrid. The ragtime craze of the 1890s to 1920, as a matter of fact, once again highlighted the American popular taste for Afro-American music. Significantly, it also provided some composers such as Scott Joplin (*Treemonisha*, from 1911) and James P. Johnson (*Yamekraw*, from 1927, and *Jazzamine Concerto*, from 1934) the opportunity to pursue a wedding of Afro-American and European forms and ideas in concert works, though of course the gulf between popular appreciation and social acceptance remained wide. In fact, ragtime's influence not only pervaded popular music of the time but also participated in the formation of jazz, blues, elements of musical theater, and even the music of classical composers. For one thing, talented and trained ragtime pianists would "rag" the classics—take a piece of classical music and perform it in ragtime's highly syncopated style—or "classicize" the rags by taking a ragtime melody and playing it in the style of European classical composers. James Weldon Johnson portrays both in *Autobiography of an Ex-Colored Man* (1912). Jelly Roll Morton demonstrates the former in his

Library of Congress recording, made in 1938 for Alan Lomax, of "The Miserere," and Fats Waller the latter in his famous composition "Honeysuckle Rose," recorded at the RCA studios in 1941.

Hughes himself wrote, in his 1951 poem "Prelude to Our Age," that "Ragtime sets the pattern for a nation's songs" (*CP* 382), and his famous poem "Negro," from 1922, names ragtime as one of the Afro-Americans' signal contributions to world culture (*CP* 24). Of course, in their own minds, many Afro-Americans did not have to associate their music with the European classics to demonstrate its value or viability. There were, of course, Afro-American classical composers in the nineteenth century, such as Edmond and Eugene Dédé and Lucièn and Sidney Lambert, who anticipated a link between European classical music and Afro-American vernacular music in their works. But these kinds of boundary-stretching genres did provide entrée for Afro-American music into popular and haute culture salons, making it harder and harder to ignore the important contributions Afro-Americans had made, were making, and could make to American culture.

2

Such cultural cross-breeding and borrowing in literature and the musical arts, however effective or successful it might have been, served to move Afro-American culture and music closer to the popular mainstream. By creating a popular interest in and an audience for Afro-American vernacular forms, these various artistic avenues helped create a blueprint for the employment of aspects of Afro-American vernacular culture in the work of classical composers such as Darius Milhaud, Igor Stravinsky, Ernst Krenek, Paul Hindemith, George Antheil, George Gershwin, William Levi Dawson, and William Grant Still, as well as in the productions of literary modernists and New Negro authors of the 1920s. However, they also established a tradition of dealing with vernacular culture against which an author would have to write. Afro-American writers like Langston Hughes would have to make their point that the older generations of Afro-Americans had great wisdom and beauty to pass on in vernacular forms if only current and future generations would recognize their value. By subverting the negative stereotypes and condescension, they could provide a corrective to the stilted portrayals and misinformation that had come before them. This was especially true when the primary reading audience was composed of people from outside the Afro-American racial group who had been schooled in the stereotypes of previous American literature and popular culture. Hughes wanted to see to it that representatives of vernacular culture were not always a laughing matter.

One of the most important elements in the dissemination of Afro-American music in the twentieth century was Thomas Edison's invention of the phonograph in 1877. It took some thirteen years for Afro-Americans to finally appear on Edison's phonograph cylinders, a quarter century for the Dinwiddie Colored Quartet to turn up on a phonograph disc, and nearly half a century for Afro-American blues to make its triumphant debut, in 1920, in the person of Mamie Smith. The implications for American culture were great, especially given the historical forces that had come together to position Americans finally to confront and deal with the "Negro problem" in a postbellum, urban, industrialized environment. The entry of the Afro-American artist into the national marketplace, even in its remotest regions, presenting the possibility of permeating the American environment with reasonably authentic representations of Afro-American style, creativity, and technical ability, meant that no longer would sheet music, mechanical piano rolls, or secondhand imitations have exclusive rule over the popular dissemination of Afro-American music. These brittle, primitive recording vehicles would prove remarkable in helping to generate an enduring modern art with significant repercussions for the folk, popular, and literary culture of the world.

During the 1920s, writers of the New Negro Renaissance, such as Hughes, Sterling Brown, and Zora Neale Hurston, were attempting to forge a new and revitalized literature that reflected the spirit and genius of Afro-American culture. They drew on the poetic inspiration of Afro-American folklore, especially, for Hughes, the blues, both in its folk forms and in the vaudeville blues get-up that had emerged on recordings in 1920 and that dominated the blues recording industry during its first decade. The early years of commercial blues recordings were dominated by women singers, from the earliest recordings of Mamie Smith, Lillyn Brown, and Lavinia Turner to the milestone recordings of Bessie Smith and Ma Rainey. John Godrich and R. M. W. Dixon report that the years 1923–1926 were the years of the ascendancy of the vaudeville blues singers, "professional singers who sang mostly for city audiences, using fairly standard song material" written often by professional songsmiths interested in altering traditional folk blues forms (33). It was these blues singers, sometimes ostentatiously dressed as exotic, feathered "hot mamas" for the stage (as opposed to singing their blues in the environment in which the genre had originally been created), that a broad, popular city audience often first identified with blues music. Indeed, these women dominated the numerous resident and traveling stage shows and revues of the twenties, indelibly fixing them as the central figures of the first blues craze, though they had already, to varying degrees, left behind aspects of their folk blues roots.

Harlem, of course, was one of the places where such commercial presentations were concocted for crowds of slumming white patrons, who flocked to places like the Cotton Club or to clubs like those mentioned in Rudolph Fisher's "The Caucasian Storms Harlem" to feed their primitivist fantasies about blacks. It was in part just such an interest on the part of wealthy white patrons—along with some sincere interest in progressive race relations, social justice, and artistic camaraderie—that helped sustain the Harlem Renaissance and in part worked to move in the direction of freeing blacks from facile, racist, delimiting stereotypes. Blues and jazz found an important place in the work of several New Negro Renaissance authors. However, not all middle-class blacks, who through their socioeconomic status were frequently centrally involved in supporting the movement, could or would accept what they deemed such ignorant and sinful creations, preferring either sacred music or imitations of white Western art products to help mainstream themselves into white American society. In an attempt to leave behind the experiences of slavery and of the Reconstruction and post-Reconstruction South for the promising urban world of race, class, and political advancement, many middle-class Afro-Americans frequently sought to bury their rural heritage.

On the other hand, Hughes, Brown, and Hurston found blues and jazz to be creations of strength and beauty, providing a rallying point for pride in heritage, in the "common Person," and in the vernacular. "The tom-tom of revolt against weariness in a white world" Hughes called jazz, in "The Negro Artist and the Racial Mountain," associating it not with resignation, defeat, or ignorance but with the racial struggle (308). Like Whitman putting the reins in the hands of a black man in *Song of Myself*, so Hughes, Brown, and Hurston place the spirit of their work in the hands of Afro-American vernacular music makers. Blues harmonica players who specialize in playing diatonic harmonicas are frequently asked how they make so much music with what is, to many, merely a ten-holed toy. The answer is threefold: you don't think of the harmonica as a toy; you don't treat it like a toy; and you allow it to become an extension of your voice. If you just let your voice come through it, it will help you say whatever you want by providing its own focus, order, and discipline, all the while maintaining an admirable flexibility. So it is with the vernacular tradition in art: the seemingly simple, uncomplicated instrument of expression becomes one of great subtlety and power.

None of these three writers, though, was wholly pleased with the commercialization of black people's music. This commercial representation of the blues was criticized by Brown, who found its "crudities" and "sophisticated smut" to be a reduction of the blues to the level of "cabaret appetizers" (Brown 1930, 339). Unfortunately, such representations were just another part of American society's feeble and misguided efforts to come to terms with and to control the progress of blacks in the twentieth century by reducing them to mere entertainments and sexual stereotypes. Of course, all of the vaudeville blues did not find themselves thus reduced, even if many were perceived that way by imperceptive whites. Ultimately, vaudeville blues singers contributed greatly to the success of the New Negro Renaissance and to the art of Langston Hughes, in direct contrast to the "high road" of Keatsianism and Victorianism employed by his friend and "rival" Countee Cullen.

Of course, behind the vaudeville blues was the folk blues tradition so familiar to Hughes, Hurston, and Brown. The latter two especially were familiar with the pioneering work done by collectors such as H. E. Krehbiel, Henry Davis, Guy Johnson, Howard Odum, Gates Thomas, John Lomax, and others in the early years of the twentieth century. Hurston herself was a valued collector of Afro-American folklore, and she and Hughes traveled together in the South for a brief period and heard a number of folk performers (*TBS* 296), culminating in their collaboration on the folk play *Mule Bone*. They were familiar, in other words, with the various styles of folk blues that began to achieve commercial success later than the vaudeville brand, though the folk blues predated the vaudeville style. During 1927–1930, the peak prewar years for the issuance of blues and gospel records (Godrich and Dixon 104–5), five hundred blues and gospel recordings were released per year. Field excursions by major record companies to Atlanta, Memphis, Dallas, New Orleans, and other locations greatly expanded the types of blues issued for the "race" market, but not for the popular (read white) market to any degree. Since the use of the words "blues" and "jazz" signified a different and broader group of musics for many Afro-American artists in the twenties (and later) than for their white Modernist counterparts, the use of those terms by Modernists must be read in the light of their familiarity with only a segment of the variety of blues and jazz music, as well as in light of their sometimes racist responses, deliberate or not, to Afro-Americans.

3

White writers had been attempting to come to terms with the meaning of Afro-American vernacular music and its relation to their writing tradition, as we have said, for many years. By the twentieth century, a number of prominent white American writers were employing aspects of that tradition. Vachel Lindsay, who helped "jump-start" Hughes's career after a chance meeting with the busboy poet in 1925, had attempted to achieve a "higher vaudeville" and to reproduce the rhythms of Afro-American music to create his own poetry. The poet Carl Sandburg, an early stylistic influence on Hughes, recalled listening to a black folk performer on the streets of Galesburg, Illinois, in his childhood. He featured folk songs at his poetry readings and recorded several items, the Afro-American ballad "Boll Weevil" among them, in 1926. One year later, he prepared *The American Songbag*, a collection of 260 American folk songs, for publication. Sherwood Anderson wrote, in *Dark Laughter*, of songs of Afro-Americans that demonstrated "an unconscious love of inanimate things lost to whites" (106) that "had sometimes a way of getting at the ultimate truth of things" (248). But Lindsay himself felt slandered as a "jazzer" (xxxii), and he focused on the "picturesquely exotic" (Brown 1937, 94–95), thus capturing some of the heat, but not the light, of jazz. Anderson's romanticized view presents Afro-Americans primarily as lovers of sex and gaudy things, cloaked in a rather laughable mysticism that looks upon "the folk" as noble savages. The decade of F. Scott Fitzgerald, the "Jazz Age," was attempting to come to terms with Afro-Americans and blues and jazz, sometimes only half seriously, as a trendy or avant-garde pose, in part as a way of effecting a literary renaissance. Fitzgerald himself felt that the Jazz Age had no interest in politics at all, obviously ignoring not only those outside his social circle, but the political implications of the actions of those within his group as well (Mellow 95). On the other hand, authors such as John Howard Lawson saw jazz as related to rebellion against the middle class, a view shared by Hughes.

Jazz had its influence on white avant-garde Modernists, as well. Daniel Joseph Singal asserts that "Modernism should be properly seen as a *culture*—a constellation of related ideas, beliefs, values, and modes of perception" (7), but the jazz that was part of this constellation was not based on an intimate and personal intellectual and emotional knowledge of the tradition as it related to blacks and their socioeconomic position. Rather, it was an intellectual and impressionistic knowledge of the commercial as it related to whites, or, for people like Lawson in *Processional*

(1925), a conception of the needs and desires of the workers expressed in "the jazz today for the glory of the working class" (Singal 7). Many writers seemed to be interested in using jazz more in an abstract rather than in a concrete and racially and historically accurate sense. Separated from the Afro-American tradition that had created it, jazz became significant to many non-black writers as analogy, for how it could be used cut loose from an Afro-American, culturally specific message. Wassily Kandinsky and his fellow theosophist Piet Mondrian both sought, for example, "to further through abstract (and hence unmaterial) art what [Kandinsky] regarded chiliastically as 'The Epoch of the Great Spiritual'" (Robinson 134). Mondrian specifically identified a correlation between his work and one segment of the vernacular music tradition: "True Booogie-Woogie [*sic*] I conceive as homogeneous in intention with mine in painting" (Bradbury 30).

But the browns of Mondrian's Parisian grids in 1910 were "colors presaging war and the sadness that follows" (Tytell 67), not the colors of Afro-Americans who created the music he conceived as being homogeneous in intention with his work. Aesthetic kinship does not always equate with social understanding and cooperation. Afro-American jazz musicians were seen as human beings paradoxically slaves in a "free" land, the dark side, the outsiders who transcend their social situation through exploitation of otherness, perceived not so much as human beings but as things, forces to be used rather than beings to be accepted. They represented a way for many white intellectuals to free themselves psychologically and aesthetically, rather than an argument for intellectuals to commit to liberating Afro-Americans. Therefore, the music was frequently perceived by white artist-intellectuals as a potent analogue for the revolution in contemporary literature in the 1920s but not, until later, for the most part, as a catalyst for revolution in contemporary race relations. Malcolm Cowley wrote, "Always, everywhere, there was jazz" (279), but it only accompanied "the long debauch that had to end" (238). It is the primitivist illusion associated with jazz that suggests that "discipline and technical mastery are unnecessary, clarity and sophistication to be avoided" (Gioia 48)—an avoidance of honest race relations rather than an attempt to deal with them, and a misrepresentation of jazz. Indeed, Ralph Ellison wrote that white writers of the twenties ignored discussing the difficulties of the racial situation in this country more than writers at any other time in the history of American literature (*Shadow and Act* 92).

4

In the midst of that Modernist revolution we know as the Harlem Renaissance or the New Negro Movement, Langston Hughes sought to change the way we looked not only at art and African Americans but also at the world. His vision was modernistic: experimental, both spontaneous and improvisatory and thoughtfully and carefully crafted, at times primitivistic, disjunctive, and cacophonous, and intent on rejecting artificial middle-class values, promoting intellectual and artistic freedom, and, above all, life- and love-affirming—self-affirming. And not only affirming of the African American self, though certainly Hughes spent a lifetime climbing the racial mountain and living and affirming an Afro-American self, but also affirming what Ralph Ellison called, in *Invisible Man*, the principle "dreamed into being out of the chaos and darkness of the feudal past" (574).

"Freedom! / Brotherhood! / Democracy!" Hughes hallelujahed in "Freedom's Plow," calling for it to grow and spread "[U]ntil all races and all people know its shade (*SP* 297). Hughes planted his feet among the Warren Street Baptists in Lawrence, with their "fiery sermons, inspired responses, and passionate, skilled singing" (Rampersad 16); among the "ordinary Negroes" of Seventh Street in Washington, D.C., where people who drew no color line "played the blues, ate watermelon, barbecue, and fish sandwiches, shot pool, told tall tales, looked at the dome of the Capitol and laughed out loud" (Hughes, *TBS* 209); among, as he called them proudly, jubilantly, "the low-down folks":

> The so-called common element, and they are the majority—may the Lord be praised! . . . They furnish a wealth of colorful, distinctive material for any artist because they still hold

their individuality in the face of American standardizations. ("The Negro Artist" 306)

For his vision of Afro-American music—sacred and secular—was comprehensively affectionate, much more so than Du Bois's, Johnson's, and Locke's, all of whom preferred spirituals to blues and jazz, Du Bois even terming jazz "caricature" (202–3). But, for Hughes, Afro-American music was elemental, primal, as his epigraph to this essay attests. The beat of the heart, the pulse—Hughes used these metaphors repeatedly in reference to the music of his people, and his work from *The Weary Blues* through *The Panther and the Lash* throbbed with ethnopoetic splendor.

The fact that Hughes could throw one arm around spiritual and gospel music and the other arm around the blues simultaneously would seem remarkable, even blasphemous, in some circles, primarily Christian ones, where blues was frequently labeled "the devil's music." But Hughes sat them rather comfortably side by side in his work and ethos: "I liked the barrel houses of Seventh Street, the shouting churches, and the songs," he wrote in *The Big Sea* (209). In the mid-fifties, his devil figure Big Eye Buddy Lomax, in both the play and the novel *Tambourines to Glory*, asserted "them gospel songs sound just like the blues," to which the holy sister managed only the feeble reply, "At least our words is different" (*FP* 126–27).

Clearly Hughes did not exalt spirituals and gospel music because of any fervent belief in Christianity. The "Salvation" chapter in *The Big Sea* outlines his traumatic (non-)conversion experience that left him doubting the existence of a Jesus who had not come to rescue him (18–21), and his poem "Mystery" describes the feelings of an uninitiated thirteen-year-old, isolated by her uncertainty, yoking *"The mystery / and the darkness / and the song / and me"* (*CP* 416). In "To Negro Writers," he called upon his Afro-American colleagues to "expose the sick-sweet smile of organized religion . . . and the half-voodoo, half-clown face of revivalism, dulling the mind with the clap of its empty hands" (139). He recounted his "first experience with censorship" in "My Adventures as a Social Poet," reporting how a preacher directed him not to read any more blues in his pulpit (206). Years later, in the story "Gospel Singers," Simple compares churches to movie theaters, preachers to movie stars, and church services to revues during which gospel singers are "working in the vineyards of the Lord and digging in his gold mines." He jokes that when you hear gospel singers "crying 'I Cannot Bear My Burden Alone,' what they really mean is, 'Help me get my cross to my Cadillac'" (*SUS* 39). Significantly, though, Simple does not mind paying to hear the gospel singers—paying twice, even—because he feels that "the music that these people put down can't be beat" (39). For Simple, as for Hughes, it is not the meaning of the words so much as the wording of the means that carries him away. What Hughes said about the blues in "Songs Called the Blues" applies to gospel music, as well: "You don't have to understand the words to know the meaning of the blues, or to feel their sadness or to hope their hopes" (145). In the melisma and glissandi of the "wordless moan, that is the essence of gospel music" (Heilbut 23), Hughes heard the pumping drama of the life of the spirit, the human spirit. It was a spirit he tried to produce vividly in poems like the intense "Fire" and "Sunday Morning Prophecy," and in "Freedom Train," recorded by Paul Robeson in 1947, as well as in the gospel plays *Tambourines to Glory*, *Black Nativity*, *Jericho-Jim Crow*, and *The Gospel Glory*. Countee Cullen, approaching Hughes's work from quite a different aesthetic, recognized the relationship between his jazz poems and the gospel feeling, even if he didn't appreciate Hughes's poetry fully:

> Never having been one to think all subjects and forms proper for poetic consideration, I regard these jazz poems as interlopers in the company of the truly beautiful poems in the other sections of the book. They move along with the frenzy and electric heat of a Methodist or Baptist revival meeting, and affect me in much the same manner. The revival meeting excites me, cooling and flushing me with alternate chills and fevers or emotion; so do these poems. But when the storm is over, I wonder if the quiet way of communing is not more spiritual for the God-seeking heart; and in the light of reflection I wonder if jazz poems really belong to that dignified

company, that select and austere circle of high literary expression which we call poetry. (Cullen)

May the Lord be praised, Hughes was aiming not always for the
dignified, select, austere poetry that Cullen sought but for the
sensuous, visceral throb that bursts forth into human life.

Hughes heard that pulse in the blues, too, of course. Buddy
Lomax was certainly right in hearing similarities between gospel
and blues music. Richard Alan Waterman has pointed out the influence of the "Ancient African organizing principle of song and
dance" on African American music as a whole, with its "domi-
nance of a percussive performance attack . . . , propensity for
multiple meter . . . , overlapping call and response . . . , inner
pulse control . . . , suspended accentuation pattern . . . , and
songs and dances of social allusion" (Thompson xiii). It is not
surprising that one of the founding fathers of gospel music,
Thomas A. Dorsey, who came to religious prominence with the
publication of *Gospel Pearls*, in 1921, by the Sunday School Publishing Board of the National Baptist Convention, had been a
blues and hokum singer. One of Dorsey's biggest hokum hits had
been "It's Tight Like That" with singer-guitarist Tampa Red.
Eventually, though, Dorsey went from being "tight like that" to
being tight with God, penning such standards as "Precious Lord
Take My Hand" and "Peace in the Valley." It was the manner of
performing, the spirit of the performance, that transcended the
sometimes artificial sacred, secular, and profane bounds and
linked black musics together.

Certainly, Hughes wrote more about blues than he did about
gospel music in his lifetime. He recalled the first time he heard
the blues in Kansas City on the appropriately named Independence Avenue, which provided him with material for his
"Weary Blues," one of the poems, with "Jazzonia" and "Negro
Dancers," that Hughes placed beside Vachel Lindsay's plate at
the Wardman Park Hotel; the blues of Ma Rainey and the boogie-woogie and ragtime piano players on State Street in Chicago;
the blues, ragtime, and jazz of Harlem from the twenties on;
aboard the S.S. *Malone* bound for Africa, even at Le Grand Duc in
France:

> Blues in the Rue Pigalle, Black and laughing, heartbreaking
> blues in the Paris dawn, pounding like a pulse beat, moving
> like the Mississippi. (*TBS* 162)

The yoking of the pulse beat, the river, and the singing links this
description with another of Hughes's classic poems, "The Negro
Speaks of Rivers," reminding us, as Hughes wrote with Milton
Meltzer, in *Black Magic*, that the "syncopated beat which the
captive Africans brought with them" that found its first expression here in "the hand-clapping, feet-stomping, drum-beating
rhythms (related, of course, to the rhythms of the man heart)"
(4–5), is as "ancient as the world." After Le Grand Duc in Washington, D.C., and collecting with Zora Neale Hurston throughout the South—"All my life," Hughes wrote, "I've heard the
blues" ("I Remember the Blues," 152). He continued to admire its
expressive beauty, differentiating it clearly from the spirituals as
being "sadder . . . because their sadness is not softened with
tears, but hardened with laughter, the absurd, incongruous
laughter of sadness without a god to appeal to" (Van Vechten
86). To him blues songs were "sad songs sung to the most de-
spondent rhythm in the world" (review of *Blues: An Anthology*
258), at times "as absurd as Krazy Kat" (Van Vechten 86) but
nearly always conveying a "kind of marching on syncopation, a
gonna-make-it-somehow determination in spite of it all, that
ever-present laughter-under-sorrow that indicates a love of life
too precious to let it go" ("I Remember the Blues," 155), with "a
steady rolling beat that seemed to be marking somewhere to
something better, to something happy" (*FBJ* 37). Despite the differences between spirituals and blues that Hughes enumerated in
"Songs Called the Blues," he saw a greater inherent bond between the blues and spiritual and gospel music. The music, his
art, black art, was not to be isolating but ultimately unifying, and
if what Arnold Rampersad described as Hughes's "cloistered life"
(16) with Mary Langston accentuated his solitude, the visceral
drama of black music—tender, humorous, tragic, innocent, sexy,
ecstatic, mundane, playful, lively, and deadly serious—set the
stage for his emergence as an artist.

In fact, Hughes sought to infuse much of his poetry with the urgency, the immediacy, of activity and performance. Hughes delighted in reciting his poetry to musical accompaniment, seeing the performance as an occasion for meaningful group interaction that would enhance and strengthen communication. Ezra Pound wrote to Hughes about a poem Hughes had sent to him: "Thank God; at last I come across a poem I can understand" (Hentoff 27). The comment is ironic coming from Pound, but perfectly appropriate in regard to Hughes's intentions and achievement. Nat Hentoff reported Hughes's designs for his recitations with musical accompaniment:

> The music should not only be a background to the poetry, but should comment on it. I tell the musicians—and I've worked with several different modern and traditional groups—to improvise as much as they care around what I read. Whatever they bring of themselves to the poetry is welcome to me. I merely suggest the mood of each piece as a general orientation. Then I listen to what they say in their playing, and that affects my own rhythms when I read. We listen to each other. (27)

The performance of the poem, then, becomes a nexus, a dialogue, something as old as the inception of the poem but as new as the inflection of the impulse. Indeed, in the stage directions to *Tambourines to Glory*, Hughes suggested that "audience participation might be encouraged—singing, foot-patting, handclapping—and in the program the lyrics of some of the songs might be printed with an invitation to sing the refrains along with the chorus of Tambourine Temple" (184). It would not likely take much to inspire participation for, as Hughes wrote in "Spirituals," "Song is a strong thing" (CP 102).

Now Hughes had his limitations as a commentator on the blues. His discussions of the roots of the blues in African music and work songs and field hollers were often general and unsystematic early in his career, though his later work was somewhat more comprehensive. He overgeneralized a bit about the types of blues that men sang as opposed to women, and he did not adequately convey the breadth of themes or stanzaic patterns present in the blues. His lists of outstanding blues singers most often emphasized vaudeville blues singers, certainly urban blues singers at any rate, indicating a preference for sophisticated productions. Indeed, Hughes wrote that it was a desire of his to write the first libretto for a blues opera ("From the Blues to an Opera Libretto"), and he himself was ambivalent about whether he was a folk poet or a folk person, discussing the subject in equivocal terms:

> I have tried to get that quality into my, shall we call them, created blues, because of course I consciously write these, and so I guess you can't call them real folk blues, unless you want to say that I'm a folk poet, myself a folk person, which maybe I am. (*Langston Hughes Reads and Talks*)

The blues poems that Hughes wrote were often thematic rather than associative, and they contained noticeably few references to drugs, sex, and violence in comparison to blues songs recorded both in the field and in the studio, opting for something of a via media in reflecting the themes and image of the folk tradition. His language and images, in fact, are not often as stark or startling as the best blues lyrics by performers within the oral tradition, but they make excellent use of both oral and written traditions in a way that adds materially to both, making his poetry something quite familiar, yet quite new.

Of course, not all of Hughes's blues poems employed blues stanza forms. Hughes called his poem "Cross," for example, a poem whose "mood is that of the blues," although its lyric form lacks the folk repetition, for the number of measures in a stanza that makes the blues—but the feeling, spirit, attitude, and approach are there. And these, indeed, imbue much of the poetry of Langston Hughes to such an extent that the whine of a bottleneck, or the wail of a harmonica, or the trill of a piano may be regularly inferred as the subtext of his work. Behind the "Troubled Woman" who was "Bowed by / Weariness and pain (CP 42) or the "Island" toward which the speaker wishes to be taken by the "wave of sorrow" because of its fair sands (CP 376), or the question "Where is the Jim Crow section / On this merry-go-round / Mister, cause I want to ride? (CP 240), or the "Hit me! Jab Me! / Make me say I did it" (CP 370) of "Third Degree," or the words of "The Negro Mother"—"For I will be with you till no white brother / Dares keep down the children of the Negro Mother" (CP 156)—are the strains of black life and black song.

5

In fact, though some commentators have suggested that black vernacular music is frequently not political in nature or intent, Hughes's work is politically pointed and relevant, often as a result of his employment of the black vernacular music tradition. In addition to his treatments of spirituals, minstrel songs, ragtime, blues, and gospel, Hughes regular employed the ballad tradition in his work. During the 1940s, the period of his heaviest use of ballads, Hughes generated some two dozen "ballad of" poems, treating misers, sinners, landlords, and fortune tellers, as well as public figures such as Margie Polite (a woman harassed by a white policeman), Walter White, and Sam Solomon (an NAACP leader). FDR and Ozie Powell (one of the Scottsboro Boys) each rated a ballad in the 1930s, as did Booker T. Washington and Harry Moore (an NAACP leader killed when his house was bombed) in the 1950s.

There was, of course, a long tradition of both folk and literary ballads behind Hughes, which share the characteristics of being simple dramatic narratives transmitted in a limited variety of usually four line stanza patterns. This tradition perhaps achieved prominence in the twentieth century with the rise of the leftist folk song movement, given impetus by the decision of the Communist Party in the mid-1930s to employ songs of the proletariat, rather than just avant-garde classical composers, to spread leftist ideology. As Hughes's work turned more radical in the 1930s, he was drawn toward leftist ideology and political groups. The folk music movement spawned and fostered by such figures as Carl Sandburg, John and Alan Lomax, and Charles and Ruth Crawford Seeger produced a public forum for a body of folk music performers, including the Almanac Singers, Woody Guthrie, and Pete Seeger, as well as Afro-Americans such as Leadbelly, Josh White, Sonny Terry and Brownie McGhee, and Paul Robeson. Hughes, White, Terry, and McGhee had worked together as early as 1944, and in 1957 McGhee played "Gitfiddle" in Hughes's *Simply Heavenly* on Broadway. John Hammond's staging of the famed *Spirituals to Swing* concerts of 1938–1939, which featured Sonny Terry, Big Bill Broonzy, and a variety of other Afro-American performers, also reflected the interests and influence of leftist folk song admirers, as did the opening of various interracial cafés, such as Barney Josephson's Café Society. The far-reaching repercussions of this leftist folk song activity as they resounded in later decades likely helped create the environment in which the Newport Folk and Jazz Festival and a variety of blues festivals were envisioned. Of course, Hughes attended a variety of such festivals, most prominently the 1960 Newport Jazz Festival, where he co-wrote a blues song with the pianist Otis Spann that deals with the closing of the festival due to rioting.

Hughes's employment of the ballad form was yet another reflection of his interest in employing vernacular forms in the service of his aesthetic and political aims. The fact that a number of Hughes's ballads are written in the first person and lack the impersonal tone characteristic of most folk ballads reflect Hughes's aim to employ what could be called a "first-person communal" perspective in his work. This kind of personalized generic experience is evident from the beginning of his career in such works as "The Negro Speaks of Rivers," where the third person of the title modulates to the first-person voice of the poem. Hughes also provides commentary and details in such ballads as "Margie Polite" and "Sam Solomon," as well as emphatic typography in the form of capitalization and punctuation, in order to personalize and politicize his narratives. "My race! / My race! / My race!" he exults at the end of "A Ballad of Negro History" (*CP* 436), embracing not only his people but also the strenuous struggle to overcome.

6

All his life Hughes had sought to employ the variety of Afro-American vernacular musics in the service of his art and people, regularly using references to vernacular music, performers, and milieu as metaphors for the hardships, joys, defeats, and triumphs of the Afro-American experience. Numerous individual references to spirituals, minstrels, ragtime, blues, gospel, and ballads throughout his work from 1922 on testify to the centrality of this material to his work. Hughes crystallized his interest in the many facets of this music in his multivocal vernacular jam sessions *Montage of a Dream Deferred* (1951) and *Ask Your Mama: Twelve Moods For Jazz* (1961). After struggling with the demons of Nazism, Fascism, and racism abroad, Afro-Americans were now poised to turn their attentions with renewed vigor to the deficiencies and hypocrisies of American democracy. Seven years before the photographer Art Kane staged the photo of jazz performers that would be memorialized in the film *A Great Day in Harlem*, Hughes published his assemblage of Harlem's variety of great vernacular voices, kind of "A Typical Day in Harlem" to show how fruitful those voices could be. In *Montage*, Hughes combines elements of jazz, ragtime, blues, boogie-woogie, ballad, and swing into a bebop-like mix that swaps juices in a bubbling gumbo of black energy and creativity. Seeking to chart the restless drive of post–World War II Harlem as a metaphor for Afro-American retrospection, introspection, and expectation, the volume is a promenade through the multiple personalities of Afro-American experience, all of which are struggling with the central disillusionment of the deferred (Afro-)American dream. Hughes refuses to compartmentalize neatly the various attitudes and types of music, opting to reflect the diversity of thought and expression in an almost random fashion, perhaps much like Whitman's "casual" walk through the American landscape in *Song of Myself.* The volume itself has not been studied in the kind of depth it deserves. Isolating groups of poems such as the "boogie" poems reveals Hughes's close knowledge and careful modulation of themes and images—black-white, high-low, treble-bass, happiness-sadness, hearing-deafness—that bind those poems together, even as they are disseminated throughout the volume. By employing a variety of Afro-American music, a range of voices, and this type of interconnected separation, Hughes reinforces the notion of unity in diversity that finds its roots in African communal society and antiphonal patterns, as well as in democratic philosophy.

In *Ask Your Mama*, Hughes plays the dozens with America as he explores the slave quarters of an emerging Africa and Afro-American nation not yet captured on tape by Folkways Records, Moe Asch, or Alan Lomax, but arising independently through the fifties and toward the explosive decade of the sixties. It is the response to the (mis)appropriation of blues and spirituals described in "Note On Commercial Theater," a reappropriation of voice not through leftist sponsorship, capitalistic objectification, or sociological or folkloristic inquiry. This is taking back the name, and the name is an unhesitating Pan-African "Hesitation Blues": talking drum-Dixieland-rhumba-gospel-blues-bop-free jazz with a vengeance, "building," as Hughes concludes, "full blast to a bursting climax" (*CP* 525). And, of course, Hughes is right. He is building, and the basic building blocks are expressed in the music. He is representing the fullness of Afro-American music in its overwhelming power and beauty and the volume necessary to overcome the willful deafness of the world. He is, as he had been all his life, breaking through the cordons of racism and discrimination. And he is signaling the end of white hegemony as we know it. Formally, Hughes makes use of marginal comments in the work in the tradition of Vachel Lindsay's "The Congo," perhaps, or as a legacy of his dramatic and Broadway involvement. The musical directives that Hughes places in the margins of this work serve, in a sense, a double purpose: not only do they provide a soundtrack to the lives and feelings described in the poem, but also they emphasize the importance of paying attention to, of valuing, what the margins hold as essential to the meaning of the entire text. It is, after all, the entire text that Hughes wants us to read, understand, and embrace.

This, then, is the meaning of Afro-American vernacular music in the work of Langston Hughes: a reclamation of heritage, a construction of identity, an assertion of voice, and a seizure of freedom. Hughes composed out of the multitudinous resources bequeathed to him by his African, Afro-American, American, and global forebears a message to sing back to them, back to the world. It is a spiritual message; it is a physical message; it is an ancient message; it is a contemporary message; it is a personal message and a communal one. It is a corrective message confronting all the lies, deceit, and hatred attached to secondhand versions of the message. And oh so joyous in the throat of someone who knows how to sing it. And Langston, he sings.

WORKS CITED

Adams, Henry. *The Education of Henry Adams*. Boston: Massachusetts Historical Society, 1918.

Anderson, Sherwood. *Dark Laughter*. 1925. Rpt. New York: Liveright, 1970.

Apollinaire, Guillaume. *Selected Writings of Guillaume Apollinaire*. Ed. Roger Shattuck. New York: New Directions, 1971.

Bradbury, Malcolm. "The Non-Homemade World: Europeanized American Modernism." *American Quarterly* 39, no. 1 (spring 1987): 27–36.

Brown, Sterling. "The Blues as Folk Poetry." In *Folk Say I*, ed. B. A. Botkin. Norman: University of Oklahoma Press, 1930. 324-39.

———. *Negro Poetry and Drama and the Negro in American Fiction*. 1937. Rpt. New York: Atheneum, 1972.

Cowley, Malcolm. *The Exile's Return*. New York: Norton, 1934.

Cullen, Countee. "Review." *Opportunity*, February 1926.

Du Bois, W. E. B. *Dusk of Dawn*. New York: Harcourt, Brace, 1940.

Ellison, Ralph. *Invisible Man*. 1952. Rpt. New York: Vintage, 1989.

———. *Shadow and Act*. New York: Random House, 1964.

Gioia, Ted. *The Imperfect Art*. New York: Oxford University Press, 1988.

Godrich, John, and R. M. W. Dixon. *Recording the Blues*. New York: Stein and Day, 1970.

Heilbut, Tony. *The Gospel Sound*. New York: Limelight, 1992.

Hemenway, Robert. *Zora Neale Hurston: A Literary Biography*. Urbana: University of Illinois Press, 1977.

Hentoff, Nat. "Langston Hughes: He Found Poetry in the Blues." *Mayfair* (August 1958): 26, 27, 43, 45–47, 49.

Horace. "Ars Poetica." *Classical Literary Criticism*. Translated by T. S. Dorsch. New York: Penguin, 1965.

Hughes, Langston. "From the Blues to an Opera Libretto." *New York Times*, January 15, 1950.

———. "I Remember the Blues." In *Missouri Reader*. Ed. Frank Luther Mott. Columbia: University of Missouri Press, 1964. 152–55.

———. "Jazz as Communication." *The Langston Hughes Reader*. Ed. Langston Hughes. New York: Braziller, 1958. 492–94.

———. *Langston Hughes Reads and Talks*. Spoken Arts 7140, 1959.

———. "My Adventures as a Social Poet." *Phylon* 6 (1947): 205–13.

———. "The Negro Artist and the Racial Mountain." *The Nation* 122 (June 23, 1926): 692–94. Rpt. in *Voices from the Harlem Renaissance*. Ed. Nathan I. Huggins. New York: Oxford University Press, 1976. 305–9.

———. "To Negro Writers." *American Writer's Congress*. Ed. Henry Hart. New York: International, 1935. 139–41.

———. "Review of *Blues: An Anthology* by W. C. Handy." *Opportunity*, August 1926, p. 258.

———. "Songs Called the Blues." *Phylon* 2, no. 2 (1941): 143–45.

Hughes, Langston, and Milton Meltzer, eds. *Black Magic: A Pictorial History of the Negro in American Entertainment*. Englewood Cliffs, N.J.: Prentice Hall, 1967.

Oliver, Paul, Max Harrison, and William Bolcom. *The New Grove Gospel, Blues, and Jazz, with Spirituals and Ragtime*. London: Macmillan, 1986.

Rampersad, Arnold. *The Life of Langston Hughes, Volume 1: 1902–1941, I, Too, Sing America*. New York: Oxford University Press, 1986.

Robinson, Alan. *Symbol to Vortex: Poetry, Painting and Ideas, 1885–1914*. New York: St. Martin's, 1985.

Singal, Daniel Joseph. "Towards a Definition of American Modernism." *American Quarterly* 39, no. 1 (Spring 1987): 7–26.

Thompson, Big Ed. Interview with the author. Cincinnati, Ohio. 26 Aug. 1985.

Thompson, Robert Farris. *Flash of the Spirit: African and Afro-American Art and Philosophy*. New York: Random House, 1983.

Tytell, John. *Ezra Pound: The Solitary Volcano*. New York: Doubleday, 1987.

Van Vechten, Carl. "The Black Blues." *Vanity Fair* 24, no. 6 (1925): 57, 86, 92.

Wilson, Reginald. Liner Notes. *Writers of the Revolution*. Black Forum 453, 1970.

SELECTED LP AND CD DISCOGRAPHY
OF JAZZ, BLUES, AND RAGTIME PERFORMERS
MENTIONED BY AND RELEVANT TO
LANGSTON HUGHES

All listings refer to CDs except where item is identified as an LP.

Ammons, Albert. *The Chronological Albert Ammons (1936–1939)*. Classics 715.

———. *The Chronological Albert Ammons (1939–1946)*. Classics 927.

Armstrong, Louis. *Portrait of the Artist as a Young Man*. Columbia 57176 (4 CDs).

Bentley, Gladys. *Maggie Jones Vol. 2—Gladys Bentley*. Document 5349.

Carr, Leroy. *Complete Recorded Works in Chronological Order*. Vols. 1–6. Document 5134–5139.

Ellington, Duke. *The Blanton-Webster Band*. RCA 5659-2-RB (3 CDs).

———. *Early Ellington (1927–1934)*. RCA 6852-2-RB.

———. *Jazz Cocktail*. ASV AJA 5024.

Gillespie, Dizzy. *The Dizzy Gillespie Story 1939–1950*. Properbox 30.

Handy, W. C. *Memphis Blues Band*. Memphis Archives 7006.

———. *Narrates and Sings His Immortal Songs*. Mark 56 LP 684.

Hill, Bertha "Chippie." *Complete Recorded Works in Chronological Order*. Document 5330.

Holiday, Billie. *The Commodore Master Takes*. Polygram 543272.

———. *Lady Day: The Complete Billie Holiday on Columbia*. Columbia 85470 (10 CDs).

Hughes, Langston. *Rhythms of the World*. Folkways FP LP 740.

———. *The Story of Jazz*. Folkways FJ LP 7312.

———. *The Voice of Langston Hughes*. Smithsonian 47001.

———. *The Weary Blues with Langston Hughes*. Verve 841 660-2.

Jackson, Mahalia. *The Apollo Sessions (1946–1951)*. Pair PCD-2-1332.

———. *Gospels, Spirituals, and Hymns, Vol. 1.* Columbia C2K 65594 (2 CDs).

———. *Gospels, Spirituals, and Hymns, Vol. 2.* Columbia C2K 65597 (2 CDs).

Jefferson, Blind Lemon. *Complete Recorded Works in Chronological Order.* Vols. 1–4. Document 5017–5020.

Johnson, James P. *Carolina Shout.* Biograph BCD 105.

———. *The Original James P. Johnson (1942–1945): Piano Solos.* Smithsonian Folkways SF CD 40812.

———. *Snowy Morning Blues.* GRP 604.

Johnson, Lonnie. *Complete Recorded Works in Chronological Order (1925–1932).* Document 5063–5069.

———. *Complete Recorded Works in Chronological Order (1937–1947).* Document 6024–6026.

Johnson, Pete. *The Chronological Pete Johnson (1938–1939).* Classics 656.

———. *The Chronological Pete Johnson (1939–1941).* Classics 665.

———. *The Chronological Pete Johnson (1944–1946).* Classics 933.

Jones, Richard M. *Complete Recorded Works in Chronological Order (1923–1936).* Vols. 1–2. RST JPCD 1524-1525.

Jordan, Louis. *Anthology 1938–1953.* MCA 11907 (2 CDs).

———. *Let the Good Times Roll.* Bear Family 15557 (9 CDs).

Leadbelly. *Leadbelly.* Columbia CK 30035.

———. *King of the 12-String Guitar.* Columbia CK 46776.

Lewis, Meade Lux. *The Chronological Meade Lux Lewis (1927–1939).* Classics 722.

———. *The Chronological Meade Lux Lewis (1939–1941).* Classics 743.

———. *The Chronological Meade Lux Lewis (1941–1944).* Classics 841.

McGhee, Brownie. *The Complete Brownie McGhee.* Columbia C2K 52933 (2 CDs).

Memphis Minnie. *Complete Recorded Works in Chronological Order (1935–1941).* Vols. 1–5. Document 6008–6012.

———. *Complete Recorded Works in Chronological Order (1944–1953).* Vols. 1–3. Wolf 008-010.

Miller, Clarence "Big." *Did You Ever Hear the Blues?* United Artists LP 3047.

———. *Revelations and the Blues and Sings, Twists, Shouts, and Preaches.* Collectables 7453.

Morton, Jelly Roll. *The Best of Jelly Roll Morton.* EPM Musique 158012.

————. *The Jelly Roll Morton Centennial: His Complete Victor Record-ings*. RCA 2361-2-RB (5 CDs).

Parker, Charlie. *The Complete Dial and Savoy Studio Recordings*. At-lantic 92911 (8 CDs).

————. *Yardbird Suite: The Ultimate Collection*. Rhino 72260 (2 CDs).

Rainey, Ma. *Complete Recorded Works in Chronological Order*. Vols. 1–5. Document 5156, 5581–5584.

Smith, Bessie. *The Complete Recordings*. Vols. 1–5. Columbia C2K47091, 47471, 47474, 52838, 57546 (10 CDs).

Smith, Clara. *Complete Recorded Works in Chronological Order*. Vols. 1–6. Document 5364–5369.

Smith, Mamie. *Complete Recorded Works in Chronological Order*. Vols. 1–4. Document 5357–5360.

Smith, Pine Top. *Boogie Woogie and Barrelhouse Piano*. Vol. 1. Docu-ment 5102.

Smith, Trixie. *Complete Recorded Works in Chronological Order*. Vols. 1–2. Document 5332–5333.

Smith, Willie "the Lion." *1925–1937*. Melodie Jazz Classic 662.

————. *1938–1940*. Melodie Jazz Classic 692.

Spann, Otis. *Rarest Recordings*. JSP LP 1070 (includes Hughes com-mentary on blues).

Spivey, Victoria. *Complete Recorded Works in Chronological Order (1926–1937)*. Vols. 1–4. Document 5316–5319.

Taj Mahal. *Mule Bone*. Gramavision R2 7943.

Various Artists. *BeBop Spoken Here*. Properbox 10.

————. *Boogie Woogie Stomp*. ASV AJA 5101.

————. *The Greatest Ragtime of the Century*. Biograph BCD 103.

————. *Kansas City Blues*. Capitol 52047 (3 CDs).

————. *Kansas City Blues (1924–1929)*. Document 5152.

————. *Songs for Political Action*. Bear Family 15720 JL (10 CDs).

Waller, Fats. *Fats Waller in London*. Disques Swing CDXP 8442.

————. *A Handful of Keys*. Buddha 7446599603-2.

————. *The Joint Is Jumpin'*. RCA 6288-2-RB.

Washington, Dinah. *First Issue: The Dinah Washington Story*. Poly-gram 514841 (2 CDs).

————. *The Queen Sings*. Properbox 43.

Waters, Ethel. *The Chronological Ethel Waters (1921–1940)*. Vols. 1–7. Classics 796, 775, 672, 688, 721, 735, 755.

Waters, Muddy. *Muddy Waters at Newport*. Chess 1949 (includes Otis Spann singing the Hughes composition "Goodbye Newport Blues").

White, Georgia. *Complete Recorded Works in Chronological Order*. Vols. 1–4. Document 5301–5304.

White, Josh. *Complete Recorded Works in Chronological Order (1929–1944)*. Document 5194–5196, 5405, 5571–5572.

Wilson, Edith. *Johnny Dunn: Complete Recorded Works in Chronological Order (1921–1928)*. Vols. 1–2. RST JPCD 1522–1523.

Yancey, Jimmy. *Complete Recorded Works in Chronological Order (1939–1950)*. Vols. 1–3. Document 5041–5043.

Hughes and Twentieth-Century Genderracial Issues

Joyce A. Joyce

In an essay on Langston Hughes in *Blackness and the Adventure of Western Culture*, George Kent, I believe, offers useful insight into the timelessness of Hughes's literary contributions and thus answers the questions not only why Hughes was referred to during his time as the "Shakespeare of Harlem" but also why his poems and fiction continue to stimulate oral and written dialogues at the forefront of African American literature. Although Kent's comments refer primarily to Hughes's autobiographies, they also characterize what I refer to as Langston Hughes's sensibility. Kent writes, "Hughes is consistent with what I have called the *is-ness* of folk vision and tradition—life is lived from day to day and confronted by plans whose going astray may evoke the face twisted in pain or the mouth open in laughter. The triumph is in holding fast to dreams and maintaining, if only momentarily, the spirit of the self" (57).

Describing what he means by the *is-ness* of the folk tradition as he explores the black cultural tradition in Hughes's work, Kent explains, "From the animal tales to the hipsterish urban mythmaking, folk tradition has *is-ness*. Things are. Things are funny, sad, tragic, tragicomic, bitter, sweet, tender, harsh, awe-inspiring, cynical, otherworldly, worldly—sometimes, alternately expressing the conflicting and contradictory qualities; sometimes, expressing conflicting qualities simultaneously" (53). Using Kent's definition of *is-ness* and his description of *is-ness* in Hughes's poetry and fiction, I propose that it is the black women in Langston Hughes's poetry and fiction who confront their day-to-day struggles, thwarted by plans with a twisted face, with laughter, and who hold on to their dreams (sometimes momentarily and sometimes with endurance), maintaining "the spirit of the self." Hughes's description of many of the women in *The Collected Poems of Langston Hughes* and those featured in his two novels *Not Without Laughter* (1930) and *Tambourines to Glory* (1958) and in his collection of short stories *The Ways of White Folk* (1934), if compared to and contrasted with historical data regarding the social and political status of women during and after the Harlem Renaissance, confirm that Langston Hughes is indeed the first black male feminist writer of African American letters.

I

While some of the critical attention given to Hughes's work since the early 1990s focuses on Hughes's rumored homosexuality, this emphasis does not overshadow what we learn about Hughes's masculinity from exploring his depiction of black women and men in his art. It is significant that women characters have the central role in his two novels—*Not Without Laughter* and *Tambourines to Glory*—that they are the protagonists of the more moving stories in *The Ways of White Folk*, and that a black woman is the subject/protagonist of at least ninety-one poems in *The Collected Poems of Langston Hughes*.

In proposing that Hughes is a black male feminist who sustained this feminism and who did not embody accepted norms of black male masculinity from the 1920s to his death in 1967, I use Deborah McDowell's definition of feminism, as well as Sherley Anne Williams's and Delores Aldridge's comments regarding the need for a new focus in the black feminist agenda as foundations for my contention that Langston Hughes was a black male very atypical and nonrepresentative of his black male contemporaries and of societal expectations of black men. Providing a comprehensive definition of black feminist criticism, McDowell (borrowing from Annette Kolodny) says the following:

> I use the term here simply to refer to Black female critics who analyze the works of Black female writers from a feminist or political perspective. But the term can also apply to any criticism written by a Black woman regardless of her subject or perspective—a book written by a male from a feminist or political perspective, a book written by a Black woman or about Black women authors in general, or any writings by women. (153)

Embodying McDowell's definition of black feminism, Langston Hughes is a black male in whose works race and gender converge into a black male feminist perspective. Stereotypical approaches to black male creative art, stereotypical expectations of black male behavior, and stereotypical approaches to black feminist criticism have shunted attention away from Hughes's deconstruction of masculinity and his celebration/affirmation of the black woman. Although the need exists for "a thoroughgoing examination of the works of black male writers, . . . much of the scholarship [of black feminist scholars] has been limited to discussions of the negative images of black women found in the works of these [black male] authors" (158).

Broadening Alice Walker's concept of *womanism*, Sherley Anne Williams makes a distinction between womanism and feminism that suggests the need for a merger of race and gender in discussions of black male creativity:

> Womanist inquiry, on the other hand, assumes that it can talk both effectively and productively about men. This is a necessary assumption because the negative, stereotypical images of black women are only a part of the problem of phallocentric writings of black males. In order to understand that problem more fully, we must turn to what black men have written about themselves. (74)

My examination then of Langston Hughes's feminism emerges as a text reflecting double focalization, for this exploration of the gender and genderracial issues in Hughes's work illuminates the feminist literary critic's perspective of what Hughes's work suggests about his masculinity and, at the same time, deconstructs his depictions of black women.

This idea of double focalization reflects both the beauty and the caution of contemporary literary or historical analysis of works representative of an earlier social, economic, and political period. Thus, in order to assess Hughes's treatment of gender and genderracial issues, we must look at his work in the context of his time period, as well as from the advantages of contemporary intellectual advancements made possible because of his earlier work. In *Focusing: Black Male-Female Relationships*, the sociologist Delores P. Aldridge addresses the "macroanalytical framework of institutional capitalism, racism, sexism and Judeo-Christian ethic" that I use to contexualize Hughes's poetry and fiction written between the 1920s and 1967:

> Society, with its institutional arrangements, influences significantly the interaction between Black men and women. The racism, sexism, capitalism, and Judeo-Christian ethic has impacted differently upon Black males and females than it has for other race-gender groups within American society. The interplay of the structural or institutional aspects of Black life rooted in an oppressive ideology, as well as the psychological forces that individuals bring to intimate relationships, provides all the fundamental components necessary for "focusing" on the Black male-female dyad. Thus, any attempt to study male-female relationships among Black Americans that fails to place the interpersonal within the broad institutional context falls short of providing a macroanalytical model. (78)

Aldridge provides for me a comprehensive framework for a new historicist overview (one that places Hughes's creative works in the context of their times) of the genderracial and black male-female dyad in Langston Hughes's poetry and fiction.

Because Hughes's treatment of black women is impressively voluminous, as I have noted above, and thus because I shall not give attention to all of his work that addresses black women

and/or their relationship with black men and their place in society, I have divided his treatment of women into the following
thematic threads: the black woman prototype, which manifests in the strong black woman with Christian ethic, the black
woman who internalizes negative social norms, Hughes's condemnation of the black male's mistreatment and exploitation of
black women, Hughes's nonjudgment of prostitution and other
societal taboos, Hughes's empathy with black women's shortcomings, and his romanticization of black women.

My method here will be neither to provide a critical analysis
of the poems that reflect these themes nor to cite all of the
poems responsible for my deductions. I shall instead address how
selected poems and the primary characters from Hughes's fiction
reflect the merger of gender, racial, and Christian ethics in his
works, how this merger illuminates the societal conditions for
black women, and how Hughes emerges as a black male literary
feminist of the twentieth century.

Maria Miller Stewart's second speech, given in New England
before the Boston Anti-Slavery Society on September 21, 1832,
sets up the model for Christian ethics that describes the religious
black women who appear slightly less than one hundred years
later in Hughes's poetry and fiction. In Stewart's speech, entitled
"Religion and the Pure Principles of Morality, the Sure Foundation on Which We Must Build," Stewart functions as the historical prototype for poems such as "The Negro Mother," "Prayer
Meeting," "Southern Mammy Sings," and "Spirituals," as well as
the characters Aunt Hager in *Not Without Laughter* and Essie in
Tambourines to Glory. Stewart says:

> O, ye daughters of Africa, awake! Awake! Arise! No longer
> sleep nor slumber, but distinguish yourselves. Show forth to
> the world that ye are endowed with noble and exalted facul-
> ties. . . . Where is the maiden who will blush at vulgarity?
> And where is the youth who has written upon his manly brow
> a thirst for knowledge; whose ambitious mind soars above tri-
> fles, and longs for the time to come, when he shall redress the
> wrongs of his father and plead the cause of his brethren? Did
> the daughters of our land possess a delicacy of manners, com-

bined with gentleness and dignity; did their pure minds hold
vice in abhorrence and contempt; did they frown when their
ears were polluted with its vile accents, would not their influence become power-full? Would not our brethren fall in love
with their virtues? (27)

Maria Stewart's words demonstrate the merger of religion or
Christian ethic, the emotional power of the black woman, and
her strength.

Langston Hughes's "The Negro Mother" and "Aunt Sue's Stories" are prototypes for the black woman's survival, nurturing
skills, virtue, and Christian faith. Aunt Sue is a keeper of memories, who converts her life experiences as a slave into stories that
become the strength of future generations. "The Negro Mother"
explains that "God put a song and a prayer in [her] mouth," a
dream like steel in her soul. Because she is the seed of the "coming Free," no white brother dares keep her children down (*CP*
155–56). Similarly, "Spirituals," embodiments of Christian faith,
are the firm roots of the trees and thus the foundation for the
black woman's strength.

Aunt Hager, in *Not Without Laughter*, nurses the sick, both
black and white. She is the fictional counterpart to the Negro
mother and Aunt Sue. "All the neighborhood, white or colored,
called his [Sandy's] grandmother when something happened.
She was a good nurse, they said, and sick folks liked her around.
Aunt Hager always came when they called, too, bringing maybe
a little soup that she had made or a jelly. Sometimes they paid her
and sometimes they didn't" (25). While Aunt Hager is a totally
self-sacrificing and unwavering Christian, Essie, in *Tambourines to
Glory*, emerges as a more balanced religious figure, who recognizes that she is both good and bad. Challenging her friend
Laura's notion that she is perfect, Essie says, "I wrestles with
temptation, too, Laura, in my heart. But somehow or another, I
always did want to try to be good. Once I thought—just like you
said about me—being good was doing nothing, I guess, so I done
nothing for half my life. Now, I'm trying to do *something*—and be
good, too. That's harder. It's easy to preach holy, but hard to live
holy" (*FP* 120).

If Hughes's canon were limited to his description of virtuous, Christian black women with strong religious faith and whose goal is to "uplift" the race, his depiction of these women would be suspiciously stereotypical and would appear insincere. However, Hughes balances his depiction of the Maria Stewart picture of "piety, morality, and virtue" with his characterizations of black women's internalization of negative social norms and his condemnation of black men's negative treatment of black women. The empathy reflected in Hughes's prodigious treatment of diverse black women suggests an identification with black women's pain and depth.

Though his biography of Langston Hughes's life is remarkably detailed and reflective of scholarly brilliance, Arnold Rampersad, I believe, misunderstood Hughes's reaction in a story related by Roy DeCarava, one of Hughes's closet friends. DeCarava said:

> I remember once when he [Hughes] was telling me about a man who had beaten his woman and dragged her down a flight of stairs. . . . I was appalled by the story, but even more appalled by the fact that Langston was telling it as a big joke, complete with howls of laughter. I think his laughter had nothing to do with laughter, and everything to do with impotence. If I ever spoke of pain to Langston, he would become uncomfortable and turn away in embarrassment. It was obvious to me that he had been hurt a great deal but refused to face the fact in a way that might, just might, have resulted in healing. He was serious sometimes but his seriousness was oblique. Mostly he laughed. You could not get to him. (Rampersad 338)

The consistencies in Hughes's portraits of black women, by deductive reasoning, suggest not that he was "heartless" but rather that he possessed an unusually acute sensitivity regarding the maltreatment of black women.

Both Faith Berry and Arnold Rampersad, Hughes's biographers, and Hughes's two autobiographies, *The Big Sea* and *I Wonder as I Wander*, make it clear that Hughes was not forthcoming about his emotional self, despite his obvious castigation of racism and his political writing, which increased as American politics became more severe as the country confronted World War II, the McCarthy era, and the years leading to the Vietnam War. Hughes's mixture of the "funny, sad, tragic, tragicomic, bitter, sweet, tender, harsh, awe-inspiring, cynical, otherworldly, worldly," as described by George Kent, is no more prominent in any of his work than it is in his treatment of the black male's exploitation or abuse of black women in his poems, in his characterization of Jimboy in *Not Without Laughter*, and in Laura's relationship with Buddy in *Tambourines to Glory*. What appears "heartless" and resistant to healing to DeCarava reflects the breadth and depth of Hughes's comprehension of the self-effacing, self-destructive sacrifices some black women make for black men and his aversion for the men who exploit black women.

At the same time that Hughes is keenly aware of the gender-racial conditions that stifle black women's lives and the vulnerability associated with their social and political conditions, he gives most, but not all, of his black women a uniquely rebellious, witty, and tender personality that deepens their humanity. Most of Hughes's black women, like Aunt Hager, earn a living by doing domestic work for whites. Yet, in spite of their harsh working conditions, they manage to find solace in religion, in love, in alcohol, or in the jazz club. Providing the backdrop for the urban life experiences of Hughes's characters, both David Levering Lewis, in *When Harlem Was in Vogue* (1979), and Cary D. Wintz, in *Black Culture and the Harlem Renaissance* (1988), detail thoroughly the sociological and political conditions responsible for the migration of large numbers of blacks from the rural South to the urban North between 1900 and 1920. These newcomers from the South lived in congested housing in Harlem between 126th and 155th Streets and between the Harlem River and Amsterdam Avenue. Wintz and Lewis provide the general details regarding housing conditions, the formation of black churches, restaurants, the emergence of black intellectuals, newspapers, civil rights organizations, night clubs, theaters, crime, education, literary productivity, and many other issues that describe the activities within the black city inside New York City. When real estate prices dropped, numerous houses in Harlem became vacant. The few black real estate developers and the white owners began to rent to the migrating blacks. Not only did whites move out of the once middle-class neighborhoods of Harlem, but "During the 1920s the vast majority of Harlem's retail establishments would only hire blacks for menial jobs such as porter, maid, or elevator operator. As a result of this and similar job discrimination most of Harlem's residents lived, at best, on the verge of poverty, a situation which contributed to the emergence of this area as the city's leader in vice, crime, juvenile delinquency, and drug addiction" (24).

Claudia Jones's "An End to the Neglect of the Problems of the Negro Woman," published in 1947, particularizes the experiences of women that we find in Hughes's poetry. She writes:

> Following emancipation, and persisting to the present day, a large percentage of Negro women—married as well as single—were forced to work for a living. But despite the shift in employment of Negro women from rural to urban areas, Negro women are still generally confined to the lowest-paying jobs. The Women's Bureau, U.S. Department of Labor, *Handbook of Facts for Women Workers* (1948, Bulletin 225), shows white women workers as having median earnings more than twice as high as those of non-white women, and non-white women workers (mainly Negro women) as earning less than $500 a year! In the rural South, the earnings of women are even less. . . .
>
> The low scale of earnings of the Negro woman is directly related to her almost complete exclusion from virtually all fields of work except the most menial and underpaid, namely, domestic service. (110)

An overwhelming number of Langston Hughes's poems about women focus on the black male's mistreatment and/or exploitation of the black woman, many of whom are domestic workers or perform in clubs or work as prostitutes. Even a selected list of poems is astounding: "To Certain Brothers," "Midwinter Blues," "Gypsy Man," "Ma Man," "Love Song for Lucinda," "Minnie Sings Her Blues," "Listen Here Blues," "Fortune Teller Blues," "Misery," "Beale Street Love," "Suicide," "Po' Boy Blues," "Bad Man," "Free Man," "Evil Woman," "Black Gal," "Early Evening Quarrel," Ballad of the Girl Whose Name Is Mud," "50-50," "Faithful One," "Honey Babe," "Stranger in Town," and "To Artina."

Any reading of these poems reveals Hughes's indirect condemnation of the black men who exploit black women who need and love black men, who make selfless sacrifices for them, and who recognize, accept, and forgive the men's weaknesses. In treating the interaction between black men and women and between black women and white men in these poems, Hughes follows the prescription of the Combahee River Collective's black feminist statement (1977): "The most general statement of our politics at the present time would be that we are actively committed to struggling against racial, sexual, heterosexual, and class oppression and see as our particular task the development of integrated analysis and practice based upon the fact that the major systems of oppression are interlocking" (13). A brief discussion of five of the more moving of the poems listed illuminates why Hughes's laughter regarding the black man who had beaten his wife and dragged her down the stairs, as DeCarava describes, does indeed reflect his "impotence" in improving black women's lives and the depth of his identification with the black woman's impotence. Hughes's behavior illustrates the folk saying about "laughing to keep from crying."

In "Evil Woman," the male lover asserts that he will kill "his" woman lover the next time she makes him "sore." He says that, although he treats her kind, she doesn't treat him right and quarrels almost every night. He refers to her as a "blue gummed" woman he brought from the South and says that he is going to send her back or use her head for a carpet tack (*CP* 120). Like Williams Carlos Williams, Hughes in his poetry does not present us with a direct statement of the thing; instead, we get the thing itself. In other words, Hughes allows the black man to speak for himself; the man's violent attitude toward "his" woman indirectly explains why she quarrels every night—because her lover mistreats her. And her dark skin and southern training have made her strong and intolerant of maltreatment.

Again, in "Black Gal," the black woman is a "workin' girl" who treats her men "fine," but they always leave her for a "yaller gal," even though she buys them "suits o' clothes." And even though her Albert has left her for a "rinny yaller" gal, she wants her "sweet, brownskin boy" back (*CP* 121). Adding the issue of the black male's preference for light-skinned rather than dark-skinned black women, Hughes includes another layer to his empathy with the plight of black women. Interestingly enough, the Combahee River Statement is not correct when it asserts that, before the appearance of this statement in 1977, "No one before [had] ever examined the multilayered texture of black women's lives" (17).

Dorothy, in "Ballad of the Girl Whose Name Is Mud," shares Harriet's strength in *Not Without Laughter* and stands in contrast to Laura in *Tambourines to Glory*. Dorothy, who had a lot of "raising," became involved with a "no-good man," to whom she "gave her all" and who "Dropped her with a thud." Despite her being castigated by the "decent people" in her community, she never "shed a tear," and she has said that if she had the chance "She'd do it agin' (*CP* 256)! Despite being mistreated, Dorothy keeps the conviction of joy and love in the same way that Aunt Hager, in *Not Without Laughter*, stays firm in her religious convictions. Dorothy and Aunt Hager find joy and strength in different contradictory sources, reflecting what George Kent refers to as the "worldly" and "otherworldly" and the "conflicting and contradictory qualities of Hughes's work."

"Faithful One" and "50-50" characterize men whose prototype we find in Jimboy, in *Not Without Laughter*, and in Buddy, in *Tambourines to Glory*. While the male speaker in "Faithful One" describes a woman who is faithful despite his many varied transgressions, the male speaker in "50-50" explains that he wants all and that he will not bring his half to a relationship. He wants the woman to share her bed *"And your money, too"* (*CP* 262). It is not by accident that Hughes italicizes *"And your money, too."* For the black men in these poems consciously and heartlessly exploit black women, both emotionally and financially.

Though he uses natural images frequently to suggest his critical attitudes, his poems taken as a whole reveal strong, indirect criticism of black male socialization. While Hughes is unflinchingly committed to a black perspective in his art, he does not embody the sexism of the black male nationalist. Poems such as "Young Prostitute," "Ballad of Gin Mary," "Red Silk Stockings," "Cabaret Girl Dies on Welfare Island," and "S-sss-ss-sh" demonstrate that though he is fully aware that moral social statutes or sanctions are very severe for black women who fail to follow Maria Stewart's model of virtue, the tone of his poetry does not judge black women negatively.

Hughes does not judge Harriet, the youngest of Aunt Hager's three daughters in *Not Without Laughter*. Like some of the women in the poems earlier, Harriet does not adhere to the religious standards of virtue and morality prescribed by Maria Stewart and Aunt Hager. Harriet loves jazz, dancing, and having fun. To escape domestic work, she becomes a prostitute, and after the death of her mother she begins to earn a promising reputation as a jazz singer when we leave her in Chicago. She has come a long way from having been arrested for prostitution in her hometown in Kansas. Like Dorothy, Harriet wants to focus on the joy life has to offer, yet she is not unaware of what George Kent refers to as the tragic and the bitter.

Annjee, Harriet's sister, on the other hand, is much like Laura in *Tambourines to Glory*; the weaknesses in their character reinforce Hughes's celebration of and empathy with black women despite their shortcomings. Annjee has an almost masochistic, irrational love for Jimboy, who never keeps a steady job and who spends his time traveling around the Midwest rather than raising his son, Sandy, and functioning as partner for his wife. When Annjee is working in the kitchen for the whites who employ her, she denies her hungry son the food that she is saving to take home to Jimboy, who sits around the house all day playing his guitar. When Jimboy is bored and ready for traveling, he leaves for Detroit, and Annjee follows him, leaving her son with her aging mother. When Jimboy takes his son fishing, Jimboy gives advice to Sandy about women, which makes clear Hughes's critique of the politics of masculinity:

"Don't never let no woman worry you," said the boy's father softly, picking the moist wriggling worms from the up-turned loam. "Treat 'em like chickens, son, Throw 'em a little corn and they'll run after you, but don't give 'em too much. If you do, they'll stop layin' and expect you to wait on 'em." (*NWL* 72)

Though Jimboy's advice to his son is totally irresponsible and reprehensible, Jimboy is not as abusive to Annjee as Buddy is to Laura in *Tambourines to Glory*. Early in the novel, Laura is charac-terized as a woman who spends her money on men, who craves the presence and body of man, and who drinks too much, par-ticularly when a man is not around on whom to put her atten-tion. After she and Essie are successful at moving into their store-front church, which started on the street corner, Buddy, who is a young, good-looking, completely unprincipled hustler who works for a mob boss, shows up in their church, and he and Laura mutually seduce each other. Once Buddy convinces Laura to make all the illegal changes in their church services, including running a "holy" numbers racket, he flaunts a younger woman around Harlem. When Laura confronts him, he cruelly and vilely responds:

"You? I'll slap the hell out of you, if you fool with me! A woman like you is supposed to put out some dough—if you want to keep a guy like me around. I don't mean peanuts. Be-lieve me, baby, now that you've got me, *you gonna keep me*. I ain't gonna give you up. Besides, I'm a partner in this deal—from the Holy Water and the Lucky Texts to the tam-bourines." (*NWL* 165)

Most of the black men in the poems and fiction discussed in this essay embody the negative male behavior that has been decon-structed primarily by black feminist scholars, rather than by black male literary critics or creative writers. Hughes is indeed atypical for his time (and for ours), and his works are atypical among the works of black male writers in the amount of space they give to the treatment of black women and especially atypi-cal in their presentation of a black man's identification with a black woman's response to her environment or her way of being.

While some poems, such as "Fascination," "Songs to the Dark Virgin," and the more familiar "Harlem Sweeties," suggest a romanticization of black women, an overview of Hughes's oeuvre reveals an impressive affirmation of the strength, beauty, vulnerabilities, victimization, wisdom, creative talent, and sensuality of black women that is unmatched in the writings of any other black man before, during, or after Hughes's time period.

3

When addressing the idea of Langston Hughes as a black male feminist, this essay would be incomplete without some discussion of Hughes's relationship with Zora Neale Hurston, his characterization of Jesse B. Semple, and his alleged homosexuality. Robert Hemenway, Arnold Rampersad, Cheryl Wall, and Faith Berry are just a few of the scholars who have recorded their versions of the dispute between Hurston and Hughes over the ownership of their collaborative play, *Mule Bone*. The consensus in these scholars' versions of the breakdown in communication and in the friendship between Hurston and Hughes is that Hurston was angered by Hughes's addition of Louise Thompson, the typist for the manuscript, as a collaborator. It is also generally agreed that Alain Locke, who shared Charlotte Osgood Mason as a patron with Hurston and Hughes, fueled Hurston's anger with Hughes because Locke wanted to solidify his relationship with Mason, who was angry with Hughes for asserting his independence from her. Having read the play as it appears in Henry Louis Gates Jr.'s edition of *Langston Hughes and Zora Neale Hurston: Mule Bone, A Comedy of Negro Life* and having read the many versions of the *Mule Bone* controversy, I propose that Hurston may have easily been in love with Hughes. Robert Hemenway explains that Hurston told Arna Bontemps, perhaps Hughes's closest black friend, that she was jealous of Louise Thompson. Hemenway writes:

In a letter to Hughes, dated January 29, 1931, Zora said, with some feeling: "Now get this straight, Langston. You are still dear to me. I don't care whom you love nor whom you marry, nor whom you bestow your worldly goods upon. I will never have any feeling about that part. I have always felt that if you had married anyone at all it would make no difference in our relationship. I *know* that no man on earth could change me towards you." (143)

The letter to which Hemenway refers, collected in Charles H. Nichols's *Arna Bontemps–Langston Hughes Letters, 1925–1967*, provides very useful insight into how two male writers—Bontemps and Hughes—discussed Hurston in private. Hughes's discussions of Hurston in his autobiographies are written with a public audience in mind. His private interaction with Bontemps may have been less guarded. Having talked with Hurston during his visit to North Carolina College, Bontemps, on November 24, 1939, writes to Hughes of his visit:

> To top it all, Zora [Neale Hurston] was there. She lectured there a year ago and got her hooks in so good she is now on the faculty, teaching dramatics. She gave me a wonderful time. Zora is really a changed woman, still her old humorous self, but more poised. She told me that the cross of her life is the fact that there has been a gulf between you and her. She said she wakes up at night crying about it even yet. . . . She said, or intimated, that the whole thing could be traced to old-fashioned female jealousy between her and Louise, jealousy over the matter of influence over you. When you look at it this way, it is hard to blame poor Zora. She can't help it if she's a woman. (Nichols 44)

With regard to the *Mule Bone* controversy, women scholars must acknowledge that Hurston played a role, if not a major role, in the dissolution of her relationship with Hughes. Hughes's reaction to Hurston, therefore, may appropriately be labeled self-defensive rather than sexist.

No matter what the truth behind the personal problems between Hughes and Hurston, he had a tremendous amount of respect for the quality and nature of Hurston's work. In relation to James Baldwin's *Go Tell It on the Mountain*, Hughes says, in a letter to Bontemps, dated February 18, 1953, "If you'll tell me what Dick Wright's book is like (since I haven't read it) I'll tell you about James Baldwin's *Go Tell It on the Mountain* which I've just finished: If it were written by Zora Neale Hurston with her feeling for the folk idiom, it would probably be a *quite* wonderful book. Baldwin over-writes and overpoliticizes in images way over the heads of the folks supposedly thinking them . . ." (Nichols 302). Hughes here indirectly characterizes his poetry and fiction: his love of the common folk and of black culture in general manifests in his perfect ear for the folk idiom and his empathy for the multilayered plight of black people, especially black women. Whether Hughes is correct or not, he suggests here that Baldwin creates unrealistic situations (overpoliticized situations) and that the reader is unable to psychically walk in Baldwin's characters' shoes.

Despite his affirmation of black women in his poetry and his balanced characterizations of black women in his fiction, Langston Hughes was not perfect. In the letters exchanged between him and Bontemps, he comments on Katherine Dunham's "getting fat where she sits down at" (Nichols 187); he makes a snide comment about Margaret Walker's being in "lecturable condition" because "She said NO more babies" (Nichols 329). Yet, in spite of comments that may be taken negatively, he evidences his concern that Gwendolyn Brooks and Margaret Walker, younger writers than he, were not producing as he wanted them to. His comment reflects his recognition of their creative skill. He says, in a letter dated February 8, 1953, "Both Margaret [Walker] and Gwendolyn [Brooks] never write a living word—and it would do no good for me to 'prod' them. But I might try anyhow" (Nichols 301). Having expressed in his letters his respect for the fine quality of Carson McCullers's and Katherine Anne Porter's fiction and their productivity, we can deduce that Hughes wanted Brooks and Walker to be as prolific as these white women were in the 1950s.

4

Because Langston Hughes's characterization of Jesse B. Semple demonstrates that Hughes walks comfortably in Simple's shoes, some readers may mistakenly identify Hughes with Simple. Yet, a close reading of the stories collected in *The Best of Simple* ("Simple on Indian Blood" explains the difference between *Semple* and *Simple*) reveals that, at the same time that Hughes's perfect representation of the folk idiom suggests his immersion into or identification with black folk culture, Hughes also seriously criticizes Simple's sexism. At least twenty-five years before Norman Lear popularized Archie Bunker as the king of malapropism, Hughes created the character Jesse B. Semple. Behind Simple's humorous malapropisms is a narcissistic, exploitative, boastful, penurious sexist with an overwhelming double standard in his relationship with women.

Any reader familiar with the Simple stories is aware that all the stories are interconnected around the main characters Simple; Hughes (or the writer who engages Simple in conversation and occasionally drinks with Simple); Isabel, Simple's first wife; Zarita, his woman on the side; and Joyce, the woman whom he loves and whom he eventually marries. Although Simple wants to marry Joyce, he refuses, for years, to pay to divorce Isabel. He continues to refuse even after Isabel pays one-third and her husband-to-be pays one-third as well. Simple agrees to pay the final third only after Joyce threatens that she will find another suitor if Simple does not marry her. Though everyone, including Joyce, knows that Simple uses Zarita sexually, Simple is not aware of the double standard that separates his misplaced positive self-image from his disrespect for Zarita. When the writer-conversationalist says that Simple should like Zarita a lot since he "likes a woman with experience," Simple responds, "I do and I don't. Zarita is strictly a after-hours gal—great when the hour is late, the wine is fine, and mellow whiskey has made you frisky" (*TBOS* 112). And, despite Simple's long-term sexual exploitation of Zarita, he is unflinching in differing expectations for men and for women. When Joyce takes a vacation and purposely does not tell Simple where she is when she writes to him, a conversation between Simple and the writer reveals Simple's sexism. Guessing that Joyce went to Atlantic City, Simple says,

> "I better not go down there and find Joyce setting up in no night club."
>   "What have you got against night clubs?"
>   "Nothing. It's what I got against guys who take girls to night clubs. I would not take no woman to a cabaret and spend all that loot on her that I did not intend to take further. A man is always thinking ahead of a woman." (*TBOS* 159)

Of course, when Simple is not with Joyce, he lives in nightclubs, and most frequently he is with Zarita until Joyce pressures him by threatening to refuse to see him.

The relationship between Langston Hughes, the author, and Langston Hughes, Simple's conversationalist in the stories, is at once simple and complex. In the "Foreword: Who Is Simple?" to *The Best of Simple*, Hughes explains that the Simple stories are "about no specific persons as such" (vii) but are based on the many characters that he meets in Harlem. While Simple on the surface may appear to be stereotypically drawn, Hughes gives him a depth and a complexity that are hidden behind his overshadowing sexism. Hughes also uses Simple to comment stealthily on the sociological, economic, and political laws that stifle black lives. In the story "There Ought to Be a Law," Simple explains that while whites set up laws to protect animals, they fail to institute laws or designate "Game Preserves for Negroes." These laws, according to Simple, would have signs that read "NO LYNCHING." He explains, "That is what I mean by Game Preserves for Negroes—Congress ought to set aside some place where we can go and nobody can jump on us and beat us, neither lynch us nor Jim Crow us every day. Colored folks rate as much protection as a buffalo, or a deer" (62). Despite his humorously wise critique of racism, Simple emerges as a quintessential sexist. In Simple, Langston Hughes creates a black male character whose attitude toward life and women reflects the same masculine perspective as that of the men in Hughes's poetry and other fiction. Hughes's (the writer-conversationist's) responses to

Simple's comments about women, on the other hand, subtly, and without Simple's recognition, undermine Simple's sexism.

5

It is ironic that someone who was as private about his feelings and intimate relationships as Hughes was could have been as successful as he was in revealing what I refer to as his female sensibility. I am not implying here that I am convinced that Langston Hughes was a homosexual. Despite the recent commentary that addresses his rumored homosexuality and the reflection of this homosexuality in his works, I find no definitive proof of this position.[1] Again, Hughes's response to one of James Baldwin's works obfuscates the issue of homosexuality, rather than clarifies it. Explaining Hughes's response to James Baldwin's *Another Country*, Rampersad says:

> Langston deplored what he saw as the absence in it of emotional and intellectual depth. *Another Country* was a novel about love that "will probably be widely read. Its subject is tormented love: love between men and women, homosexuals, whites and Negroes. . . . All these people are hopelessly involved in each other, and with themselves, and search for love in each other generally in physical ways. . . . The ending is a tragic and inconclusive general dissolution in which truth destroys love." (Rampersad 334–35)

Given the contemporary respect for Baldwin's creative genius, we learn more about Langston Hughes from his comments on Baldwin than we learn about Baldwin. One key to Hughes's dislike for Baldwin's *Another Country* lie in Hughes's idea that Baldwin's characters are "hopelessly involved" and that truth in the novel "destroys love." In contrast, the women characters in Hughes's fiction and in his poetry, despite their disappointment and pain, maintain, for the most part, an unwavering faith in the joy of love, rather than its "hopelessness." In Hughes's work, "truth does not destroy love." Laura's fall into perdition when confronted with the truth about Buddy is not typical of Hughes's women's characters. For most of Hughes's women, like Janie in *Their Eyes Were Watching God*, the dream is the truth, and they, too, like Harriet, live accordingly.

Hughes's reaction to Baldwin's novel about homosexuality and his referral to Baldwin's novel as a depiction of "tormented love" suggest that if Hughes was indeed homosexual, as some critics believe, he may have deliberately chosen to protect his privacy not only because of societal condemnation of homosexuality but also because of the intricacies of a gay lifestyle. Rampersad cites a number of people who knew Hughes quite well, including a young woman who indicated that Hughes may have been bisexual; in her opinion, he was definitely not homosexual. Arna Bontemps, who knew Hughes well, and Richard Bruce Nugent, a homosexual, assert that Hughes was not gay. Though it was generally agreed among Hughes's contemporaries that he was very elusive about his sexuality, Rampersad writes, "What also seems clear, however, is that Hughes found some young men, especially dark-skinned men, appealing and sexually fascinating. . . . Virile young men of very dark complexion fascinated him" (Rampersad 336).

While, according to Rampersad, "Hughes's reputation as a homosexual is based exclusively on rumor and suspicion" (Rampersad 337), his artistic sensibility is more feminine—though not necessarily gay—than masculine. And he chose not to marry, though Faith Berry and Arnold Rampersad describes Hughes's intimate relationships with Anne Coussey, Si-lan Chen, Natasha, and Elsie Roxborough. It may be true, as Rampersad suggests, that Hughes allowed his sexuality to "evaporate." Hughes's personality emerges to be much like that of the "Madam" in his "Madam" poems. The seventeen "Madam" poems create a rebellious, witty, grassroots, cagey black woman who defies a diverse range of societal norms. Because men and women have been socialized drastically differently and because of gendered constructions of reality, the Madam emerges as a persona who reflects Langston Hughes's defiance of gendered constructions of reality. The predominance of his poetry with black women as subject, his identification with these women, his refusal to judge these women, his indirect condemnation of the "norm" of black male masculinity, and his elusive, private attitude toward his sexuality deconstruct our stereotypical expectations of gender and emphasize the distinction between sexuality and gender that is now the subject of women's studies and feminist discourse.

It is this stereotypical notion of gender that is responsible for the hostility among black men to Alice Walker's characterization of black men in *The Color Purple*. Too many male readers have focused too narrowly on one novel selected from Walker's canon and have refused to admit that too many black men do indeed abuse black women. This same narrow focus and limited expectation have caused Hughes's readers to overlook the amount of time and space Hughes devotes to black women. Though he wrote poems with black men as subject, these poems, such as "Johannesburg," "Park Benching," and "Minstrel Man," emerge as generalized treatments of racism and thus the black condition in general. We have failed to note and ask why Hughes wrote such a large number of poems about black women. The answer to the puzzle of his enigmatic attitude toward his sexuality, perhaps, is hidden behind or within the subtext of these poems, in which the majesty and vulnerabilities of rural and urban black women are captured in the merger of race and gender. The majority of his canon unarguably makes him the prototype of contemporary feminist intellectuals such as Audre Lorde, bell hooks, and Beverly Guy-Sheftall, who critique the politics of difference and the effect of race and gender on the black woman's concept of self.

NOTE

1. For discussion of Hughes's alleged homosexuality, see Anne Borden, "Heroic 'Hussies' and 'Brilliant Queers': Genderracial Resistance in the Works of Langston Hughes," *African American Review* 28 (autumn 1994): 333–345; Gregory Woods, "Gay Re-Readings of the Harlem Renaissance Poets," *Journal of Homosexuality* 26 (1993): 127; and Craig Hickman, "Servin' Shade," *Harvard Gay and Lesbian Review* 3 (1996): 36.

WORKS CITED

Aldridge, Delores P. *Focusing: Black Male-Female Relationships*. Chicago: Third World, 1991.

"A Black Feminist Statement: The Combahee River Collective." In *But Some of Us Are Brave*, ed. Gloria T. Hull, Patricia Bell Scott, and Barbara Smith. Old Westbury, N.Y.: Feminist Press. 13–22.

Hemenway, Robert. *Zora Neale Hurston: A Literary Biography*. Urbana: University of Illinois Press, 1977.

Jones, Claudia. "An End to the Neglect of the Problems of the Negro Woman." In *Words of Fire: An Anthology of African American Feminist Thought*. Ed. Beverly Guy-Sheftall. New York: New Press, 1995. 108–23.

Kent, George. *Blackness and the Adventure of Western Culture*. Chicago: Third World Press, 1972.

Lewis, David Levering. *When Harlem Was in Vogue*. New York: Knopf, 1981.

McDowell, Deborah E. "New Directions for Black Feminist Criticism." *Black American Literature Forum* 14 (winter 1980): 153–59.

Nichols, Charles, ed. *Arna Bontemps–Langston Hughes Letters, 1925–1967*. New York: Dodd, Mead, 1980.

Rampersad, Arnold. *The Life of Langston Hughes, Volume II: 1941–1967, I Dream a World*. New York: Oxford University Press, 1988.

Stewart, Maria Miller. "Religion and the Pure Principles of Morality, the Sure Foundations on Which We Must Build." In *Words of Fire: An Anthology of African American Feminist Thought*. Ed. Beverly Guy-Sheftall. New York: New Press, 1995. 26–29.

Williams, Sherley Anne. "Some Implications of Womanist Theory." In *Reading Black, Reading Feminist: A Critical Anthology*. Ed. Henry Louis Gates Jr. New York: Meridian, 1990. 68–75.

Wintz, Cary D. *Black Culture and the Harlem Renaissance*. Houston, Tex.: Rice University Press, 1988.

The Adventures of a Social Poet

Langston Hughes from the Popular Front
to Black Power

James Smethurst

One of the peculiar things about critical assessments of Langston Hughes's career is the still pronounced tendency to think of Hughes as primarily a Harlem Renaissance writer. In recent years there have been critical efforts to rethink Hughes's post–Harlem Renaissance work, particularly that of his "revolutionary" period in the 1930s and his work during the civil rights and Black Power eras. However, critics still quite commonly regard the "red" poetry as second-rate didactic efforts lacking the lyricism and nuance of voice found in other periods of Hughes's work and dismiss the early Black Power–period poems as weak and opportunistic efforts to repackage Hughes's work in order to find a niche in changing times (Ford; Sundquist; Vendler). What is peculiar about these assessments is that the later Hughes resonates with popular African American audiences so strongly, the fame of such early poems as "The Negro Speaks of Rivers" and "Mother to Son" notwithstanding. It is largely the later poetry, drama, fiction, and sketches, the "Simple" stories, such poems as "Harlem," "Theme for English B," and "Let America Be America," such plays as *Black Nativity* and *Simply Heavenly*, that have made Hughes among the most beloved writers for a general black readership—and for many post–World War II black artists and intellectuals. In fact, one might say that the work of Hughes not only appealed to a general black audience but in no small part created that audience for a serious, often formally difficult, vernacular-based and politically radical African American literature that engaged the forms and resources of popular culture.

Hughes's work at the beginning of the 1930s was in three distinctive registers aimed at three relatively discrete audiences. This division of Hughes's work into three basic modes can be seen as a reflection of the relative weakness of the Left within the broader African American community in the early 1930s at the same time that the political, cultural, and economic impact of the Great Depression and a new Communist Party engagement with "Negro Liberation" drew African American intellectuals and artists further into the circles of the communist Left. One register might be thought of as the emphatically "literary" in a modernist vein. The primary audience for this work was the relatively small, interracial (though largely white) group(s) of readers who habitually read "serious" modern literature. Hughes's writing in this mode included not only the lyrics collected in *Dear Lovely Death* (1932) but also his early short stories, which were largely modeled on the short fiction of D. H. Lawrence. These lyrics and stories are suffused with feelings of alienation, fragmented identity, and failed attempts to constitute or reconstitute family and community. Perhaps the most representative stories in this regard are those based on Hughes's experiences as merchant seaman in the early 1920s. As with Melville's Ishmael, the African American narrator who has shipped out on a freighter bound for West Africa with a polyglot crew of "Greeks, West Indian Negroes, Irish, Portuguese, and Americans" finds an "America" in which normative bonds of race, nationality, and ethnicity are at times temporarily transcended, redrawn, and reconfirmed— tellingly, the Americans, black and white, are not always clearly marked by race. An African American narrator frequently searches for an organic connection to an African heritage but finds himself strangely rejected and assigned to another community in which he is an outsider when the indigenous people see him indistinguishable from his "white" (and "brown") mates. At the same time, "American" customs are sometimes upheld in a context that totally changes their meaning, as in "The Little Virgin." In that story, Mike, an older sailor from Newark, New Jersey, strikes an African prostitute for spilling his beer in a waterfront bar in Senegal. A younger sailor, "The Little Virgin," who is a sort of protégé of the older man, deranged by loneliness and a loss of community, attacks Mike. The story ends with "The Little Virgin" deliriously chanting over and over, "He oughtn't to hit a woman." The African American narrator's understated outrage over the injustice of colonialism, racism, sexual exploitation, and the miserable treatment of merchant seaman mixes with a confusion of racial, gender, class, and national lines that results from his own implicit alienation and lack of community. Hughes would take up this irony again later in a far more humorous vein in the 1946 story "Who's Passing for Who."

Another mode of Hughes's writing was what might be thought of as African American uplift. This mode consisted largely of dramatic monologues, such as "The Negro Mother," "The Colored Soldier," and "The Black Clown," collected as *The Negro Mother and Other Dramatic Recitations* (1932), that served as much of the basis for Hughes's early reading tours across the South. These readings, largely at African American educational institutions, were predominantly attended by "middle-class" African American audiences (Rampersad 1986, 223–34). This material consisted largely of formally conservative poems of black pride and perseverance leavened by the occasional humorous piece, such as "Broke."

Interestingly, "Broke" draws on the conventions of African American vaudeville that had their origins in black or "Ethiopian" minstrelsy:

> Aw-oo! Yonder comes a woman I used to know way down
>   South.
> (Ain't seen her in six years! Used to go with her, too!)
> She would be alright if she wasn't so bow-legged, and cross-
>   eyed,
> And didn't have such a big mouth.
> Howdy-do, daughter! Caledonia, how are you? (*CP*, 150)

Drawing on the resources of minstrel-derived comic theater seems at odds with several of the "serious" uplift poems, such as "The Black Clown" and "The Big-Timer," in which minstrel images serve as metonymies for black false consciousness. In some respects, this contradiction mirrors traditional African American divides of secular and sacred, of uplift and popular entertainment. Few other black writers, with the exception of Helene Johnson, were willing to take on the representation of this divide without devaluing one side or the other. One could see the coexistence of "Broke" with the uplift poems as a gesture by Hughes toward the split of Paul Laurence Dunbar in "We Wear the Mask" and elsewhere. It also anticipates Hughes's future attempts to put different African American voices, different discourses really, in conversation with each other.

The final sort of work Hughes wrote in the early 1930s was his "revolutionary" poetry, prose, and drama. Hughes's revolutionary writing includes the many poems that he published in such journals associated with the communist Left as *New Masses*, the *Daily Worker*, and the *Harlem Liberator*. In fact, Hughes's work probably appeared more frequently in the communist Left press than that of any other writer. Of course, Hughes had published poetry in leftist journals since the mid-1920s. However, the combination of the economic crisis of the Great Depression, which struck the black community particularly hard, and the single-minded devotion to the causes of "Negro Liberation" and anticolonialism on the part of the Communist Party of the United States of America drew Hughes into a much closer relationship with the communist Left in the early 1930s. He served as president of the League of Struggle for Negro Rights and participated prominently in the Left-led struggle to save the nine Scottsboro defendants from execution, as well as in other Left-initiated campaigns.

One of Hughes's most widely circulated radical pieces of the period was his jazz-inflected semiverse play "Scottsboro Limited." This play was performed in a variety of locations around the country by leftist theater groups as part of the campaign to save the Scottsboro defendants. It ended with black and white workers joining the newly revolutionary Scottsboro defendants, each now the "new red Negro," in smashing the electric chair—and, by extension, racist and capitalist oppression. While Hughes's shorter revolutionary lyrics of the 1930s seem to draw away from the vernacular language- and music-based pieces of the 1920s, "Scottsboro Limited" is a testament to Hughes's embryonic attempts to imagine an African American popular radical art that would appeal to a broad black audience beyond a relatively small cadre of organized radicals.

Hughes's project of creating a popular radical art that would appeal to a wide African American (as well as non-African American) audience found new opportunities with the rise of the Popular Front era in the mid-1930s. A full description of the features and events of the Popular Front are beyond the scope of this essay. However, some general comments on the Popular Front and on Popular Front aesthetics and literary practices are in order. As to periodization, while the official era of the Popular Front as a policy of broad-based antifascist coalition building by the Communist International might be marked from the Seventh Comintern Congress, in 1935, to the Hitler-Stalin Pact, in 1939, the Popular Front approach dominated the communist Left, particularly in what was known as the "cultural work," until at least 1948. One of the most notable, and most noted, features of Popular Front aesthetics is a conscious mixing of genres and media—of "high" and "low," of "popular" and "literary," of Whitman and Eliot, of folk culture and mass culture, of literary and nonliterary documents.

Another important of feature of much Popular Front art was an interest in race and ethnicity and the relation of racial identity and ethnic identity to an American identity. Some commentators have considered the Popular Front to be a retreat from earlier communist concerns with ethnic and national identity, particularly with the African American "nation," promoting instead a sentimental and blandly assimilationist multiculturalism. While there is some evidence for this argument, when one considers the poetry of Sterling Brown, Frank Marshall Davis, Langston Hughes, Waring Cuney, and Margaret Walker in the second half of the 1930s, narratives such as Donato DiPietro's *Christ in Concrete*, Jerre Mangione's *Mount Allegro*, Daniel Fuchs's Williamsburg trilogy, Carlos Bulosan's *America Is in the Heart*, H. T. Tsiang's *And China Has Hands*, Richard Wright's *Native Son*, the famous "Spirituals to Swing" concerts of 1939, and paintings by Jacob Lawrence, Ben Shahn, Aaron Douglas, and Jack Levine, to name but a few of many, many examples, it is clear that race and ethnicity remained overriding concerns during the Popular Front. It is true that these concerns were often as much about transformation, interaction, and hybridity as they were about tradition, distinction, and separate development. This interest in race, ethnicity, and nationality within artistic, literary or quasi-literary works of the Popular Front was frequently linked to a strong sense of community and region and the relationship of place, particularly (though not exclusively) the urban neighborhood, to American identity.

While the poetics of the Popular Front shaped (and were shaped by) Hughes's poetry, especially in such poems as "Broadcast on Ethiopia," "Air Raid over Harlem," and "Seven Moments of Love," as well as his "poetry-play" (and musical) "Don't You Want to Be Free?" the foremost examples of Hughes's Popular Front approach (and perhaps the premier literary achievement of the Popular Front) are his "Simple" stories. Of course, the composition and publication of these stories spanned several literary/political/historical periods, from the late Popular Front to the McCarthy era to the civil rights period to the early stirring of the Black Power/Black Arts era. The "Simple" stories (named after their protagonist, Jesse B. Semple, aka "Simple") first emerged as part of Hughes's "From Here to Yonder" *Chicago Defender* column in 1943 and continued to appear until 1965. While the home paper of the stories was the *Defender* (and, at the very end of the series' life, the *New York Post*), the stories were syndicated to a wide range of papers, including such nationalist journals as *Muhammad Speaks*.

These stories were shaped by the cultural conversations of World War II and Cold War America, particularly among African Americans, and how in turn they attempted to push the boundaries of acceptable political and aesthetic discourse in the Cold War era or at least to retain some shred of Popular Front poetics and politics. Hughes is adamant about avoiding political and artistic marginalization in the Simple stories, as in much of his work, both in terms of the African American community and American society generally. Instead, Hughes is determined to place, or re-place, the African American speaker, and his or her voice, at the center of some of our society's primary defining stories.

These stories were molded by late Popular Front aesthetics (of which, as noted, Hughes was one of the chief creators) of the World War II era but were adapted brilliantly to the Cold War. World War II provided African Americans unprecedented opportunities to break through the legal and extralegal barriers of Jim Crow segregation, particularly in the areas of housing and employment. These opportunities occurred for what might be thought of as ideological as well as practical reasons—not that you can completely separate the two. On a practical level, the vastly increased demand for labor in the war industries, which included everything from meat packing to making bombs, and the vastly decreased availability of white male workers, many of whom enlisted or were drafted into the military, opened up to African Americans jobs that had previously been thought of as "white." This, along with a continued decline in the tenant farmer system in southern agriculture, accelerated the migration of African Americans to urban centers, such as Chicago, Detroit, Baltimore, St. Louis, Memphis, Birmingham, Los Angeles, and, of course, New York.

On an ideological level, the system of Jim Crow and the American ideology of white superiority were obviously uncomfortably close to the tenets of Nazi Germany and to notions of Aryan superiority. The civil rights movements, significantly led by communists, socialists, Trotskyists, and other sorts of leftists during World War II, spent much time emphasizing to great effect the contradiction inherent in supporting white supremacy while fighting Nazism. Also, a certain ideological space for the fight against racism was created by actual and feared antiwhite propaganda appeals by the Japanese to African Americans, whom the U.S. government feared might see the early victories of Japan over the the United States, Britain, France, and the Netherlands as victories over the ideology of white superiority.

In short, a combination of guilt, fear, and contradiction allowed civil rights organizations to argue effectively against racism to an extent not seen since the end of Reconstruction. This is not to say that it was easy or that Jim Crow did not remain the law of much of the land, including much of the North, only that it was possible for movements, such as the labor and civil rights leader A. Philip Randolph's March on Washington movement in 1942, to make large demands on a national and local level and to achieve significant results, such as Roosevelt's executive order banning discrimination in federal employment and the establishment of the Fair Employment Practices Commission.

It is worth noting that this sort of thing had happened before, if not to this extent. During World War I, labor shortages also opened up new jobs to African Americans, prompting the beginning of what we now call the "Great Migration" of African Americans from the South to the North. And, while in that conflict the United States was not at war with an explicitly racist enemy, it did mobilize for the war with a rhetoric of democracy that civil rights leaders, such as W. E. B. Du Bois, felt provided an opportunity for African Americans to argue against institutionalized racism. However, in what might be thought of as the racial reconversion process after the war, such hopes were dashed to a large extent. Many African Americans lost their wartime jobs once the First World War was over. The Ku Klux Klan grew into a national organization with millions of members in the late 1910s and 1920s. And, even before the war ended, a wave of racist violence began, ranging from lynchings, often of black soldiers in uniform, to race riots in East St. Louis, Chicago, Omaha, Knoxville, and many other American cities, where white mobs attacked black neighborhoods. The often frankly stated purpose of the violence was to remind African Americans of "their place," whether in terms of jobs, housing, public accommodations, or general demeanor. This violence was carried out with a minimum of federal interference despite the activities of civil rights organizations, such as the "silent parade" of 1917, in which ten thousand African Americans marched down New York's Fifth Avenue to protest lynchings and assaults on black communities such as the East St. Louis riot of 1917.

What made the post–World War II era different from the period after World War I was the interrelated phenomena of the Cold War and decolonization in Asia, Africa, the Caribbean, and Latin America. The post–World War II period was characterized by competition and conflict between what might be thought of as a capitalist bloc of nations led by the United States and a communist bloc of nations led by the Soviet Union, or, as it was often put in the United States, democracy versus communism. The period of the late 1940s, 1950s, and early 1960s was also marked by a huge upsurge in anticolonial struggles, both violent, as in China, Algeria, Cuba, the Philippines, Malaya, Kenya, and Indochina, and relatively peaceful, as in India, Ghana, South Africa (until the 1960s), and Guyana. These anticolonial struggles complicated the Cold War for the United States in that the bloc of nations led by the United States included the leading colonial powers—Britain, France, the Netherlands, Portugal, Belgium, and the United States itself. The situation was further complicated by the fact that many anticolonial struggles were led by communists and/or other sorts of leftists who were relatively open to Communism. While the United States on occasion directly supported the old colonial powers, as in Indochina and in the Portuguese colonies in Africa, more and more the United States's policy vis-à-vis decolonization tended to be the support of anticommunist alternatives to Left-led anticolonial movements. The result was that the battle for the hearts and minds of what we sometimes refer to as the Third World (a term that has its origins in the era of Cold War decolonization) became a crucial aspect of the Cold War and American international policies.

American racism and the institutions of Jim Crow became hugely important factors in this struggle for hearts and minds. In the first place, while not exactly the same as U.S. racism, the ideological underpinning of colonialism rested to a large extent on notions of white supremacy. As a result, the peoples of European and American colonies and neo-colonies were extremely interested in and identified with the conditions and struggles of black people in the United States where the fight against white supremacy had been sharper and antiracism more clearly articulated than in any other country. And, of course, these same peoples remained very suspicious of U.S. claims for American-style democracy while the glaring contradictions of Jim Crow remained. Left-led movements and the bloc of communist nations were not slow in pointing these contradictions out. For example, when the militant Florida NAACP leader Harry Moore was assassinated by the Ku Klux Klan in 1951, the Soviet ambassador to the United Nations denounced Moore's murder on the floor of the UN General Assembly. Similarly, Soviet premier Nikita Khrushchev repeatedly raised the issue of racial discrimination in the United States with Vice President Richard Nixon in their famous 1959 "Kitchen Debates." And, African Americans here in the United States also noted the contradictions between U.S. rhetoric abroad and the U.S. reality for African Americans at home—as seen in various of Hughes's works, such as the early Cold War–era story "When a Man Sees Red," in which the narrator, Simple, imagines himself denouncing the John Martin Wood, the Georgia congressman and open Ku Klux Klan member who chaired the House Un-American Activities Committee and who conflated African American equality and communism (*RS* 84–86).

Thus, it is not surprising that many of the actions of various branches of the federal government, such as the U.S. Supreme Court's decision in *Brown vs. the Board of Education*, specifically cited the Cold War as a justification for the ending or restricting of various aspects of Jim Crow segregation. This is not to say here that the federal government was completely sympathetic to the civil rights movement—or that these victories did not require tremendous struggle, organization, courage, and sacrifice on the part of the civil rights activists, only that the Cold War provided African Americans with new leverage to fight against Jim Crow, and prevented, at least partially, the sort of racial reconversion that followed World War I. And, in much the same way that the earlier struggles of African Americans influenced contemporary anticolonial movements, the liberation movements in Asia, Africa, and Latin America galvanized African Americans. At the same time, the rapid changes worldwide brought on by the anticolonial movement around the world inspired a sense of impatience in many more activist African Americans who found the rate of change in the United States much too slow by comparison.

The late 1940s and early 1950s witnessed high-profile federal interrogation and/or persecution of many of the African Americans who were, or had been, most prominently linked to the Communist Party, such as the leading black Communists Benjamin Davis and Henry Winston, W. E. B. Du Bois, the singer and actor Paul Robeson, and Hughes himself. In addition to high-profile trials, hearings, jailings, deprivation of citizens' right to travel, and so on, the period also featured lower-profile (and sometimes covert) disruptions of the lives of various black artists and intellectuals deemed "disloyal." At the same time, Left-led black organizations, such as the Southern Negro Youth Congress, the National Negro Labor Council, the Civil Rights Congress, and the Southern Conference for Human Welfare, were denounced as "communist fronts," isolated, and destroyed.

Of course, the Communist Party created plenty of its own problems during the period and was torn apart by Khrushchev's 1956 revelations about the extent of Stalin's murderous activities and the Soviet-led invasion of Hungary. But it is worth recalling how limited political discourse in the United States was once the domestic Cold War really intensified around 1947. Thus, you had an ironic situation in which the Cold War, with its international competition with communism, provided new opportunities to challenge Jim Crow practically and ideologically, as in the campaign that resulted in President Truman's 1948 order abolishing segregation in the armed forces, while at the same time the actual organizations and individuals that had led the struggle for African American equality during the 1930s and 1940s were destroyed, discredited, isolated, or forced to bend over backward to prove their anticommunist purity, as in the case of the NAACP, which supported the government persecution of W. E. B. Du Bois. On an ideological level, an anticommunist consensus of liberals and conservatives is declared; individualism becomes emphasized, and forms of group identification, especially of class and race, are considered passé, if not downright un-American; the notion of ideological struggle in which Marxism, communism, and socialism are legitimate positions is attacked, and even the word "ideology" itself becomes suspect.

Thus, the "Simple" stories grew out of the late Popular Front moment and Popular Front hybrid, multigeneric, multimedia aesthetics but were used by Hughes to engage the cultural moment of the Cold War. For example, the story "Temptation," Simple's working-class, African American revisionist take on *Genesis*, first appeared in book form in the 1950 collection *Simple Speaks His Mind*. A partial list of the texts, movements, institutions, figures, and events that this short and seemingly "Simple" piece references the Bible, African American folk religion, popular American religious culture, Milton's *Paradise Lost*, an array of African American religious figures from fifty years of Harlem history, African American nationalism (particularly Marcus Garvey's Universal Negro Improvement Association and its religious arm, the African Orthodox Church), the Cold War and the arms race, the antinuclear weapons gospel song "Atom and Evil" by the Golden Gate Quartet, Bing Crosby, the 1936 film *The Green Pastures*, African American variety-show comedy (with the generally unnamed narrator as the straight man), the African American rhetorical practices of capping (or ritualized insult) and toasting (a form of rhymed and often bawdy narrative oratory), and what might be thought of as the ur-text of American racism from which black people as full humans are absent. Perhaps the most frequent "high culture" reference is to the most iconic canonical English writer, Shakespeare, recalled by Simple's nutty and often free-associative rants, which frequently make disturbing sense (as in the jump from apple to atom), more sense generally in the context of political and cultural politics during the high Cold War than the pronouncements of the more "reasonable" narrator. The most overt invocation appears in the narrator's typically stiff world-as-stage comment at the end of the story: "I trust you will not let your rather late arrival on our contemporary stage distort your perspective." (Simple tersely and with perfect timing answers, "No") (*TBOS* 28). This obvious reference to Shakespeare and Hamlet's famous speech recalls also the clown-gravediggers of *Hamlet* and their comments on Adam, thereby connecting Simple with the Shakespearean fool who speaks truth, albeit often obliquely—a useful ability in the Cold War era.

The issue of audience, imagined and real, is crucial to our un-

derstanding of what Hughes is doing in the Simple stories. To
start with the stories in their original context of the *Chicago Defender*, one needs to note that the *Defender* and the more repu-
table journals of the African American press and their readers
were not necessarily in sympathy with the street culture embodied by Jesse Semple, who is definitely one of what Amiri Baraka,
in his play *Dutchman*, called "all these blues people" (Baraka 98).
For example, other than accepting ads for new record releases,
the *Defender* was notably unengaged with the blues boom of the
1920s and early 1930s. While this was somewhat less true later,
the attitude of the *Defender* and many of its readers, to generalize
broadly, was a lot like that of Simple's wife Joyce, who is always
taking Simple to lectures, "classical" European music concerts,
poetry readings, and the Episcopal church in hopes of "improving" him, without notable results.

Thus, Hughes uses Simple to make an intraracial (as opposed
to interracial) argument against a Eurocentric model of cultural
value that enshrines dead or near-dead white people at the expense of the culture of the majority of African Americans. This
model of cultural value is bad, Hughes argues through Simple,
because it ignores living African American "high" artists unless
they have been certified by white taste makers—as seen in "Banquet in Honor," where an elderly African American artist takes
an "elite" black gathering to task for not supporting him until he
was called a genius by the *New York Times* (*TBOS* 46).

Hughes also criticizes this Eurocentric model because it ex-
cludes the vast majority of African American cultural expression
and, by extension, the producers and consumers of this expression such as Simple. Such an approach is seen as elitist, pessimistic, and self-hating. Simple does not completely reject
"high" culture but instead explicitly proposes a model in which
African American popular expression, particularly music, is integrated, so to speak, with "high" culture. This approach is seen as
far more optimistic, self-affirming and democratically inclusive of
the entire African American community:

A jazz band like Duke's or Hamp's or Basie's sure would of
helped that meeting. At least on Saturday afternoon, they

could have used a little music to put some pep into the pro-
ceedings. Now just say for instant, baby, they was to open
with jazz and close with jam—and do the talking in between.
(*TBOS* 244)

Simple's construct of the African American popular tradition
is one that stretches from the "classic" blues of the 1920s, as seen
in the story "Shadow of the Blues," to the big band jazz of the
1930s, as seen in "Jazz, Jive, and Jam," to the bebop of the 1940s as
seen in "Bop"—from Ma Rainey to Duke Ellington to Dizzy
Gillespie. As he did so often in his career, Hughes is making an
argument for the fundamental continuity of African American
expressive culture. Here Hughes is making not only an intraracial argument but also an interracial argument. Once again, the
issue of audience, imagined and real, comes into play. While the
audience for the columns in the *Defender* was almost entirely
African American, the audience for the collections, especially *The
Best of Simple* (1961), was another thing. In the 1940s and 1950s,
various schools of white critics and listeners adopted jazz for
their different cultural purposes. This period featured a "Dixieland Revival" in which versions of early New Orleans jazz were
promoted as the "real" jazz; there were similar champions of Big
Band jazz; finally there was a bohemian or "avant-garde" school
that adopted bebop as its badge of rebellion (Gennari 1991). By
featuring so prominently stories that proclaim the continuity of
African American music—and, by extension, African American
culture—Hughes pointedly argues against appropriations of
African American culture that would remove pieces of that culture from their larger context. And, of course, the notion that
African American popular culture had a place within Euro-
American "high" culture—and Euro-American popular culture—
was also directed as much to white audiences as black and so
became a prominent part of the collections, especially *The Best of
Simple*.

The arguments Hughes makes here are not simply sociological, political, or even broadly cultural but are also literary in that
he is polemicizing against what might considered the "high" neo-
Modernist approach that arose in American letters during the

1950s. What this neo-Modernism consisted of, for the most part, was a stripped-down "high" modernism derived from a fairly restricted reading of European and American "high" literary modernism of the early twentieth century, such as the works of Eliot, Yeats, and the early Joyce, a neo-Modernism that was formally conservative and aspiring toward a sort of "universality" that tended to avoid or decry the concerns with popular culture, ethnicity, race, and locale that animated the Popular Front. While we most prominently associate the "high" neo-Modernist styles championed by the New Critics and the New York Intellectuals with such diverse poets as Robert Lowell, Delmore Schwartz, John Berryman, and Allen Tate and with fiction writers such as Saul Bellow, Schwartz, and Mary McCarthy, it also had a huge influence on African American letters in the work of such writers as Ellison, Robert Hayden, Gwendolyn Brooks, and Melvin Tolson. Of course, Ellison is very difficult to pigeonhole because he adopts the radical and largely abstract individualism that marks much neo-Modernist art during the 1950s while retaining the engagement with folk culture and popular culture that was a hallmark of many of the early works of the literary Left in which Ellison, as well as Hughes, participated. Hughes, instead, argued through these "Simple" stories, and in his poetry, for a style that was popular and modern, even postmodern, and that drew on the resources of mass culture.

This is not to say that the essence of Hughes's argument translates into a simplistic style for a debased audience. On a formal level, the Simple stories are quite complex. The metaphor of conversation appears so much in this essay because it arises organically from these texts, which are often literally a series of conversations, say between Simple and the narrator, which in turn often describe a dizzying spiral of interlocking conversations. Consider the levels of narration in the Simple stories for a minute. For example, in a number of stories, you have Simple's Cousin Minnie or Joyce or the "old gentleman" artist of "Banquet in Honor" speaking through Simple speaking through the narrator speaking through Langston Hughes the author whose presence as author is established by the forewords of the various collections. Such a plethora of overlapping narratorial voices reminds us that the Simple stories foreground, are in fact virtually nothing but, the overt representation and recreation of a wide range of African American speakers. These stories, as is virtually all of Hughes's work, are characterized by the representations and re-creation of diverse black voices and white voices. This much resembles the Russian literary critic Mikhail Bahktin's notion of heteroglossia in what Bahktin calls dialogic fiction, in which different voices contained within a text represent different, and often conflicting, social groups (Bahktin 1984). (One might also raise the formal principle of antiphony, or call and response, which characterizes much vernacular [or folk] African and African American culture.) Hughes allows the voices to remain in all their diversity and conflict while insisting on an ultimate community between these integral African American speaking subjects. In short, this is, as Simple says, not quite simple.

Other formal aspects of the Simple stories are worth mentioning. First, there is the obvious influence of music, not only thematically, as in the genealogy of the blues cited by the narrator and Simple in "Shadow of the Blues," but in the diction and syntax of Simple's speech. Not only does Simple quote fragments of blues, but the blues often inflect Simple's speech:

> But Zarita has ruint my life. You don't know how it feels, buddy, when somebody has gone that you never had before. I never had a woman like Joyce. I *loved* that girl. Nobody never cared for me like Joyce did. (*TBOS* 83)

Not only does this passage engage the sensibility and the thematics of the blues, but the repeated "never" gives the flavor of a three-line blues stanza.

Simple's speech is similarly inflected by folk and popular African American expressive forms, including jokes, the dozens, tall tales, badman stories, and toasts. And, of course, probably the most important influence on the form of the story is black vaudeville, with the stories resembling a comic routine in which the narrator plays the straight man to Simple's clown. (It is worth mentioning that the vaudeville-style variety show survived in the African American community until the late 1960s [at the Apollo

Theater, in New York City, the Regal Theater, in Chicago, the Howard, in Washington, D.C., and so on].) While in some respects the impact of African American popular music on the form of the Simple stories is more clearly foregrounded, it is hard to overemphasize the crucial connection between the Simple stories and African American vaudeville comedy. While it is one of the most difficult formal elements to analyze, in part because it is so invisible so to speak, the translation of vaudeville comic timing and rhythm onto the page in the stories is among the most brilliant accomplishments of Hughes.

Obviously, these stories, after the manner of most newspaper columns, take on many of the topical concerns of the day and respond to immediate events. One of the uses of a character as goofy as Simple is that Simple allowed Hughes to make points that were difficult to make during the Cold War. Hughes, as readers may know, was called before Joseph McCarthy's Senate committee in 1953. Hughes, unlike Paul Robeson, and unlike Simple in "When a Man Sees Red," written before Hughes's appearance, essentially apologized for his earlier radical activities and proclaimed his patriotism—though he did not name names, as they said back then. Hughes lay very low politically for quite a while after that. This is important to our understanding of the shape and content of the *Best of Simple*, which appeared in 1961. The collection features the illustrations of Bernhard Nast, a German artist who first illustrated a German edition of the Simple stories. Nast's drawings put Simple in a depoliticized frame, emphasizing the aspects of Simple as a lover and hanger-around, rather than as a worker and commentator on race and class relations. After 1953, Hughes also toned down, though he did not eliminate, his criticism of the various communist-hunting government committees. Hughes did not include even this muted criticism in *The Best of Simple*. Neither did he comment on anticolonial struggles much in *The Best of Simple*, though he often mentioned these struggles in his *Defender* stories even after 1953.

Nonetheless, even in *The Best of Simple*, Simple makes many points, including the right to armed self-defense against racists in "A Toast to Harlem," and refers to the Cold War in such stories as "Radioactive Red Caps" and "Temptation" in ways that might have been considered subversive. After the manner of fools in Shakespeare's plays, Simple plays the clown who speaks the truth for discerning listeners (readers) to hear. That Simple speaks the truth to an often ambiguous and ambivalent narrator who is sometimes identified with Hughes further suggests the nature of Hughes's own mask during the McCarthy era.

The Cold War clearly shaped not only the subjects and the denotative meaning of the stories but also the formal choices that Hughes made—even down to the selection of stories and illustrations for *The Best of Simple*. However, while shaped by many of the same concerns and pressures as other artists, Hughes argues against much of Cold War culture. Hughes, like many artists of that era, is much concerned with the relation between individual identity and group identity. As vivid a personality as Simple is, Hughes nonetheless makes the claim in the Foreword to *The Best of Simple* that "it is impossible to live in Harlem and not know at least a hundred Simples." The point here is that Simple is both a type and an individual and that there is not necessarily a contradiction between individual identity and group identity—whether of race, class, or gender. This is obviously different from such diverse cultural products of the Cold War era as Ralph Ellison's novel *Invisible Man*, the abstract expressionist painting of William De Kooning, Jackson Pollock, and Franz Kline, and the films *High Noon*, *Invasion of the Body Snatchers*, and *Rebel Without a Cause*, to name a few of the most famous high-art and popular-culture works of the era, which emphasized a heroic but somewhat abstract individualism (as indicated semantically by the names of the most famous James Dean movie [*Rebel Without a Cause*] and the dominant movement in the visual arts [abstract expressionism]). Thus, on the level of formal construction, Hughes pushes the limits of Cold War end-of-ideology culture. In this, we have an excellent example of how formal choices have a certain cultural meaning and how particular arguments, including what constitutes literary value, cultural value, and political value, are advanced by the shifting diction, the complex layering of narration, the incorporation of the forms, subjects, and inflections of African American folk culture and popular culture, and a huge range of literary, musical, folkloric, sociological, political, and

historical allusion seamlessly compressed into a "Simple" style—
a style so "Simple" that it seems to be a natural expression and
not the sort of literary production that, like the most critically
valued postwar fiction, say *Invisible Man*, wears its literariness on
its sleeve.

Hughes's poetry in the late 1940s and early 1950s, particularly
Montage of a Dream Deferred (1951), also in many ways continues a
Popular Front sensibility in a Cold War context, though it is
more clearly engaged with "neo-Modernist" poetics than his
short fiction. "Neo-Modernist" here refers to the powerful trend
among black and white writers, such as Delmore Schwartz, John
Berryman, Robert Lowell, Allen Tate, Randall Jarrell, Gwendolyn Brooks, Melvin Tolson, and Robert Hayden, to propose
the "high" Modernist work of the early twentieth century, particularly the work of Eliot and Pound, and, to a lesser extent, of
Stevens and Crane, as the necessary ground of any truly serious
contemporary literature. Hughes is mentioned less often with
this neo-Modernist aesthetic. If one looks for a "high" Modernist
analog of Hughes's *Montage*, it would be found in the work of
William Carlos Williams, rather than that of Eliot, Pound,
Stevens, or even Hart Crane—though Crane's *The Bridge* certainly has some affinities to Hughes's poetic sequence. (Hughes's
Montage could be productively paired with William Carlos
Williams's *Paterson,* though that is beyond the scope of this
essay.) Certainly, the fact that Hughes's text is rooted in African
American rhetoric—song lyrics, jokes, turns of speech—and is,
as announced in the prefatory note, organized formally with the
"conflicting changes, sudden nuances, sharp and impudent inter-
jections, broken rhythms" of bebop in mind—makes problematic the model of the neo-Modernist text that draws back from
the vernacular-influenced diction and "social realism" that characterized much of the poetry of the 1930s and early 1940s (*CP*
387). Unlike other forms of American neo-Modernist art, abstract
expressionist painting for example, Hughes's work not only re-
tains the stance of rebellion but also makes rebelliousness and
potential rebellion quite explicit, most famously in "Harlem,"
which both psychologically contextualizes the Harlem riots of
1935 and 1943 and also predicts future unrest.

At the same time it is necessary to point out that Hughes's choice of the word "montage" in the title of the poem signals his desire to connect his work with an earlier era of artistic modernism. Of course, Hughes's use of a montage-like technique has in its origins in his earliest work, such as the 1925 "The Cat and the Saxophone," and can be clearly seen in such poems of the 1930s as "Radio Broadcast on Ethiopia" and "Air Raid over Harlem." But Hughes took this polyvocal technique further in *Montage* than he did in any of his earlier works, with the possible exceptions of his verse plays, notably the 1938 semimusical "Don't You Want to Be Free?" And, even in these plays, the juxtaposition of the voices is less radical and the transitions between scenes is usually less abrupt than the transitions of the *Montage* sequence. Of course, one can read a number of Hughes's earlier collections, notably the 1927 *Fine Clothes to the Jew* and the 1942 *Shakespeare in Harlem*, as essentially polyvocal montages of black America, but even in those collections there is a sense that the individual poems stand on their own far more than those of *Montage*, despite the relative fame of the poem "Harlem." That Hughes included *Montage* in its entirety in his *Selected Poems*, with one significant change that will be noted later, indicates that he too saw this work as a single long poem or a poetic sequence, rather than a collection.

The use of the word "montage" in the title indicates a connection to an earlier era of modernist art, notably the overtly Left side of German expressionism and the early Soviet cinema, especially the films and criticism of Sergei Eisenstein. However, the claim that the sequence is formally influenced by bebop—a claim thematized in many of the sequence's poems—argues for a new, politically engaged African American modernism based on postwar urban African American experience and expressive culture. While the protest elements of the sequence are often quite explicit, as in "Freedom Train," which was removed from the "Montage" section of the *Selected Poems* by Hughes and placed in the "Words Like Freedom" section, more often they are explicitly implicit, or, to put it another way, anger is linked with fear and concealment so that the concealment of anger becomes the dominant theme of the sequence. Thus, the first poem of the sequence, "Dream Boogie," provides a guide to reading the rest of the text:

> Listen to it closely:
> Ain't you heard
> something underneath
> like a—
>
> *What did I say? (CP 388)*

There is an obvious connection with the longstanding African American notions, both in literature and in the folk culture, of the need to conceal one's true identity from white people, particularly those who can exercise direct power over one. *Montage* is in many respects a perfect poem for the Cold War era, as well as a revision of Paul Laurence Dunbar's bitter rondeau from the early Jim Crow period, "We Wear the Mask." (In fact, when one considers his later testimony before Joseph McCarthy's communist-hunting Senate Permanent Sub-Committee on Investigations, in which Hughes disavowed his earlier radical poems under aggressive questioning, it becomes almost heartbreaking) (Rampersad 1988, 209–21). In this poem are sounded the themes of discontent transvalued into "nonsense" syllables and "wild" music ("*Hey, pop! / Re-bop! / Mop!*") in the face of a consensus compelled by force on those unwilling to accept it otherwise (*CP* 388). It both thematizes and embodies the enforcement of this consensus while making its shortcomings with respect to African Americans obvious. It maintains a link with Hughes's earlier "communist" poetry both in its representation of the Harlem community and its problems, which in many respects is quite "realistic," and in the implication of a coming explosion of the "dream deferred," which, while not perhaps quite as ideologically delineated as in his earlier work, is quite consonant with the calls for and predictions of social revolution in such works as "Air Raid over Harlem," "Scottsboro Limited," and "Don't You Want to Be Free?" In addition, one can also say that Hughes is making an argument for how such themes may be expressed in the Cold War era before the civil rights movement, when it is not only dangerous to express radical political positions directly but also difficult in that the institutions—whether *The New Masses*, which under the pressures of the period had retrenched from a weekly journal to a monthly and merged with the journal *Mainstream* in 1947, or the National Negro Congress, which folded in 1946—that had provided both forums and forms for such sentiments had collapsed or were becoming increasing isolated.

In many ways, Langston Hughes was himself a national African American literary institution during the 1950s and 1960s. His constant reading and lecture tours, his network of contacts across the United States (and the world), his syndicated "From Here to Yonder" column (though its home was in the *Chicago Defender*, the column, which often featured Hughes's "Simple" stories, appeared widely in the black press, from the most conservative to *Muhammad Speaks*), his work as editor of the poetry anthologies *Poetry of the Negro* (1949 and 1970) and *New Negro Poetry* (1964), and his prolific letter writing were among the many factors that made Hughes far more than a regional figure.

Nonetheless, despite his national status, from the late 1930s, at least, Hughes was strongly associated with Harlem as its most famous permanent literary resident in whose work the literary landscape of Harlem figured prominently. If Harlem retained its place as an iconic African American landscape that was both special and typical, it was in no small part through the poetry, columns, short stories, and plays of Hughes during the 1940s and 1950s. The "Simple" stories and the poetry sequence *Montage of a Dream Deferred* were particularly influential in maintaining Harlem as a literary site where the somewhat conflicting figurations of the neighborhood as a place of refuge, home, and prison intersect.

In many respects, it was the work of Hughes that made Harold Cruse's claims for Harlem as the necessary locus of the new black revolution in *Crisis of the Negro Intellectual* (1967) and Amiri Baraka's (and that of other proto–Black Arts intellectuals in the East) initial sense of Harlem as "home" plausible. The move of Baraka and other African American artists and intellectuals (either physically or in terms of orientation, since many, including Sun Ra and other "new thing" musicians, continued to live downtown) from Greenwich Village or the Lower East Side to Harlem gained much of its power from the work of Hughes.

Hughes was also an influential model for those artists and intellectuals who were trying imagine and define a "Black Aesthetic." Hughes, after all, had been investigating the possibilities of a distinctly African American literary diction and literary forms for decades. As noted, Hughes had written poems, sketches, and stories that drew on the formal resources of jazz, the blues, gospel, r & b, toasting, badman stories and songs, tall tales, black vaudeville humor, the dozens and other forms of "signifying," street corner and barbershop conversations, sermons, and so on since the 1920s. For those black artists and intellectuals, particularly such East Coast intellectuals as Baraka, Touré, and Larry Neal, who imagined a continuum of African American culture from Africa to the United States present, including folk, popular, and avant-garde elements, Hughes was the great predecessor. Hughes's work had long been distinguished by his willingness to draw on folk blues, popular music, and various "art" music traditions simultaneously. This can be seen during the 1950s not only in his explicit formal and thematic references to bebop generally in *Montage of a Dream Deferred* but specifically in his great utopian poem "Projection," from *Montage*, where the speaker dreams that "Paul Robeson / will team up with Jackie Mabley" (*CP* 404).

Beyond Hughes's work as a writer and editor was the impact that he had as a tireless supporter of younger black writers, both formally and informally. On a formal level, Hughes (like his close friend Arna Bontemps) was constantly writing (often without solicitation by the artist) recommendations, letters of support, and so on, to gain grants, fellowships, and other sorts of institutional support for young black writers, such as Amiri Baraka, Ron Milner, and Conrad Kent Rivers, as well as for older writers who would play significant roles in the Black Arts Movement, such as Margaret Danner (Bontemps and Hughes 53; Rampersad 1988, 310–11). Hughes was also famous for writing letters of encouragement to young writers (and not so young writers) who published what Hughes considered to be strong work. Hughes also made an effort to appear on programs with younger and/or less-known writers and to meet with groups of these writers on his reading trips (Smith 107–11). Hughes was a particularly strong supporter and presence in New York for such proto-Black Arts institutions as the Market Place Gallery readings organized in Harlem by Raymond Patterson and the Umbra group, based primarily on the Lower East Side (Rampersad 1988, 311). On a less formal level, Hughes, as he had for decades, constantly introduced writers and intellectuals to each other, extending circles of acquaintance and interest at social gatherings in a seemingly offhand way.

Some Black Arts activists did sharply criticize Hughes and his basic commitment to integrationism, as well as his use of popular culture (O'Neal). However, it is easy to see why so many cite him as a crucial influence, as evidenced by memoirs, introductions, and dedications to volumes, poems (e.g., Larry Neal's "Don't Say Good-Bye to the Porkpie Hat" and Etheridge Knight's "For Langston Hughes"), and tributes, such as Woodie King's "On Langston Hughes," which appeared in two major Black Arts journals, *Negro Digest* (later renamed *Black World*) and *Black Theatre*. Hughes's work as a writer, columnist, and editor, his formal and informal support of younger writers, and his tireless effort to build and extend networks of black artists and intellectuals (and to connect those artists to an audience) were crucial in the emergence of the new black writing, especially in New York City. If New York was an early center of the emerging Black Arts Movement, it was in no small part because of Hughes.

Like a number of the most politically engaged older black writers and intellectuals, such as Margaret Burroughs, Margaret Walker, John O. Killens, and Melvin Tolson, Hughes maintained a stance of critical support toward the emerging Black Arts Movement in his work. Some have read Hughes's final collection, *The Panther and the Lash* (1967), as a largely unconvincing attempt to repackage himself so as to advance his career (Ford). Others have seen it, in the final analysis, as a repudiation of the new black poetry (Rampersad 1988, 412).

However, the collection, which combines new politically militant poems with older radical poems from the 1930s and 1940s, is both a critique and a gesture of support. A large part of Hughes's project in the collection was to encourage younger poets and activists while reminding them of earlier moments of African American cultural and political radicalism. In this, Hughes was like a number of older writers, such as Dudley Randall, Margaret Walker, and John O. Killens, who became associated with the Black Arts Movement, as Hughes might have had he lived long enough.

Another aspect of it seems to be an attempt to rethink Hughes's own career, and by extension those of the radicals and former radicals of his generation, within the frame of the new militants. The ending of "Stokely Malcolm Me" may not be, as Arnold Rampersad suggests, a parodic "beat" critique of Black Power and the new black poetry:

> Stokely,
> did I ever live
> up your
> way?
> ???
> ??
> ?
>
> (*CP* 561)

While it is possible that Hughes was lampooning the Beats and the Student Non-Violent Coordinating Committee (SNCC) leader Kwame Turé (Stokely Carmichael), the shape of the poem's end mirrors the ending of Hughes's "Elderly Leaders" (first published in 1936 as "Elderly Race Leaders"), which appeared in the first section of *The Panther and the Lash*:

> They clutch at the egg
> Their master's
> Goose laid:
> $$$$$
> $$$$
> $$$
> $$
> $$
>
> (*CP* 194)

As Arnold Rampersad points out, the former poem was composed in the aftermath of a bitter debate around the term (and concept) of "Black Power," which had been popularized by Turé. This debate featured the forceful denunciation of the idea of Black Power by "elderly race leaders," notably Hughes's friend Roy Wilkins, of the NAACP. This criticism was met by often personally vituperative responses on the part of Black Power supporters such as Amiri Baraka, who threatened "to stick half my sandal up / his ass" (Rampersad 1988, 411). However, it is worth noting that Hughes's critique in the later poem is hardly less cutting, if less verbally violent, than Baraka's. It is telling that the dollar signs of the earlier poem are replaced by the question marks of the later work. The dollar signs are linked to the denounced race leaders of the earlier poem, while the question marks are connected to the later poem's speaker. The relation of the pronouns in the later poem are telling in this regard. If Hughes were simply critiquing Turé (you) and the Black Power advocates, and if the "I" ("me") referred to the voice of an African American everyman/woman, as often was the case in Hughes's poetry, then Hughes could suggested a distance between Black Power and "the people" by saying "Did you ever live up my way?"—much as Simple criticized "race Leaders" "I have not laid eyes on" in "Letter to Mr. Butts" (*STW* 1953).

However, instead the speaker asks if he or she ever lived "up your way." In other words, the speaker could be Hughes, or his generation of engaged artists and intellectuals, trying remember when he lived in something like Turé's ideological neighborhood and criticized "elderly race leaders" in much the same spirit that the Black Power activists did Wilkins. In short, rather than simply critiquing Turé and his generation of militants for their extremism and lack of historical perspective, Hughes could also be chiding his generation, and himself, for their failure of political imagination (and memory) and their own lack of historical perspective. In this way, again like others of his generation who engaged Black Arts and Black Power, Hughes was genuinely a bridge between different moments of cultural activism, prodding, chiding, reminding, supporting, and honoring.

The notion of Ralph Ellison and others that Hughes in the

end was a limited artist because he did not "grow" is clearly mistaken (Rampersad 1988, 286). There does seem to be a core to Hughes's work, especially after the early 1930s, that is fairly constant. That core consists of a sense of the importance of popular African American culture to the black literary artist (and a sense of the cultural continuum between different eras of black cultural expression) and a commitment to the freedom struggles of African Americans. In fact, Hughes is notable among his contemporaries not only for his distinguished efforts in so many genres over so many years but for his efforts to negotiate, renegotiate really, changing cultural and political eras while remaining basically true to his core. This project, in fact, forced Hughes's work to change while he attempted to retain links to the past. In part, that is why one Simple story, "Bop," retells the popular story of the relationship between bebop and police violence (*TBOS* 118) in one sketch and renders what is essentially a prose praise poem to Ma Rainey in another (*TBOS* 168). It is this drive to remain current while being cognizant of the past, along with a recognition of the need to rethink his core values and poetics and their relationship to the present moment, that made Hughes's work so powerful and so popular with audiences beyond what is normally thought of as the market for "serious" literature.

WORKS CITED

Bahktin, Mikhail. *Problems of Dostoevsky's Poetics*. Edited and translated by Caryl Emerson. Minneapolis: University of Minnesota Press, 1984.

Baraka, Amiri. *The LeRoi Jones/Amiri Baraka Reader*. Edited by William J. Harris. New York: Thunder's Mouth, 1991.

Bontemps, Arna, and Langston Hughes. *Letters, 1925–1967*. Selected and edited by Charles H. Nichols. 1980. Rpt. New York: Paragon, 1990.

Ford, Karen Jackson. "Making Poetry Pay: The Commodification of Langston Hughes." In *Marketing Modernisms: Self-Promotion, Canonization, Rereading*. Edited by Kevin J. H. Dettmar and Stephen Watt, 275–96. Ann Arbor: University of Michigan Press, 1996.

Gennari, John. "Jazz Criticism: Its Development and Ideologies." *Black American Literature Forum* 25, no. 3 (fall 1991): 449–523.

Hughes, Langston. "Don't You Want to Be Free?" *One Act Play Magazine* 2 (October 1938): 359–93.

———. *Short Stories of Langston Hughes*. Edited by Akiba Sullivan Harper. New York: Hill and Wang, 1996.

O'Neal, John. "Black Arts: Notebook." In *The Black Aesthetic*. Edited by Addison Gayle, Jr., 46–56. New York: Anchor, 1972.

Rampersad, Arnold. *The Life of Langston Hughes, Volume I: 1902–1941, I, Too, Sing America*. Oxford: Oxford University Press, 1986.

———. *The Life of Langston Hughes, Volume II: 1941–1967, I Dream a World*. Oxford: Oxford University Press, 1988.

Smith, Suzanne E. *Dancing in the Street: Motown and the Cultural Politics of Detroit*. Cambridge, Mass.: Harvard University Press, 1999.

Sundquist, Eric. "Who Was Langston Hughes?" *Commentary* 102, no. 6 (December 1996): 55–59.

Vendler, Helen. "The Unweary Blues." Review of *The Collected Poems of Langston Hughes*. *New Republic*, March 6, 1995, pp. 37–42.

ILLUSTRATED
CHRONOLOGY

Hughes's Life

1902 James Langston Hughes is born February 1, in Joplin, Missouri, later moving to the Lawrence, Kansas, home of his grandmother Mary Langston with his mother, Carrie, when his father departs for Cuba. Hughes stays primarily with his grandmother during his early childhood while his mother moves about seeking jobs.

1908 Hughes moves briefly to Topeka to live with his mother and enroll in school but returns to his grandmother in Lawrence the following year.

1915 Hughes leaves Lawrence upon the death of his grandmother, joining his mother, her second husband, Homer Clark, and his stepbrother Gwyn "Kit" Clark in Lincoln, Illinois, where Hughes starts the eighth grade.

1916 After graduating eighth grade with the honor of being named class poet, Hughes moves to Cleveland, Ohio, with his family and enrolls in Central High School, where he publishes poetry and prose influenced by Walt Whitman and Carl Sandburg in the school magazine.

1918 In the summer, Hughes goes to visit his mother, who has left his stepfather and moved to Chicago.

Historical Events

1902 Paul Laurence Dunbar, *The Sport of the Gods*.

1903 W. E. B. Du Bois, *The Souls of Black Folk*; eighty-four African Americans reported lynched.

1904 Calls for a New Negro renaissance sounded by the *AME Church Review*; Abbey Theatre founded.

1905 Edith Wharton, *The House of Mirth*; Sinn Fein Party founded in Dublin; Niagara Movement founded by Du Bois and others; first issue of the *Chicago Defender* published; Theodore Roosevelt inaugurated as president; fifty-seven African Americans reported lynched.

1906 Upton Sinclair, *The Jungle*; hair care business established by the future millionaire Madame C. J. Walker.

1907 First cubist exhibition in Paris; Ivan Pavlov studies conditioned reflexes.

1908 Ford produces the first Model T; major race riot in Springfield, Illinois; Jack Johnson becomes first African American world heavyweight boxing champion; eighty-nine African Americans reported lynched.

1920 Hughes graduates in June. On the train en route to spend a year with his father in Mexico, he composes "The Negro Speaks of Rivers," his first artistic triumph.

1921 Two poems are published in the children's magazine *The Brownie's Book*, prompting Hughes to submit "The Negro Speaks of Rivers" for publication in *The Crisis*, the official publishing organ of the NAACP. Hughes enters Columbia University in September with the reluctant financial support of his father. More important, Hughes strikes up acquaintances with Jessie Fauset, W. E. B. Du Bois, and the poet Countee Cullen.

1922 Hughes withdraws from Columbia after refusing to travel to Mexico to assist his convalescing father. Hughes's poems continue to appear in *The Crisis* as he supports himself in such mundane positions as delivery boy and messman.

The Niagara Movement, an interracial organization founded in response to the accommodationist and conciliatory policies of Booker T. Washington, was organized in 1905. Special Collections and Archives, W. E .B. Du Bois Library, University of Massachusetts–Amherst.

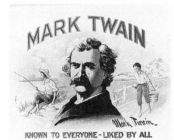

KNOWN TO EVERYONE - LIKED BY ALL

Mark Twain's death in 1910 marked the passing of an author that Hughes grew to admire deeply. From the collection of Steven C. Tracy.

1909 Gertrude Stein, *Three Lives*; William Howard Taft inaugurated as president; Sigmund Freud lectures on psychoanalysis in the United States; Robert E. Peary and Matthew Henson reach the North Pole; NAACP founded.

1910 National Urban League founded; beginning of the Great Migration of some two million southern African Americans to northern cities; sixty-seven African Americans reported lynched.

1923   Hughes writes "The Weary Blues," inspired by a visit to a Harlem cabaret and his memory of the first blues verse he had ever heard as a child back in Lawrence. Seaman Hughes sails aboard the steamship *West Hesseltine* in June after impulsively and unceremoniously dumping all of his books into the harbor save for his copy of Whitman's *Leaves of Grass*. Hughes visits a variety of ports on the west coast of Africa before returning in October. On ship, Hughes experiences his first homosexual encounter.

Oswald Garrison Villard, a journalist, author, reformer, and owner of the New York Evening Post *and the* Nation, *co-founded the NAACP and wrote a highly praised biography of John Brown. Special Collections and Archives, W. E. B. Du Bois Library, University of Massachusetts–Amherst.*

Bert Williams and George Walker sought to leave behind the coon stereotype for a less degrading image. Williams was recognized as a seasoned comic actor and mime with brilliant timing whose work was eventually featured in the Ziegfeld Follies. From the collection of Steven C. Tracy.

1911   Arnold Schoenberg, *Manual of Harmony.*

1912   James Weldon Johnson, *The Autobiography of an Ex-Colored Man;* Hart Wand's "Dallas Blues" and W. C. Handy's "The Memphis Blues" are the first blues published as sheet music; *Titanic* sinks on its maiden voyage; sixty-one African Americans reported lynched.

1924 Voyaging to Europe aboard the *McKeesport* as a seaman once again, Hughes leaves the ship and settles into a job in the kitchen of the Montmartre night club Le Grand Duc. There he enjoys the company of expatriate African American jazz musicians. On a month-long vacation in Italy, Hughes winds up stranded in Genoa without his passport and writes the Whitman-influenced poem "I, Too."

1925 Hughes works in a variety of jobs in Washington, D.C., while living with his mother, including working in the office of African American historian Carter G. Woodson. Upon winning first prize in the Urban League's *Opportunity* poetry contest for "The Weary Blues," Hughes meets Carl Van Vechten, who arranges for the publication of Hughes's first volume of poetry by Alfred A. Knopf. Among other important contacts Hughes makes at the time are Alain Locke, who includes some of Hughes's work in his seminal anthology *The New Negro* (1925), Zora Neale Hurston, and Arna Bontemps. A highly publicized encounter between the "busboy poet" Hughes and the renowned poet Vachel Lindsay results in more press.

James Weldon Johnson, educator, songwriter, poet, novelist, essayist, editor, national organizer for the NAACP, and the first African American to head that organization. Special Collections and Archives, W. E. B. Du Bois Library, University of Massachusetts–Amherst.

1913 D. H. Lawrence, *Sons and Lovers*; "Armory Show" introduction of cubism and postimpressionism in New York; premiere of Igor Stravinsky's controversial *Le Sacre du Printemps*; Niels Bohr generates theory of atomic structure; death of Harriet Tubman.

1914 Vachel Lindsay, *The Congo*; James Joyce, *The Dubliners*; Robert Goddard initiates rocketry experiments; World War I breaks out.

1926   *The Weary Blues* is published in January to positive reviews. A benefactress, Amy Spingarn, assists Hughes financially so that he can attend Lincoln University in Pennsylvania. Hughes publishes his bold manifesto "The Negro Artist and the Racial Mountain" in June in *The Nation* and contributes to the incendiary but short-lived magazine *Fire!!*

In 1913, W. E. B. Du Bois produced for the National Emancipation Exposition in New York the elaborate "Star of Ethiopia" pageant, depicting in music and stories 10,000 years of the history of the Negro race. Special Collections and Archives, W. E. B. Du Bois Library, University of Massachusetts–Amherst.

Mary White Ovington, a New York Socialist, author, and longtime associate and admirer of W. E. B. Du Bois. Special Collections and Archives, W. E. B. Du Bois Library, University of Massachusetts–Amherst.

1915   Marcel Duchamp generates the first Dadaist paintings; D. W. Griffith's film *Birth of a Nation* premieres; Einstein postulates his general theory of relativity; Alexander Graham Bell places the first transcontinental telephone call; KKK receives charter from Fulton County, Georgia, Superior Court; Carter G. Woodson establishes the Association for the Study of Negro Life and History and the *Journal of Negro History*; fifty-six African Americans are reported lynched.

Marcus Garvey, who founded the UNIA in 1914 in his native Jamaica, is now treated there as a national hero, as evidenced by his presence on the nation's currency. From the collection of Steven C. Tracy.

1927 Hughes is berated in the African American press for his focus on what some consider the uninhibited and tasteless behavior of the "low down folks" portrayed in Hughes's *Fine Clothes to the Jew*. Locke arranges a poetry reading by Hughes in Washington, D.C., where Hughes performs accompanied by a blues pianist, placing him at the forefront of the poetry and musical performance tradition. Locke also introduces Hughes to "Godmother" Charlotte Mason, who acts as Hughes's patron over the next three years and immediately supports his travels in the South with another of her protégés, Zora Neale Hurston.

1929 Hughes works on completing his first novel following his graduation from Lincoln in June.

1916 Angelina Weld Grimke, *Rachel*; Carl Sandburg, *Chicago Poems*; first birth control clinic opens in the United States; Marcus Garvey arrives in the United States and establishes the Universal Negro Improvement Association (UNIA).

1917 C. G. Jung, *Psychology of the Unconscious*; first jazz recordings made by the white Original Dixieland Jazz Band; Woodrow Wilson inaugurated as president; United States enters World War I; ten thousand march down New York's Fifth Avenue to protest lynchings and racial injustice; thirty-six African Americans reported lynched.

1918 Georgia Douglas Johnson, *The Heart of a Woman*; Oswald Spengler, *The Decline of the West*; Max Planck introduces quantum theory; race riots continue to break out; sixty African Americans are reported lynched.

The World War I Hospitality League provided segregated hospitality. Special Collections and Archives, W. E .B. Du Bois Library, University of Massachusetts–Amherst.

Ten thousand African Americans, decrying the lynchings and race riots that were occurring during and after World War I, participated, on July 28, 1917, in a silent protest parade down New York's Fifth Avenue. Special Collections and Archives, W. E. B. Du Bois Library, University of Massachusetts–Amherst.

1930 Hughes visits Cuba, where he fraternizes with many writers and artists. Back in the States, Charlotte Mason suddenly drops him, apparently over aesthetic disagreements, and Hughes also clashes with and separates himself from Hurston and Locke. Meanwhile, his novel *Not Without Laughter* is published, and he receives the Harmon Foundation Medal for his contributions to American literature.

1931 Following his breakup with Mason, Hughes goes to Haiti for six weeks. He also begins to follow more intensely a leftist turn in his writing, publishing prose and poetry in the radical magazine the *New Masses*. *Dear Lovely Death* is published in a small edition by Amy Spingarn's Troutbeck Press. During a reading tour of the South, Hughes visits the Scottsboro Boys in prison. *The Negro Mother* is published by Golden Stair Press, the publishing company formed by Hughes and the artist Prentiss Taylor.

1932 Hughes's press publishes *Scottsboro Limited*, while Knopf releases two children's books, *The Dream Keeper* and *Popo and Fifina*, the latter written in collaboration with Bontemps. In June, Hughes travels to the Soviet Union with a group of twenty-two African Americans to participate in a film about U.S. race relations, which is ultimately not produced.

1919 Sherwood Anderson, *Winesburg, Ohio*; W. E. B. Du Bois organizes the first Pan-African Congress; *Gospel Pearls* published by the National Baptist Convention; American Communist party established; Prohibition enacted; eighty-three African Americans are reported lynched in the "Red Summer of Hate."

1920 Eugene O'Neill, *The Emperor Jones*; Nineteenth Amendment grants women's suffrage; Mamie Smith first African American to record blues songs commercially; Mahatma Gandhi becomes leader in India's struggle for independence.

1921 KKK activities become brazenly violent across the South; *Shuffle Along* opens in New York City; Warren G. Harding inaugurated as president; fifty-nine African Americans reported lynched.

1922 James Joyce, *Ulysses*; T. S. Eliot, *The Waste Land*; Sinclair Lewis, *Babbitt*; James Weldon Johnson, ed., *The Book of American Negro Poetry*; Claude McKay, *Harlem Shadows*; Meta Vaux Warrick Fuller's *Ethiopia Awakening* exhibited in New York; Dyer antilynching bill passed in the House but filibustered in the Senate; discovery of the tomb of Tutankhamen; fifty-one African Americans reported lynched.

Bessie Smith captivated both black audiences and white intellectuals and music aficionados flirting with the African American music scene in the 1920s. From the collection of Steven C. Tracy.

The naming of a trendy nightspot after the "prototypical" African American blues singer Blind Lemon Jefferson demonstrates how far the genre had penetrated the American consciousness by the decade of Hughes's death. From the collection of Steven C. Tracy.

1923   Jean Toomer, *Cane*; Wallace Stevens, *Harmonium*; *Runnin' Wild* introduces and popularizes the Charleston; George Gershwin premieres *Rhapsody in Blue*; Calvin Coolidge succeeds Harding as president.

1924   Jessie Fauset, *There Is Confusion*; Walter White, *Fire in the Flint*; Ida Cox records "Wild Women Don't Have the Blues"; James Van Der Zee begins a photographic series dealing with Marcus Garvey and the UNIA; Lenin dies (b. 1870).

1925   F. Scott Fitzgerald, *The Great Gatsby*; Alain Locke, ed., *The New Negro*; Countee Cullen, *Color*; Howard W. Odum and Guy B. Johnson, *The Negro and His Songs*; Bessie Smith and Louis Armstrong record W. C. Handy's "St. Louis Blues"; Calvin Coolidge inaugurated as president; Scopes "Monkey Trial" takes place.

1926   Ernest Hemingway, *The Sun Also Rises*; Carl Van Vechten, *Nigger Heaven*; Blind Lemon Jefferson records his first blues for Paramount Records; Aaron Douglas embarks on the "Emperor Jones" series of illustrations; twenty-three African Americans reported lynched.

This Christmas greeting from a prominent label with its own "race" series, initiated in 1926, reflected the industry's desire to capitalize on the burgeoning interest in black music, as well as its caution in segregating black artists in their own separate catalog and categories. From the collection of Steven C. Tracy.

1927   James Weldon Johnson, *God's Trombones*; Countee Cullen, ed., *Caroling Dusk*; Duke Ellington takes up residence at the Cotton Club; the first talking motion picture, *The Jazz Singer*, premieres; Charles Lindbergh flies the *Spirit of St. Louis* nonstop from New York to Paris; the Harlem Globetrotters are formed; Sacco and Vanzetti executed.

1928   Claude McKay, *Home to Harlem*; Nella Larsen, *Quicksand*; Stephen Vincent Benét, *John Brown's Body*; Maurice Ravel's *Bolero* premieres; Oscar DePriest elected first African American congressman from a northern state; Archive of American Folk Song established.

1933   Hughes travels through the Soviet Union to China and Japan but returns to California in August. Noel Sullivan supports Hughes for a year in Carmel while Hughes is developing a group of short stories influenced by D. H. Lawrence.

The compositions of Duke Ellington, which first came to national prominence in the 1920s through his recordings and his residency at the famed Cotton Club in Harlem, now place him among the greatest American composers of the twentieth century. Irving Mills, a music publisher, composer, and lyricist, was Ellington's manager and business partner. From the collection of Steven C. Tracy.

1934   Knopf publishes the highly praised short-story collection *The Ways of White Folks*. Unfortunately, labor turmoil in California leads to the specter of antisocialist violence directed against Hughes, so Hughes leaves Carmel and, in November, travels to Mexico after his father's death.

1935   A sensationalized version of Hughes's play *Mulatto* is prepared for production unbeknownst to Hughes, who arrives in New York in time to see it open on Broadway to harsh reviews.

1936   A nine-month Guggenheim Foundation Fellowship fails to produce anything substantial, but Hughes's work as a playwright bears fruit with the Karamu Players in Cleveland, where *Little Ham* and *Troubled Island* are produced.

1937   Following Karamu's production of *Joy to My Soul*, Hughes works as a correspondent covering the Spanish Civil War for a number of African American newspapers. While in Europe, he meets Pablo Neruda, W. H. Auden, Bertolt Brecht, and Ernest Hemingway. He addresses the Writer's Congress in Paris in July, travels in Spain with Nicolás Guillén, and translates a number of poems by Federico García Lorca.

1929   Jessie Fauset, *Plum Bun*; Wallace Thurman, *The Blacker the Berry*; Virginia Woolf, *A Room of One's Own*; William Faulkner, *The Sound and the Fury*; Archibald Motley paints *Blues*; Albert Einstein propounds the "unified field theory"; "Black Friday" stock market crash; Herbert Hoover inaugurated as president.

1930   Hart Crane, *The Bridge*; Mike Gold, *Jews Without Money*; Augusta Savage sculpture *Gamin* completed; Grant Wood paints *American Gothic*; Pluto is discovered; Nation of Islam founded by W. D. Fard.

Laura C. Boulton's long career collecting and studying world musics is represented by significant recordings of African music in the 1930s. From the collection of Steven C. Tracy.

Hughes covered the Spanish Civil War for various Afro-American newspapers in 1937, meeting, in Madrid, a variety of prominent writers and intellectuals, Mikhail Koltzov, Ernest Hemingway, and Nicolás Guillén among them. Yale Collection of American Literature, Beinecke Rare Book and Manuscript Library.

1938 Hughes founds the leftist Harlem Suitcase Theatre, which produces *Don't You Want to Be Free?* His pamphlet *A New Song* is published by the International Workers Order. On June 3, Hughes's mother dies in New York. The following month, Hughes addresses the International Association of Writers in Paris. In Cleveland, Karamu stages *Front Porch* in November, but by year's end Hughes has left for California.

1939 Hughes writes the movie script for *Way Down South*. After addressing the Third American Writers Congress, in New York, in June, he settles in Carmel once again at the home of Noel Sullivan.

1931 George S. Schuyler, *Black No More*; James Weldon Johnson, *Black Manhattan*; Edgar Varèse premieres *Ionisation*; Scottsboro Boys convicted of raping two white women in Alabama.

1932 Aldous Huxley, *Brave New World*; Sterling Brown, *Southern Road*; Wallace Thurman, *Infants of the Spring*; Amelia Earhart first woman to fly solo across the Atlantic.

1933 W. B. Yeats, *Collected Poems*; James Weldon Johnson, *Along This Way*; Nathaniel West, *Miss Lonelyhearts*; Leadbelly makes his first recordings for the Library of Congress; Franklin Delano Roosevelt inaugurated as president; Adolf Hitler appointed German chancellor; Roosevelt's New Deal programs initiated.

1940   Publication of *The Big Sea* is eclipsed by the success of Richard Wright's novel *Native Son* earlier in the year. Picketing targeted at his poem "Goodbye Christ" at a Pasadena literary luncheon influences Hughes to leave his reviewer's job at the Hollywood Theatre Alliance to retreat to the relative safety of Carmel. Hughes's subsequent public repudiation of the poem elicits attacks from the communist press.

1941   Hughes wins a Rosenwald Fund fellowship to support playwriting activities and leaves California for Chicago, ultimately settling in New York in December with Toy and Emerson Harper.

1942   Veering off the radical path, Hughes's *Shakespeare in Harlem* harks back to Hughes's oral tradition aesthetic of the 1920s in style and subject matter. The Skyloft Players stage *The Sun Do Move* in Chicago in April, and in August Hughes is the first invited African American writer at the Yaddo writers' and artists' colony. Hughes also finds time to generate material for the Office of Civil Defense in support of U.S. war activities and, more important, initiates his weekly "Here to Yonder" column in the *Chicago Defender*.

1934   Nancy Cunard, ed., *Negro, an Anthology*; Aaron Douglas paints *Aspects of Negro Life*; Du Bois resigns position at NAACP.

1935   Clifford Odets, *Waiting for Lefty*; Zora Neale Hurston, *Mules and Men*; George Gershwin premieres *Porgy and Bess*; Roosevelt signs Social Security Act; Mary McLeod Bethune founds the National Council of Negro Women; Federal Writers Project established (1935–1939).

1936   William Faulkner, *Absalom, Absalom!*; Archibald Motley paints *Saturday Night Street Scene*; Jesse Owens wins four gold medals at the Berlin Olympics; Mary McLeod Bethune receives the first major appointment of an African American woman in the federal government, as director of Negro affairs of the National Youth Administration; Federal Theatre Project established (1936–1939).

1937   Zora Neale Hurston, *Their Eyes Were Watching God*; Pablo Picasso, *Guernica*; Jacob Lawrence's *Toussaint L'Ouverture* series begun; Frank Whittle builds first jet engine; William H. Hastie becomes first African American federal judge; Joe Louis becomes world heavyweight boxing champion.

Acutely aware of the ironies of fighting racism and fascism overseas in World War II while Jim Crow was in force in the United States, Hughes urged the full partici-pation of Afro-Americans in the voting process in 1944 as a way to help end dis-crimination at home. Yale Collection of American Literature, Beinecke Rare Book and Manuscript Library.

1943   Hughes's masterful comic creation Jesse B. Semple makes his first appearance in Hughes's *Defender* column on February 13. "Freedom's Plow" is published by Musette and *Jim Crow's Last Stand* by the Negro Publishing Society of America. An honorary doctorate from Lincoln University received alongside Carl Sandburg is followed by another residency at Yaddo in July.

1944   Hughes's high-profile participation in a nationally broadcast radio debate concerning segregation is followed by increased FBI surveillance, harassment by the House Special Committee on Un-American Activities, and newspaper attacks. Still, Hughes manages to emcee the Fifth Annual Negro Music Festival in Chicago and to visit a circuit of New York and New Jersey high schools for the Common Council of American Unity before preparing to leave on a national speaking tour that extends into 1945.

1945   Hughes collaborates with Mercer Cook on a translation of Jacques Roumain's novel *Masters of the Dew* and with Kurt Weill and Elmer Rice on a musical adaptation of *Street Scene*; the recording *Poems by Langston Hughes* appears on the Asch label.

1938   Thornton Wilder, *Our Town*; Richard Wright, *Uncle Tom's Children*; first *From Spirituals to Swing* concerts at Carnegie Hall; Supreme Court rules that University of Missouri Law School must admit African Americans due to lack of other facilities in area; establishment of the forty-hour workweek in the United States.

1939   John Steinbeck, *The Grapes of Wrath*; World War II (1939–1945).

1940   Ezra Pound, *Cantos*; Richard Wright, *Native Son*; Eugene O'Neill, *Long Day's Journey into Night*; Robert Hayden, *Heart-Shape in the Dust*; Lascaux caves with prehistoric wall paintings discovered in France; troop integration ruled out for morale reasons by FDR; Benjamin O. Davis appointed first African American general in the U.S. armed forces.

1941   Supreme Court rules that separate railroad car facilities must be substantially equal; United States enters World War II after attack on Pearl Harbor; threat of protest march by African Americans prompts FDR to issue Executive Order 8802 prohibiting discrimination in defense industries.

W. E. B. Du Bois, Mary McLeod Bethune, and Horace Mann Bond, three prominent educators, scholars, and race leaders of the twentieth century. Special Collections and Archives, W. E. B. Du Bois Library, University of Massachusetts–Amherst.

1946   The American Academy of Arts and Sciences awards Hughes $1,000 in recognition of his writing contributions.

1947   *Street Scene* is greeted enthusiastically upon its Broadway opening on January 9. Following a speaking tour, Hughes teaches a semester at Atlanta University and sees his book of poetry *Fields of Wonder* published to unimpressed reviews. At this time, Hughes also begins his collaboration with Jan Meyerowitz on an operatic treatment of his play *Mulatto*.

1942   Margaret Walker, *For My People*; Albert Camus, *L'Etranger*; first issue of *Negro Digest* published; development of the first automatic computer in the United States; Congress of Racial Equality (CORE) organized in Chicago.

1943   First one-man show by Jackson Pollack; Paul Robeson stars in Theatre Guild production of *Othello* on Broadway; singer-saxophonist Louis Jordan dominates rhythm and blues charts for the next eight years; race riots break out in Mobile, Beaumont, Detroit, and Harlem; zoot suits and jitterbugging gain widespread popularity.

1948   In June, Hughes takes up residence in a townhouse in Harlem bought with proceeds from his lucrative *Street Scene* collaboration. The Harpers move in with him, Mrs. Harper running the household and renting rooms.

1949   *The Poetry of the Negro 1746–1949*, a collaborative effort with Arna Bontemps; his poetry collection *One Way Ticket*; and *Cuba Libre: Poems by Nicolas Guillen*, translated with Ben Frederic Carruthers, are published. In Chicago, Hughes teaches at the Laboratory School (K–12) for a semester. The City Center in New York City premieres *Troubled Island*, his opera written in collaboration with William Grant Still. Hughes is attacked by *Life* magazine following his participation in an international conference sponsored by a leftist organization.

1950   The Hughes-Meyerowitz collaborative opera *The Barrier* opens to critical praise, though it bombs when it reaches Broadway in November. A collection of Simple sketches, *Simple Speaks His Mind*, is a critical and financial success. Hughes is attacked in *Red Channels: The Report of the Communist Influence in Radio and Television*. In Washington, D.C., in October, Hughes visits his old acquaintance Ezra Pound at St. Elizabeth's Hospital for the Criminally Insane.

The boogie-woogie craze that emerged in the 1940s not only brought that music into the American mainstream but also introduced it to socially prestigious establishments like this Chicago opera house. From the collection of Steven C. Tracy.

1944   Lillian Smith, *Strange Fruit*; Melvin B. Tolson, *Rendezvous with America*; Aaron Copland, *Appalachian Spring*; Supreme Court rules that "white primaries" excluding African Americans are unconstitutional; Adam Clayton Powell elected first African American congressman from the East.

1945   George Orwell, *Animal Farm*; Richard Wright, *Black Boy*; Gwendolyn Brooks, *A Street in Bronzeville*; Guggenheim Museum designed by Frank Lloyd Wright; FDR dies and is succeeded by Harry Truman; United States drops atomic bombs on Hiroshima and Nagasaki; end of World War II; "Charlie Parker's Reboppers" record for the Savoy label.

1951 Hughes's poetry collection *Montage of a Dream Deferred* fails to excite reviewers. *Beloit Poetry Journal* publishes a chapbook number consisting of Hughes's translations of Lorca's *Gypsy Ballads*. Hughes uses his October 6 *Defender* column to defend the beleaguered W. E. B. Du Bois, who, like Hughes, is under attack by right-wing forces and is on trial.

1952 Hughes publishes the short-story collection *Laughing to Keep from Crying*, and his children's book *The First Book of Negroes* initiates a period of concentration on books aimed at educating and bolstering the self-image of children and young adult readers. Hughes provides a lively introduction to the centenary edition of *Uncle Tom's Cabin*.

1953 On March 26, Hughes is interrogated in front of television cameras by Senator Joseph McCarthy's subcommittee on subversive activities, where Hughes admits and deprecates his radical past but avoids implicating others. Hughes's heartfelt defense of Walt Whitman appears in the *Defender*, and a collection of Simple sketches, *Simple Takes a Wife*, appears to heady reviews but disappointing sales. With anticommunist attacks still not subsiding, Hughes travels to Carmel to vacation at Noel Sullivan's farm.

1946 William Carlos Williams, *Paterson I*; Ann Petry, *The Street*; Mahalia Jackson does the first of her recordings for the Apollo label; Supreme Court bans segregation in interstate bus travel; Truman creates Committee on Civil Rights; first session of UN General Assembly held in London.

1947 Tennessee Williams, *A Streetcar Named Desire*; Robert Lowell, *Lord Weary's Castle*; Alan Lomax tapes interview / discussion with Big Bill Broonzy, Memphis Slim, and Sonny Boy Williamson in New York City; discovery of the Dead Sea Scrolls; transistor invented by scientists at Bell Laboratories; Jackie Robinson becomes the first African American major league baseball player in modern times.

Independent labels like the trumpeter Dizzy Gillespie's Dee Gee Records were frequently in the forefront in terms of issuing cutting-edge blues, jazz, and country music in the postwar era. From the collection of Steven C. Tracy.

The editors of The Encyclopedia of the Negro. *Special Collections and Archives, W. E. B. Du Bois Library, University of Massachusetts–Amherst.*

1954   The Hughes-Meyerowitz oratorio *Five Foolish Virgins* premieres at Town Hall in Manhattan. Two more children's books, *Famous American Negroes* and *The First Book of Rhythms*, are published. Hughes becomes a judge for the short-story competition sponsored by *Drum: Africa's Leading Magazine*.

1955   *The First Book of Jazz* and Hughes's collaboration with the photographer Roy De Carava, *Sweet Flypaper of Life*, are published. At Carnegie Hall, the premiere of the Hughes-Meyerowitz Easter Cantata *The Glory around His Head* receives rave reviews. Folkways releases the LPs *The Glory of Negro History* and *Rhythms of the World*, with narration by Hughes. Hughes records narration for the LP *The Story of Jazz*.

1948   Norman Mailer, *The Naked and the Dead*; Theodore Roethke, *The Lost Son and Other Poems*; Dorothy West, *The Living Is Easy*; Alan Paton, *Cry, the Beloved Country*; World Council of Churches organized; Alfred C. Kinsey, *Sexual Behavior in the American Male*; equal treatment in the armed forces mandated by Truman in Executive Order 9981.

1949   George Orwell, *Nineteen Eighty-Four*; Truman inaugurated for full term as president.

1950   Gwendolyn Brooks is first African American to win Pulitzer Prize (for *Annie Allen*, 1949); Ralph Bunche is first African American to receive Nobel Peace Prize; emergence of anticommunist demagogue Joseph McCarthy; anti-apartheid riots in Johannesburg; outbreak of Korean War (1950–1953).

1956 Hughes and Jobe Huntley collaborate on the gospel musical *Tambourines to Glory*, which Hughes also publishes as a novella. Another children's book, *The First Book of the West Indies*, is followed by the second volume of Hughes's autobiography, *I Wonder as I Wander*, and, in collaboration with Milton Meltzer, of *A Pictorial History of the Negro in America*.

1957 *Esther*, the three-act opera by Hughes and Meyerowitz, premieres at the University of Illinois at Urbana-Champaign. A novelized version of *Simple Stakes a Claim* is published in May, and the musical play *Simply Heavenly* opens off-Broadway and moves to Broadway for a brief run.

1958 Hughes records *The Weary Blues and Other Poems*, with instrumental accompaniment by Charles Mingus, Henry "Red" Allen, Sam "the Man" Taylor, and others. Hughes publishes *The Langston Hughes Reader*, his translation *Selected Poems of Gabriela Mistral,* the children's book *Famous Negro Heroes of America*, and, edited with Arna Bontemps, *The Book of Negro Folklore*.

1951 J. D. Salinger, *Catcher in the Rye*; Benjamin Britten, *Billy Budd*; Ralph Bunche appointed undersecretary to the United Nations.

1952 Ralph Ellison, *Invisible Man*; Ernest Hemingway, *The Old Man and the Sea*; Marianne Moore, *Collected Poems*; Samuel Beckett, *Waiting for Godot*; Revised Standard Version of the Bible published; according to a Tuskegee report, for the first time in seventy-one years, no lynchings reported in the United States.

1953 Arthur Miller, *The Crucible*; Melvin B. Tolson, *Libretto for the Republic of Liberia*; Gwendolyn Brooks, *Maud Martha*; James Baldwin, *Go Tell It on the Mountain*; execution of the Rosenbergs as spies; Simone de Beauvoir, *The Second Sex*; segregation banned in Washington, D.C., restaurants by Supreme Court; Eisenhower inaugurated as president.

1954 Tennessee Williams, *Cat on a Hot Tin Roof*; segregated schools declared unconstitutional in *Brown v. Board of Education* decision; first annual Newport Jazz Festival held; Elvis Presley cuts his first commercial sessions for Sun Records.

Hughes's poetry-with-jazz recording session produced the 1958 release The Weary Blues with Langston Hughes, *with Henry "Red" Allen, Charles Mingus, Vic Dickenson, Horace Parlan, and Sam "the Man" Taylor. From the collection of Steven C. Tracy.*

1959   *Selected Poems* is published in March to a notably condescending review from James Baldwin. Hughes attends African Freedom Day at Carnegie Hall and records some of his poems for the Library of Congress in May. The LP *Langston Hughes Reads and Talks about His Poems* is released on Spoken Arts. After writing an introduction for *The Tragedy of Pudd'nhead Wilson* and liner notes for a recording of spirituals sung by Harry Belafonte, Hughes travels to Trinidad to lecture, where he meets Derek Walcott and C. L. R. James.

1955   James Baldwin, *Notes of a Native Son*; Flannery O'Connor, *A Good Man Is Hard to Find*; Marian Anderson debuts at the Metropolitan Opera House; Supreme Court orders school integration "with all deliberate speed"; Rosa Parks refuses to give up her seat on a Montgomery, Alabama, bus and triggers a 382-day-long bus boycott.

1960 Hughes experiences bomb threats related to his alleged communist sympathies while on a book tour. A play entitled *Shakespeare in Harlem*, based on Hughes's work, runs briefly on Broadway. In June, Hughes receives the Spingarn Medal from the NAACP. The following month, Hughes writes "Goodbye Newport Blues," performed at the Newport Jazz Festival by Otis Spann with the Muddy Waters Blues Band. *The First Book of Africa* and *An African Treasury: Articles, Essays, Stories, Poems by Black Africans* are published. After the Hughes-Meyerowitz opera *Port Town* premieres at the Tanglewood Festival, in Massachusetts, Hughes visits Nigeria, Rome, Paris (where he visits the ailing Richard Wright just before Wright's death), and London.

1961 Hughes is inducted into the National Institute of Arts and Letters. Later, he attends a luncheon at the White House for the president of Senegal, Léopold Senghor, who is also a poet. *Ask Your Mama* and *The Best of Simple* are published. Hughes completes the gospel musical *Black Nativity* (a resounding success at a Broadway theater and later released on LP) and the gospel play *The Prodigal Son*. In Lagos, Nigeria, Hughes performs at a concert sponsored by AMSAC.

1956 Eugene O'Neill, *A Long Day's Journey into Night*; Allen Ginsberg, *Howl and Other Poems*; Montgomery bus boycott leader Martin Luther King, Jr.'s home is bombed; African American artists and writers attend first international conference at the Sorbonne; Sudan becomes an independent state.

Joel E. Spingarn was a Jewish philanthropist and university professor, founder of the American branch of New Criticism in literature, and, beginning in 1914, chairman of the board of the NAACP. Along with his wife, Amy, he established, in 1914, the Spingarn Medal for unique and distinguished achievements by American Negroes. Special Collections and Archives, W. E. B. Du Bois Library, University of Massachusetts–Amherst.

No matter how famous Hughes became, or how congenial the company he kept, racial prejudice continued to provide a backdrop for the black experience in America. Yale Collection of American Literature, Beinecke Rare Book and Manuscript Library.

1962   Hughes begins a weekly column for the *New York Post* and travels in Africa, where he meets Chinua Achebe and Wole Soyinka, and Italy, where *Black Nativity* is greeted enthusiastically at Gian Carlo Menotti's Festival of Two Worlds. *Fight for Freedom: The Story of the NAACP* is published. Hughes attends the first national poetry festival at the Library of Congress.

1957   Jack Kerouac, *On the Road*; Dr. Seuss, *The Cat in the Hat*; Leonard Bernstein, *West Side Story*; Southern Christian Leadership Conference organized; Ghana becomes independent state; Civil Rights Act of 1957 establishes a civil rights commission and division in the Justice Department;

1963 *Something in Common and Other Stories*, *Five Plays by Langston Hughes*, and *Poems from Black Africa, Ethiopia, and Other Countries* are published. An honorary doctorate from Howard University and completion of the gospel play *Jericho-Jim Crow* precede vacationing and a cruise in Europe. The Theatre Guild premieres *Tambourines to Glory* on Broadway to negative reviews.

1964 *Jericho-Jim Crow* opens to high acclaim at a Greenwich Village theater. Hughes is honored by the Poetry Society of America. The anthology *New Negro Poets: U.S.A.* is published. In Europe, Hughes collaborates on an eighteen-part BBC series dealing with African Americans, takes part in the Berlin Folk Festival, and recites his poetry at the University of Hamburg.

1965 Hughes revises *The Poetry of the Negro* to include more contemporary writing, opens his play *The Prodigal Son* in Greenwich Village, and offers lectures and recitations in Europe at the behest of the U.S. State Department. Hughes contributes to a television script entitled "The Strollin' Twenties," publishes *Simple's Uncle Sam*, and attends the premiere of *Let Us Remember*, a cantata written in collaboration with David Amram.

Arkansas governor Orval Faubus orders the National Guard to turn away African American students from a Little Rock high school, prompting Eisenhower to send in federal troops to enforce desegregation orders.

1958 John Barth, *The End of the Road*; Archibald MacLeish, *J. B.*; bluesman Muddy Waters tours England and influences British musicians whose work will help feed American blues into the pop music mainstream in the 1960s and 1970s; first moon rocket launched by United States.

1959 Lorraine Hansberry, *A Raisin in the Sun*; Eugene Ionesco, *The Rhinoceros*; Newport Folk Festival influences generations of folk music performers by introducing such artists as Sonny Terry and Brownie McGhee, Lightnin' Hopkins, John Lee Hooker, Son House, Mississippi John Hurt, Skip James, Sleepy John Estes, and others on stage over the next eight years; Miles Davis, *Kind of Blue*; Berry Gordy, Jr., establishes Motown Records; Fidel Castro becomes premier of Cuba.

1960 Harper Lee, *To Kill a Mockingbird*; sit-in movement initiated at Woolworth lunch counter in North Carolina; Student Non-Violent Coordinating Committee (SNCC) organized; Civil Rights Act of 1960 passed by Congress; numerous sections of Africa proclaimed independent.

1966   Hughes's last "Simple" column appears in the *Defender*. After vacationing in Europe, Hughes publishes *The Book of Negro Humor*, and *Street Scene* is revived at the New York City Opera. President Johnson appoints Hughes to travel to Dakar for the First World Festival of Negro Arts.

1961   Joseph Heller, *Catch-22*; Leroi Jones, *Preface to a Twenty Volume Suicide Note* and *Dutchman*; James Baldwin, *Nobody Knows My Name*; Ornette Coleman records LP *Free Jazz*; John F. Kennedy inaugurated as president; Bay of Pigs affair; Berlin Wall erected; "Freedom Riders" harassed and attacked in Alabama and Mississippi.

The racism that was so much a part of the scene, in the form of lynching, Klan activities, and Jim Crow laws and customs, at the time of Hughes's birth was still reflected in the newspaper The Thunderbolt, subtitled "The White Man's Viewpoint." From the collection of Steven C. Tracy.

1967 Hughes publicly registers his opposition to the Vietnam War. *The Best Short Stories of Negro Writers from 1899 to the Present* and a French translation of *The Best of Simple* are published. Entering the New York Polyclinic Hospital on May 6, Hughes undergoes prostate surgery on May 12 and dies of complications following surgery. At a memorial service on May 25, Randy Weston and a rhythm section perform Duke Ellington's "Do Nothing 'Til You Hear from Me" and an original blues composed by Weston. Hughes's works *The Panther and the Lash* and *Black Magic: A Pictorial History of the Negro in American Entertainment* (in collaboration with Milton Meltzer) are published posthumously.

1962 Edward Albee, *Who's Afraid of Virginia Woolf*; Robert Hayden, *A Ballad of Remembrance*; James Baldwin, *Another Country*; John Glenn orbits the Earth in a spacecraft; *Telstar* launched; Rachel Carson, *Silent Spring*; Supreme Court rules that the University of Mississippi must admit James Meredith; executive order issued by JFK bars discrimination in federally financed housing.

1963 Leroi Jones, *Blues People*; Martin Luther King, Jr., "Letter from Birmingham Jail"; Pop Art exhibition at the Guggenheim; Medgar Evers assassinated; JFK assassinated; March on Washington culminates in a series of speeches at the Lincoln Memorial, including Martin Luther King, Jr.'s "I Have a Dream" speech.

1964 Saul Bellow, *Herzog*; Melvin B. Tolson, *Harlem Gallery*; Ralph Ellison, *Shadow and Act*; B. B. King records classic LP *Live at the Regal*; Organization of Afro-American Unity founded by Malcolm X; Civil Rights Act of 1964 includes public accommodations and fair employment sections; race riots widespread; Martin Luther King, Jr., wins the Nobel Peace Prize; Cassius Clay / Muhammad Ali becomes world heavyweight boxing champion; the Beatles initiate the "British Invasion" by musical groups.

1965   Malcolm X and Alex Haley, *The Autobiography of Malcolm X*; John Berryman, *77 Dream Songs*; Black Arts Movement initiated by Leroi Jones/Amiri Baraka and others in Harlem; Lyndon Baines Johnson inaugurated for a full term as president; Malcolm X assassinated; LBJ signs Voting Rights Bill; United States delivers military support to South Vietnam.

1966   Sylvia Plath, *Ariel*; Thomas Pynchon, *The Crying of Lot 49*; Indira Gandhi becomes prime minister of India; Dakar, Senegal, hosts first world festival of African art; Stokely Carmichael named chairman of SNCC; Black Panther Party and National Organization for Women established; CORE and SNCC espouse "Black Power" concept.

1967   William Styron, *Confessions of Nat Turner*; Ishmael Reed, *The Freelance Pallbearers*; Christiaan R. Barnard performs first human heart transplant; major race riots take place in Detroit, Newark, and Chicago; LBJ nominates Thurgood Marshall as first African American Supreme Court justice.

Langston Hughes

A Bibliographic Essay

Dolan Hubbard

Throughout four decades of literary creativity that are virtually unrivaled in American letters, Langston Hughes wrote in a diversity of genres—poetry, drama, autobiography, history, fiction, prose comedy, juvenile literature, newspaper columns, librettos—and assembled anthologies, perfected the black gospel song-play, and collaborated on translations. Hughes wrote more than fifty books with one central purpose: "to explain and illuminate," in his words, "the Negro condition in America" (qtd. in Emanuel and Gross, *Dark Symphony* 1968: 191). He presents us with a captivating multidimensional portrait of black America. He shows us how the discourse of black America informs and alters our understanding of cultural history and our appreciation of aesthetic value.

The Langston Hughes Papers

The James Weldon Johnson Memorial Collection and the Beinecke Rare Book and Manuscript Library at Yale University include letters, manuscripts and typescripts of published and unpublished work, lecture notes, and various magazine and newspaper clippings and pamphlets. Additional materials are in the

Schomburg Center for Research in Black Culture of the New York Public Library; the library of Lincoln University, in Pennsylvania; the Moorland-Spingarn Research Center, at Howard University; the Fisk University Library; the Library of Congress; the Bancroft Library, at the University of California, Berkeley; the Bibliothèque Nationale, in Paris; the Kenneth Spencer Research Library, at the University of Kansas; the New York Center for Visual History; the American Institute of Marxist Studies; the archives of the Federal Bureau of Investigation; the Lenin Library, in Moscow; and the Western Reserve Historical Society, in Cleveland, Ohio.

Standard Edition

Thirty-five years after the death of Langston Hughes, the University of Missouri Press is publishing the standard edition, titled *The Complete Works of Langston Hughes*, edited by Arnold Rampersad, Dolan Hubbard, Leslie Catherine Sanders, and Steven C. Tracy (18 volumes, 2001–).

The Langston Hughes Society

Founded in 1981, the Langston Hughes Society, the first literary society in the United States named in honor of a black writer, is a national association of scholars, teachers, creative and performing artists, students, and lay persons. The Society emerged during the Langston Hughes Study conference held in Joplin, Missouri, Hughes's birthplace, 13–14 March 1981. Sponsored by Missouri Southern State College and funded by the Missouri Committee for the Humanities, the conference attempted to assess the status of Langston Hughes in contemporary American literature and attracted scholars from across the country, as well as students and the general public.

The biannual publication of *The Langston Hughes Review*, the official publication of the Langston Hughes Society, concretely reflects the growing interest in Hughes and his work. First published in 1982, with Therman B. O'Daniel as editor (1982–1983), the journal began with fewer than fifty original subscribers. Currently housed at the University of Georgia, the *Review* enjoys a circulation of nearly two hundred, including members in several foreign countries. In addition to publishing articles devoted to all aspects of the man and his work, the *Review* publishes book reviews, research notes, and announcements that are relevant to a critical study of the Hughesian tradition. The computer literate can also keep in touch with the latest in the field by visiting web sites devoted to the author on the Internet and the World Wide Web.

Biographies of Hughes

There are three major biographies of Langston Hughes, each expanding the horizon of Hughes studies: James A. Emanuel, *Langston Hughes* (1967); Faith Berry, *Langston Hughes: Before and Beyond Harlem* (1983); and Arnold Rampersad, *The Life of Langston Hughes*, 2 vols. (1986–1988). Emanuel, who wrote his doctoral dissertation on Hughes, presents a very workmanlike introduction to Hughes. Berry, who concentrates on Hughes's development before he moved to Harlem in the 1940s, uncovers unknown facts about his life and the missing links in his autobiographical volumes, *The Big Sea* (1940) and *I Wonder as I Wander* (1956). With the publication of his two-volume biography of Hughes, Rampersad transformed Hughes studies and provided succeeding generations of scholars with new avenues of intellectual inquiry on Hughes, as well as on American life and culture. He offers the reader "a full-scale portrait" of Hughes, though some would take issue with his thin treatment of Hughes's sexual orientation (Rampersad 1989: 195). The study of Hughes has now been divided into a pre- and post-Rampersad world. Future generations of Hughes scholars will acknowledge his monumental biographies. Four of the finest short biographical overviews of Hughes's life are Therman B. O'Daniel's Introduction to *Langston Hughes: Black Genius* (1971); Arthur P. Davis's "Langston Hughes," in *Dictionary of American Negro Biography* (1982); R. Baxter Miller's "Langston Hughes," in *The Dictionary of Literary Biography* (Vol. 51, 1987); and Arnold Rampersad's "Langston Hughes," in *The Oxford Companion to African American Literature* (1997).

Letters

For Hughes's letters, collections include *Arna Bontemps–Langston Hughes Letters, 1925–1967*, ed. Charles H. Nichols (1980), and *Remember Me to Harlem: The Letters of Langston Hughes and Carl Van Vechten, 1925–1964*, ed. Emily Bernard (2001).

Early Growth and Development of Hughes Scholarship

From the 1920s to the 1940s, Hughes's work was critiqued by leading luminaries such as W. E. B. Du Bois, James Weldon Johnson, Alain Locke, Jessie Fauset, Vachel Lindsay, Countee Cullen, William Stanley Braithwaite, George Schuyler, Carl Van Vechten, Du Bose Heyward, Herbert Gorman, and Richard Wright. Both Cullen, Hughes's rival as poster child for the New Negro, in "Poet on Poet" (1926), and Johnson, in *Black Manhattan* (1930), saw Hughes as rebel in content and form (Miller 1978: x). In "Forerunner and Ambassador" (1940), Wright, in a trenchant observation, noted that Hughes had freed "Negro literature" from timidity as Theodore Dreiser had freed American literature from puritanism. V. F. Calverton, "possibly the most often quoted reviewer of Hughes' work" (Miller 1978: xii) prior to mid-century, saw him as a significant voice in American letters, writing with a freshness often absent from the work of other black writers. In "I Teach Negro Literature" (1941), Nick Aaron Ford declared that Hughes was the "most original of Negro poets."

Hughes began to receive sustained scholarly attention in the 1950s and 1960s. Led by members of the College Language Association, founded in 1937, the academy took serious note of his contribution to American and African American letters. His major scholars were John W. Parker and Arthur P. Davis. Parker not only reviewed books almost as quickly as Hughes published them but also was among the first to note, in "Literature of the Negro Ghetto" (1952), that Hughes's creative genius consisted in blending a humor of characterization with a humor of situation. In "The Harlem of Langston Hughes's Poetry" (1952), Davis sharpens the reader's appreciation for Harlem as the center of Hughes's aesthetic universe. He notes that Hughes wrote about Harlem more often and completely than any other poet; Harlem became literary shorthand for talking about black ghettos in America. A critic of another generation, James de Jongh, in *Vicious Modernism: Black Harlem and the Literary Imagination* (1990), traced the Harlem theme in the poetry of Hughes.

Much of the scholarship of the 1950s and 1960s treated the character Jesse B. Simple, one of Hughes's most enduring literary creations. J. Saunders Redding predicted that the day would come when Simple "would take his place among the great folk hero-gods in the American pantheon" (1966). James A. Emanuel and Theodore Gross observed that Simple was "the one great fictional character" Hughes offered to the literary world (1968: 195). Arthur P. Davis called him Hughes's "greatest single creation" (1974: 69). Blyden Jackson observed that he represented the "Black everyman" (1971: 119)—"an ordinary working black man," who, as Akiba Sullivan Harper notes, is "representative of the masses of black folk in the 1940s"(1995: 3–4). The 1950s concluded with a rush in criticism of Hughes, led by Robert Bone's *Negro Novel in America* (1958); the celebrated *New York Times Book Review* "Sermons and Blues," by James Baldwin, of *Selected Poems* (1959), that chastises Hughes for "having done so little with his genuine gifts"; and "A Golden Mean for the Negro Novel," by Blyden Jackson, who discusses *Not Without Laughter* (1930) within the context of other novels that treat the emerging black middle class. In a later assessment of Hughes, Jackson, one of the most astute critics of African American letters, called Hughes "the Great Impressionist" (1974: 57) of black American literature.

The 1960s witnessed the emergence of perhaps the two key figures in the promulgation of Hughes studies: James A. Emanuel and Therman B. O'Daniel. Beginning with his Columbia University dissertation, "The Short Stories of Langston

Hughes" (1962), Emanuel proved to be one of the most astute interpreters of Hughes. Soon after completing his dissertation, Emanuel, in *Langston Hughes* (1967), set the standard in Hughes criticism with his discussion of the sea as a metaphor, the blues poems as a new form of literature, and American Négritude. Through his prolific writing on Hughes, Emanuel quickly established himself as a critic of record on Hughes, who captured the warp and woof of black life.

A good friend and longtime admirer of Hughes and a fellow Lincoln University of Pennsylvania alumnus, O'Daniel served as the founder and first editor of the influential *CLA Journal* (1957–1978) and later as the first editor of *The Langston Hughes Review* (1982–1983). A little over a year after Hughes's death, O'Daniel published six essays in the June 1968 issue of the *CLA Journal* dedicated to the memory of Hughes. These articles formed the critical spine of the landmark book *Langston Hughes: Black Genius: A Critical Evaluation* (1971). It included twelve essays, eleven of which were written by members of the College Language Association, in the first sustained scholarly study of Hughes.

These African American scholars evaluated Hughes as poet, novelist, playwright, and translator. Among the most incisive of the essays are "The Good Black Poet and the Good Gray Poet: The Poetry of Hughes and Whitman," by Donald B. Gibson; "*Not Without Laughter* but Without Tears," by William Edward Farrison; "A Word about Simple," by Blyden Jackson; "Rhetorical Embellishments in Hughes's Simple Stories," by Harry Jones; "Langston Hughes as Translator," by John F. Matheus; and "Langston Hughes and Afro-American Folk and Cultural Tradition," by George E. Kent.

James A. Emanuel contributed two articles to *Langston Hughes: Black Genius*: "The Short Fiction of Langston Hughes" and "The Literary Experiments of Langston Hughes." The latter piece originally appeared in *Freedomways* magazine (1968). Anticipating the future direction of Hughes studies, Emanuel notes that while many people praise Hughes as an innovator of the blues and jazz and the gospel-song play, this "Poet Laureate of the Negro People" (171) had just begun to attract scholarly study.

Emanuel then proceeds to give a tour de force literary review of Hughes as an artistic innovator, who throughout his career redrew the boundaries of African American letters. Emanuel's insights into the art and imagination of Hughes still reverberate in Hughes studies. O'Daniel's *Langston Hughes: Black Genius*, a landmark publication, stands first among equals on a Hughes studies citation index. R. Baxter Miller wrote a Hughes primer in "Langston Hughes" (1987), an incisive overview that complements the work of Emanuel and O'Daniel.

The ensuing years have witnessed the development of a variety of methodological and interdisciplinary initiatives in Hughes scholarship: cultural criticism, black studies, deconstruction, gender studies, new historicism, and postmodernist studies. These critical initiatives offer a telling refutation to those critics who considered his work shallow or transparent. Moreover, many in the academy have overlooked the work of Hughes, who, along with Claude McKay, as Amiri Baraka notes in his Foreword to the 1986 edition of *The Big Sea* (1940), "catalyzed black literary development internationally" (1986: i). As we enter the twenty-first century, the scholarship on Hughes has matured, and the tributary of articles in the wake of his death more than thirty-five years ago has become a veritable river of scholarly interest, domestical and international.

The Treatment of Hughes in the Journals

For a broad look at Hughes in the context of cultural studies, *Opportunity* was a particularly valuable journal in the 1920s, as *Phylon* would be in the 1940s and 1950s. Locke, who attended to Hughes's development as a poet from the 1920s to early 1950s, was one of the most perceptive commentators. Locke's comments in the annual literary surveys in *Opportunity* and *Phylon* reveal much about his philosophy of creative literature. Near the time of Hughes's death, in 1967, the *CLA Journal*, *Freedomways*, *Crisis*, and *Présence Africaine* all brought out special issues worthy of scholarly consideration (Miller 1989: 5). *The Langston Hughes Review* has published issues on a range of topics related to

Hughes and his milieu: Langston Hughes in translation (4, no. 2; fall 1985); the African Diaspora (5, no. 1; spring 1986); the critical reception of Hughes in Cuba, Haiti, Japan, and France (6, no. 1; spring 1987); black women as cultural conservators (7, no. 2; fall 1988); a selection of writings by James Weldon Johnson (8, nos. 1–2; spring/fall 1989); George H. Bass, poet, playwright, scholar, and executor of the Hughes estate (9–10: 1–2; 1990–1991); Darwin T. Turner (11, no. 2; fall 1992); Frank Marshall Davis and the Chicago Renaissance (14, nos. 1–2; spring–fall 1996); Hughes as a playwright (15, no. 1; spring 1997); and Dorothy West (16, no. 1; spring 1998).

Critical Studies

Readers who want 365 days of Hughes should consult *A Langston Hughes Encyclopedia* (2002), by Hans Ostrom. It chronicles the life and writings of Langston Hughes through hundreds of alphabetically arranged entries, many including bibliographical information. For the study of Hughes's writings, see Thomas A. Mikolyzk, *Langston Hughes: A Bio-Bibliography* (1990), Donald C. Dickinson's *A Bio-Bibliography of Langston Hughes, 1902–1967* (1967), and R. Baxter Miller's *Langston Hughes and Gwendolyn Brooks: A Reference Guide* (1978). Dickinson is useful as a bibliographical source but not as a critical work. Extending the work of Dickinson and Miller, Mikolyzk presents the first annotated bibliography devoted to the life work of Langston Hughes and also provides a concise biography of this important writer. Peter Mandelik and Stanley Schatt noted revisions in Hughes's work, including the omission of Dunbar-like dialect and political references to the thirties, in a *Concordance to Langston Hughes* (1975). Schatt's "Langston Hughes: The Minstrel as Artificer" (1975) continues his discussion of the extensive revisions in Hughes's poetry, especially *Selected Poems*. To know the score on Hughes as a poet-musician, see *The World of Langston Hughes Music: A Bibliography of Musical Settings of Langston Hughes's Work with Recordings and Other Listings* (1982), by Kenneth P. Neilson.

Also see Therman B. O'Daniel, ed., *Langston Hughes: Black Ge-*

nius (1971); and idem, "An Updated Bibliography," in a special issue of *Black American Literature Forum* (1981), guest editor R. Baxter Miller. Blyden Jackson, in "Langston Hughes" (1978), and Sharynn O. Etheridge, in "Langston Hughes: An Annotated Bibliography (1977–1986)" [1992], provide the reader with useful bibliographies on Hughes. The *Modern Language Association International Bibliography*, available both in print and on CD-ROM, lists annually the most recent primary and secondary materials. There is no annual publication of a current bibliographic article that contains up-to-date checklists of criticism available on Hughes.

For a representative sampling of articles on Hughes that spans a half century, see *Langston Hughes: Critical Perspectives Past and Present* (1993), edited by Henry Louis Gates and Anthony Appiah; *Langston Hughes* (1989), edited by Harold Bloom; and *Critical Essays on Langston Hughes* (1986), edited by Edward J. Mullen. Also see Tish Dace, *Langston Hughes: The Contemporary Reviews* (1997), and C. James Trotman, *Langston Hughes: The Man, His Art, and His Continuing Influence* (1995), papers from the historic conference on Hughes at Lincoln University of Pennsylvania.

The mainstreaming of Hughes is most evident in *The Columbia Companion to the Twentieth-Century American Short Story* (2000), edited by Blanche H. Gelfant, and in *Anthology of Modern American Poetry* (2000), edited by Cary Nelson. With twenty-nine poems, Hughes is given full treatment for the first time in any comprehensive anthology. One can find additional information about Hughes at the accompanying Modern American Poetry website: http://www.english.uiuc.edu/MAPS. Last, Hughes is often the centerpiece of discussion in diverse treatments of the Harlem Renaissance such as *The Harlem Group of Negro Writers* (1940), by Melvin B. Tolson, the first academic study of the Harlem Renaissance written by an African American scholar; *Harlem Renaissance* (1971), by Nathan Irvin Huggins; *The Harlem Renaissance Remembered* (1972), edited by Arna Bontemps; *The Novels of the Harlem Renassance: Twelve Black Writers, 1923–1933* (1976), by Amritjit Singh; *When Harlem Was in Vogue* (1981), by David Levering Lewis; *This Was Harlem* (1982), by Jervis Anderson; *The Harlem Renaissance: A Historical Dictionary for the Era* (1984), edited by Bruce Kellner; *Black Culture and the Harlem*

Renaissance (1988), by Cary Wintz; *The Harlem Renaissance* (1995), by Steven Watson; and *The Harlem Renaissance: The One and the Many* (2001), by Mark Helbling.

With the exception of O'Daniel, these critical studies must be read against the backdrop of the Black Aesthetic Movement of the 1960s and 1970s. Critics who came of age in the years after the 1960s were informed by a criticism of liberation that challenged the unitary approach to reading black literature as articulated by the editors of the landmark anthology *Negro Caravan* (1941). Hearkening back to Hughes's manifesto "The Negro Artist and the Racial Mountain" (1926), their intent was to recenter African American literature. They saw Hughes as one of the legislators of black culture and as a major figure on the international stage, the engaged intellectual who aligned himself with freedom struggles in Russia, Spain, and in the African Diaspora.

For instance, in *Black Protest Poetry from the Harlem Renaissance and the Sixties* (2001), Margaret Reid analyzes Hughes within the context of the 1960s Black Arts Movement. He is both a sturdy black bridge for the generation of black poets who came of age in the 1960s and a figure to rail against for being out of touch with the tenor of the time. Robert Bone, in *Down Home: Origins of the Afro-American Short Story* (1975; rev. ed. 1988) offers a corrective to those who locate the roots of the Black Aesthetic Movement in the 1960s. Finally, Abdul Alkalimat, in "Toward a Paradigm of Unity in Black Studies" (2001), celebrates Hughes as a template for the emerging field of black studies with it emphasis on political self-determination for black America.

Poetry

Hughes published fifteen volumes of poetry, which present a veritable thesaurus of the black experience. However, accessing the full range of his poetic output has been extremely difficult because of the scattered nature of the publishing outlets for his poems. Arnold Rampersad and David Roessel's *The Collected Poems of Langston Hughes* (1994) pushed back shutters and opened windows to the poetic universe of Hughes with the publication of nearly seven hundred poems. For the first time, readers had access to all of the poems Hughes had published during his lifetime, arranged in the general order in which he wrote them and annotated by Rampersad and Roessel. In addition, Rampersad edited three volumes of Hughes's poetry for *The Complete Works of Langston Hughes* (2001).

Onwuchekwa Jemie, an Ibo from Nigeria who took his doctorate at Columbia, stresses, in *Langston Hughes: An Introduction to the Poetry* (1976), that one should evaluate Hughes from a dual perspective of folk tradition and struggle and protest. Moreover, Jemie asserts that Hughes prefigures the cultural nationalism of the 1960s and 1970s—Hoyt Fuller, Ron Karenga, and Amiri Baraka—all evolving from the work of Richard Wright.

In *Good Morning Revolution: Uncollected Writings of Social Protest* (1973), Faith Berry published a collection of prose pieces and poems by Hughes. People in progressive circles, nationally and internationally, took note of Hughes's work of the 1930s because of his political commitment on the side of the proletariat. These revolutionary writings from leftist journals of the 1930s and 1940s were suppressed from that part of the Hughes canon because they did not fit his popular image in a Right-leaning America following World War II. Hughes published a representative sampling of his work, minus his Left-leaning poetry and essays, in *The Langston Hughes Reader: Selected Writings of Langston Hughes* (1958).

Alain Locke, who attended to Hughes's development as a poet from the 1920s to early 1950s, offers the reader one of the longest unbroken critical treatments of Hughes as a poet. However, Locke's comments in the annual literary surveys in *Opportunity* and *Phylon* reveal much about Locke's philosophy of creative literature. The first genre study that focused on Hughes as a poet was written by the French critic Jean Wagner in *Les Poètes Nègres des Etats-Unis* (1962; trans. by Kenneth Douglas 1973). With a sweet irony that also reflects Hughes's standing on the international stage, this Gallic critic gives Hughes a focal treatment in his analysis of America's foremost black poet. Wagner is strongest when he discusses the later rather than the earlier Hughes.

In *Langston Hughes: The Poet and His Critics* (1977), Richard K. Barksdale wrote the first sustained scholarly treatment by an

American of Hughes as a poet. He uses a chronological and historical approach in his analysis of Hughes's development. Barksdale continued to reassess Hughes's contribution to American letters in *Praisesong of Survival* (1992). Among the six essays included are "The Humanistic Techniques Employed in Hughes's Poetry" (1981); "Langston Hughes and James Baldwin: Some Observations on a Literary Relationship" (1988); and "The Poet, the Preacher, and the Dream" (1988).

Steven C. Tracy wrote the first sustained study on Hughes and the blues in *Langston Hughes and the Blues* (1988). Written from the perspective of a "blues purist," Tracy demonstrates how blues performers such as Bessie Smith, Ma Rainey, Lonnie Johnson, Blind Lemon Jefferson, and Memphis Minnie greatly influenced Hughes. Tracy shows how Hughes combined African American oral and literary traditions to create a blues-inspired poetry that is intellectually stimulating, sociopolitically responsible, and aesthetically pleasing both as folk poetry and as literature. R. Baxter Miller reminds the reader that the aesthetic universe of the blues was compatible with Hughes's vision of himself as a social and political rebel (1989). Beginning with the premise that the Great Migration is a defining event of postemancipation African American life and a central feature of twentieth-century black literature, Lawrence Rodgers, in *Canaan Bound: The African-American Great Migration Novel* (1997), posits that Hughes is the poet of migration.

C. Barry Chabot's *Writers for the Nation: American Literary Modernism* (1997) sees Hughes as an active participant in a broad conversation about ways to restore or create feelings of belonging among his contemporaries who thought that life was becoming too abrasive and that the United States no longer afforded its citizens a viable sense of community. Chabot includes a discussion of *The Weary Blues* (1926) and *Fine Clothes to the Jew* (1927).

In his long commentary on jazz and the battle for the soul of America titled "Pulp and Circumstance: The Story of Jazz in High Places" (1998: 420–21), Gerald Early situates the Cullen-Hughes debate in the center of an unruly conversation on religion, aesthetics, and identity, or, in the words of George Hutchinson, "the nature of Americanism" (1995: 221).

Novels

Early works that treat the novels of Hughes include *The Contempo-rary Negro Novel* (1936), by Nick Aaron Ford; *The Negro in American Fiction* (1937), by Sterling A. Brown; *Negro Voices in American Fiction* (1948), by Hugh M. Gloster; *The Negro Novelist* (1953), by Carl Mil-ton Hughes; *The Negro Novel in America* (1958; rev. ed. 1965), by Robert Bone; and *The Novels of the Harlem Renaissance: Twelve Black Writers, 1923–1933* (1976), by Amritjit Singh. In *Ten Is the Age of Darkness: The Black Bildungsroman* (1995), Geta LeSeur places Hughes's *Not Without Laughter* (1930) in a global context. She shows how the circumstances of colonialism, oppression, race, class, and gender make the maturing process of young black pro-tagonists different from that of their white counterparts.

Short Fiction

For a discussion of Hughes's short fiction, see *Down Home: Ori-gins of the Afro-American Short Story* (1975; rev. ed. 1988), by Robert Bone. In the vein of Ralph Ellison and Albert Murray, Bone ap-proaches the blues as an American art form that took roots at the edge of the frontier with its outlaw culture. Bone discusses the West Illana Series, Hughes's first published short stories that re-sulted from his experience as a mess boy in 1923 on the *S.S. Mal-one*, the *Ways of White Folk* (1934), and *Laughing to Keep from Cry-ing* (1952). Hans Ostrom wrote the first full-length study, titled *Langston Hughes: A Study of the Short Fiction* (1993), devoted to Hughes's short fiction.

Humor and Satire

In *Not So Simple: The "Simple" Stories by Langston Hughes* (1995), Donna Akiba Sullivan Harper wrote the first full historical an-alysis of the Simple stories from the 1943 appearance of the street corner philosopher deluxe in Hughes's weekly *Chicago Defender* column through his 1965 farewell in the *New York Post*.

Refining his columns, Hughes wrote six books and one play on his lovable Everyman whose insights on the human condition revealed, in the words of Richard Wright, his "complex simplicity" (1937). Most important, Harper makes gender visible in Hughes through his representation of women in the Simple stories.

Critics who discuss the representation of women in Hughes include Rita B. Dandridge, in "The Black Woman as a Freedom Fighter in Langston Hughes' *Simple's Uncle Sam*" (1974); R. Baxter Miller, in "'No Crystal Stair': Unity, Archetype, and Symbol in Langston Hughes's Poems on Women" (1975); Sandra Y. Govan, in "Black Women as Cultural Conservators: Biographers and Builders of Our Cultural Heritage" (1988); and Akiba Sullivan Harper in "Langston Hughes as Cultural Conservator: Women in the Life of a "Negro Everyman" (1988). Bernice Guillaume's "The Female as Harlem Sage: The 'Aunt Viney's Sketches'" (1987) reveals that Hughes's irrepressible black Everyman, Jesse B. Semple, actually had a female antecedent. Beth Turner, in "Simplifyin': Langston Hughes and Alice Childress Re/member Jesse B. Semple" (1997) examines the comic imagination and stereotypes. Melvin G. Williams's "The Gospel According to Simple" (1977) discusses the attitude toward God, the Bible, and the church as filtered through the consciousness of Simple, the typical Harlem dweller. In "Simple's Great African American Joke" (1984), Steven C. Tracy discusses a white America that resists taking "cultural difference" in stride.

Stepping inside the humor, Dellita Martin-Ogunsola's "Ambivalence as Allegory in Langston Hughes's 'Simple' Stories" (1988) examines the Simple stories for what they tell the reader about the ambivalence, or the "double conscious," of black people in America. Don Bertschman provides the reader with a very accessible overview of Simple in "Jesse B. Simple and the Racial Mountain: A Bibliographic Essay" (1995).

More often noted for his humor than his satire, Hughes receives treatment for his satire in *Down Home: Origins of the Afro-American Short Story* (1975; rev. ed. 1988), by Robert Bone, and in *African American Satire: The Sacredly Profane Novel* (2001), by Darryl Dickson-Carr. Bone considers Hughes a satirist "clearly of a high order" (254) in *The Ways of White Folks* (1934). Dickson-

Carr's "Satire through the Harlem Renaissance" examines Hughes's satirical and allegorical take on the racial politics of the time in *The Ways of White Folks* (1934). Dickson-Carr considers Hughes's "Everyman," Jesse B. Simple, among "the most notable, artistically successful examples of progressive debate on black issues in a satirical context to emerge from the 1940s and 1950s, their depth, breadth, and consistency equaled only in George Schuyler's columns" (89).

In "Ask Your Mama: Women in Langston Hughes's *The Ways of White Folk* (1995), Susan Neale Mayberry discusses how Hughes works to defeat the stereotypes of black women. Thadious Davis, in "Reading the Woman's Face in Langston Hughes's and Roy De Carava's *Sweet Flypaper of Life*" (1993), notes how the elderly black woman protagonist takes wings and flies above Hughes's autograph and De Carava's camera to narrate her own story.

Jon Woodson's *To Make a New Race: Gurdjieff, Toomer, and the Harlem Renaissance* (1999) asserts that readers tend to misread the deeper message embedded in the work of the Harlem literati. He explores the intense influence of the Greek-born mystic on the thinking of the Harlem literati—Jean Toomer, Zora Neale Hurston, Nella Larsen, George Schuyler, and Wallace Thurman, among others. Woodson comments on how Hughes, in "Rejuvenation through Joy," from *The Ways of White Folk* (1934), satirizes his colleagues who followed Gurdjieff, a Pied Piper with his coded philosophy that promoted "objective literature."

Drama and Theater

The experience of the black playwright on Broadway has at best been problematic, and it was no different with Hughes. In *Negro Playwrights in the American Theatre 1925–1959* (1967, 1969), Doris E. Abramson discusses Hughes's *Mulatto* (1935), which enjoyed the longest run of any play by a black writer until Lorraine Hansberry's *A Raisin in the Sun* (1959). Abramson also treats *Don't You Want to Be Free* (1938).

In "Langston Hughes as Playwright" (1968), Darwin T. Turner

wrote an early article that examined Hughes as a dramatist; he finds Hughes guilty of too much predictability. Blyden Jackson, one of the most astute critics of Hughes, issued a call for more scholarship on the plays in "Langston Hughes," in *Black American Writers: Bibliographic Essays* (edited by M. Thomas Inge, 1978). Jackson's call has been ably answered by Joseph McLaren in *Langston Hughes: Folk Dramatist in the Protest Tradition, 1921–1943* (1997) and by Leslie Catherine Sanders in *The Development of Black Theatre in America* (1988). *The Langston Hughes Review* published a special issue on Hughes and drama (1997) that included a compilation by Joseph McLaren of Hughes's dramatic works. In "Langston Hughes's Lost Translation of Federico García Lorca's *Blood Wedding* (1997), Brian D. Bethune recounts his production of *Blood Wedding* by the greatest Spanish poetic playwright of the twentieth century; Bethune considers Hughes's translation the best because it moves beyond a stilted facsimile of the original to capture the mood of the original, which was rooted in the Spanish soul. In "Memories of Langston Hughes" (1995), David Ignatow recalls the excitement associated with Hughes's translation of *Gypsy Ballads* (1928), which Ignatow published in 1951, during his tenure as editor of the *Beloit Poetry Journal*.

In his Introduction to *Mule Bone* (1991), Henry Louis Gates recaps one of the more celebrated literary disputes in African-American letters. In 1931, Hughes and Zora Neale Hurston began to collaborate on a three-act comedy because their patron, Charlotte Osgood Mason, disapproved of theatrical ventures. The collaboration produced bitter recriminations and charges of plagiarism, but no play. These two formerly good friends never spoke again. *Mule Bone* was finally produced by New York City's Lincoln Center in 1991.

Autobiographies

In "Black Autobiography and the Comic Vision" (1981) [*Langston Hughes: The Poet and His Critics* (1977)], Richard K. Barksdale examines Hughes's comic vision in *The Big Sea* (1940) and *I Wonder as I Wander* (1956). R. Baxter Miller's *The Art and Imagination of*

Langston Hughes (1989) uses Hughes's autobiographies as an important yet hitherto neglected key to his imagination and, by extension, to his contribution to American letters. Miller draws upon a variety of critical methods, including formalist, structuralist, and semiotic criticism. He finds a constant symbiotic bond between the historical and the lyrical as they unified the metaphor of Hughes the "wanderer." Miller notes the simplicity of language of Hughes, whose complex use of metaphor belied "his seemingly transparent treatment of folk life" (Miller 6).

Nonfiction Prose

For Hughes's nonfiction prose, with a focus on his Chicago *Defender* columns, in which his searing, ironic, and powerful critiques of American and international race relations can be found, see *Langston Hughes and the Chicago Defender: Essays on Race, Politics, and Culture, 1942–62*, ed. Christopher C. De Santis (1995). In *To Langston Hughes with Love* (1996), Kenneth P. Neilson published selected newspaper articles from *The New York Voice*.

Introduced to progressive politics at Central High School in Cleveland, Ohio, Langston Hughes came of age during the critical, formative period of the American Communist Party. Though Hughes never formally became a member, his public stance in regard to social injustice caught the attention of people in progressive circles in the 1930s, nationally and internationally. Michael Thurston examines Hughes's reportage from the Spanish Civil War, demonstrating Hughes's dual focus on racial issues and revolutionary politics, in "'Bombed in Spain': Langston Hughes, the Black Press, and the Spanish Civil War" (2001). Hughes entered the leftist canon with the publication of *Proletarian Literature in the United States: An Anthology* (1935), edited by Granville Hicks, Joseph North, Michael Gold, Paul Peters, Isido Schneider, and Alan Calmer. In *Good Morning Revolution: Uncollected Writings of Social Protest* (1973), Faith Berry published a collection of prose pieces and poems by Hughes.

In *The New Red Negro: The Literary Left and African American Poetry, 1930–1946* (1999), James Edward Smethurst notes that the most striking thing about Hughes's poetry in the 1930s is "the wide variety of voices, styles, and themes" (94) used by him in the late 1920s and early 1930s and addressed "to equally disparate audiences become largely unified by the end of the decade in a manner that is crucial to the development of his later work" (94). Smethurst illuminates how the ideology of the Communist Left as particularly expressed through "cultural" institutions of the literary Left significantly influenced the shape of African American poetry of the 1930s and 1940s. Specifically, he examines Hughes's evolution from using a wide variety of voices, styles, and themes in the late 1920s and early 1930s to a unified voice that is reflected in *Shakespeare in Harlem* (1942) and, ultimately, *Montage of A Dream Deferred* (1951), in which formerly distinct addresses are combined to imagine a single audience and a single subject.

Children's Literature and Juvenile Biographies

Children's literature is a new area of scholarly study. Violet J. Harris (1990, 1990) discusses Hughes within the context of African American children's literature; the young Hughes was a contributor to *The Brownies' Book*, a periodical designed to instill in black children a sense of racial pride. However, among the several juvenile biographies Hughes are *Langston Hughes* (1994), by S. L. Berry; *Coming Home: From the Life of Langston Hughes* (1994), by Floyd Cooper; *Langston Hughes: Young Black Poet* (1995), by Montrew Dunham; *Langston Hughes: Poet of the Harlem Renaissance* (1997), by Christine M. Hill; *Langston Hughes: Great American Poet* (1992), by Pat McKissack and Frederick McKissack; *Langston Hughes: A Biography* (1968), by Milton Meltzer; *Langston Hughes: An Illustrated Edition* (1997), by Milton Meltzer with the illustrator Stephen Alcorn; *Langston Hughes: Poet of His People* (1970), by Elisabeth P. Myers; *Free to Dream: The Making of a Poet* (1996), by Audrey Osofsky; and *Langston Hughes: American Poet* (1974), by Alice Walker. Steven C. Tracy's introduction to Volume 12 of *The Collected Works of Langston Hughes* discusses the biographies for children written by Hughes.

International Scholarship on Hughes

Two book-length studies aim to fill a grievous gap in the fascinating history of American expatriates who chose to live in Paris in the twentieth century. *From Harlem to Paris: Black American Writers in France, 1840–1980* (1991), by Michel Fabre, details how time and circumstances altered black Americans' experiences and expectations in France. In Chapter 5, titled "Langston Hughes and Alain Locke: Jazz in Montmartre and African Art," Fabre discusses Paris as a site of "aesthetic enjoyment" (71). In *Paris Noir: African Americans in the City of Light* (1996), Tyler Stovall illuminates how Hughes, like many in the tightly knit community of African Americans, found in Paris the artistic, racial, and emotional freedom denied them back in the United States.

As a result of his extensive travels, his Left-leaning politics, his translations, and the humanistic implication of his work, Hughes has engendered commentary from a diverse group of critical voices from the international arena. For Hughes and the Hispanic World, collections include *Nicolás Guillén y Langston Hughes* (1962), by Enrique Noble; *The Devil, the Gargoyle, and the Buffoon: The Negro as Metaphor in Western* Literature (1971), by Lemuel A. Johnson; *Langston Hughes in the Hispanic World and Haiti* (1977), edited by Edward J. Mullen; and *Harlem, Haiti, and Havana: A Comprehensive Study of Langston Hughes, Jacques Roumain, and Nicholas Guillén* (1979), by Martha K. Cobb. In addition, critical appraisals of Hughes have been published abroad: in Haiti, *Langston Hughes: Un Chant Nouveau* (1940), by Réne Piquion; in France, *Langston Hughes* (1964), by François Dodat; and in Italy, *Testo e Contesto Della Poesia di Langston Hughes* (1979), by Stefania Piccinato.

Assessing Hughes's work of the 1930s, and conveniently ignoring his "bourgeois aestheticism" in *The Weary Blues* (1926) and the class interest in *Fine Clothes to the Jew* (1927), Lydia Filatova, a Russian critic, stamped him as revolutionary writer in her long essay "Langston Hughes: American Writer" (1933). The scholarship on Hughes following the end of the Cold War moved beyond the boundary of vernacular versus formality and the proletarian versus the bourgeoisie that was prevalent in much of the criticism. David Chioni Moore is working closely with a scholar at the University of Bukhara, in Uzbekistan, on translating an article of hers, called "Langston Hughes, First American Writer Translated into Any Central Asian Language," from the Uzbek language.

Queer Studies

With the emergence of queer studies, Hughes's sexual orientation has been a point of interest as various sexual sleuths attempt to "out" him. The "outing" of Hughes is part and parcel of the discourse on how homosexuality was "invented" as a category of literary identity in the United States. Hughes figures prominently in the growing body of literature that focuses on discovering the intersections of gender, race, and sexuality. Studies that discuss Hughes in this context include Charles Nero's "Re/membering Langston: Homophobic Textuality and Arnold Rampersad's *Life of Langston Hughes*" (1997), and Siobhan B. Somerville's *Queering the Color Line: Race and the Invention of Homosexuality in American Culture* (2000). See also the discussion of the film *Looking for Langston* in the following section.

Hughes and the Visual Medium

Hughes has been the subject of a PBS documentary, produced by the New York Center for Visual History, titled *Langston Hughes: The Dream Keeper* (1988), produced by St. Clair Bourne. This historic documentary was a part of *Voices and Visions: A Television Course in Modern American Poetry* (1988), an ambitious thirteen-week celebration of the lives and works of thirteen great modern American poets. In 1997, *the Langston Hughes Review* published the transcripts. Those interviewed (in order) included Arnold Rampersad, Amiri Baraka, Louise Patterson, Raoul Abdul, George Bass, Ted Joans, Rowena Jelliffe, Gwendolyn Brooks, Faith Berry, and James Baldwin.

Hughes has also been the subject of a documentary, titled

Looking for Langston (1989), by the British filmmaker Isaac Julien. This documentary forms the backdrop of what Houston A. Baker in another context refers to as an "unruly conversation." Julien, along with Baldwin (1985) and Marcellus Blount and George P. Cunningham (1996), contests the ways in which the black man and his sexuality have been represented in the modern Western world and how existing notions of race and gender figure within American and African American culture.

The works of Julien and of Charles Nero are at variance with the observation of Rampersad, in the acknowledgments to Volume 1 of the Hughes biography, where he writes: "As for the increasingly fashionable tendency to assert, without convincing evidence, that Hughes was homosexual, I will say at this point only that such a conclusion seems unfounded, and that the evidence suggests a more complicated sexual nature" (439). *Looking for Langston* is about a memoriam to Langston Hughes and the Harlem Renaissance as reconstructed from a black gay perspective (208). It is haunted by the foreboding presence of AIDS. Though Hughes never appears in the avant-garde documentary, Julien includes a radio program taped in memoriam to Hughes upon his death in 1967 overlaid by Hughes's reading of poems from *Montage of a Dream Deferred* (1951). Nero argues that Rampersad, in denying the reader a queer Hughes, denies a full representation of Hughes.

Hughes Studies in a New Century

Since the publication of "The Negro Speaks of Rivers" (1921) and its prose soul mate, "The Negro Artist and the Racial Mountain" (1926), Langston Hughes has been the bellwether writer in black America. Through his work, he has pointed the way for others to follow in the areas of race, class, gender, migration, religion, humor, music, economics, and history, while steadfastly holding to the American Dream. The following are promising areas of Hughes scholarship in the twenty-first century: Hughes and the international stage, multicultural literature and interdisciplinary studies, gender issues, and the visual media.

Bibliography

World Wide Web Sites

Langston Hughes Society: http://www.langstonhughessociety.org
(e-mail: lhreview@arches.uga.edu)

Langston Hughes Review: http://www.uga.edu/iaas/lhr (e-mail:
lhreview@arches.uga.edu)

Primary Works

See the list of abbreviations following the contents.

Bernard, Emily, ed. *Remember Me to Harlem: The Letters of Langston
Hughes and Carl Van Vechten, 1925–1964*. New York: Oxford
University Press, 2001.

Berry, Faith, ed. *Good Morning Revolution: Uncollected Writings of Social Protest*. Westport, Conn.: Lawrence Hill, 1973.

Bourne, St. Clair, producer. *Langston Hughes: The Dream Keeper. Voices
and Visions: A Television Course in Modern American Poetry*.
Alexandria, Va.: PBS Adult Learning Service, 1988. Transcripts
published in *Langston Hughes Review* 15, no. 2 (winter 1997).

De Santis, Christopher C. *Fight for Freedom and Other Writings on Civil
Rights*. Vol. 10. *The Complete Works of Langston Hughes*. Columbia: University of Missouri Press, 2001.

———. *Langston Hughes and the Chicago Defender: Essays on Race, Politics, and Culture, 1942-1962*. Urbana: University of Illinois
Press, 1995.

Harper, Donna Akiba Sullivan. *The Early Simple Stories*. Vol. 7. *The
Complete Works of Langston Hughes*. Columbia: University of
Missouri Press, 2001.

Hubbard, Dolan, ed. *The Novels:* Not Without Laughter *and* Tambourines to Glory. Vol. 4. *The Complete Works of Langston
Hughes*. Ed. Arnold Rampersad, Dolan Hubbard, Leslie
Sanders, and Steven C. Tracy. Columbia: University of Missouri Press, 2001.

Hughes, Langston. *The Big Sea*. 1940. Foreword by Amiri Baraka.
New York: Thunder's Mouth, 1986. i–iii.

———. "The Negro Artist and the Racial Mountain. *Voices from the
Harlem Renaissance*. Ed. Nathan Irvin Huggins. New York:
Oxford University Press, 1976. 305–9.

———. Poems. In *Anthology of Modern American Poetry*. Ed. Cary Nelson. New York: Oxford University Press, 2000.

———. *Poems*. Ed. Arnold Rampersad and David Roessel. New York: Vintage, 1994.

Hughes, Langston, trans. *"Gypsy Ballads* of Federico García Lorca." 1928. *Beloit Poetry Journal* 2 (fall 1951).

Nichols, Charles H., ed. *Arna Bontemps–Langston Hughes Letters, 1925–1967*. New York: Dodd Mead, 1980.

Rampersad, Arnold, ed. *The Poems 1921–1940*. Vol. 1. The *Complete Works of Langston Hughes*. Ed. Arnold Rampersad, Dolan Hubbard, Leslie Sanders, and Steven C. Tracy. Columbia: University of Missouri Press, 2001.

———. *The Poems 1941–1950*. Vol. 2. *The Complete Works of Langston Hughes*. Columbia: University of Missouri Press, 2001.

———. *The Poems 1951–1967*. Vol. 3. *The Complete Works of Langston Hughes*. Columbia: University of Missouri Press, 2001.

Rampersad, Arnold, and David Roessel, eds. *The Collected Poems of Langston Hughes*. New York: Vintage/Random House, 1994.

Sanders, Leslie, with Nancy Johnston. *The Plays to 1942:* Mulatto *to* The Sun Do Move. Vol. 5. *The Complete Works of Langston Hughes*. Columbia: University of Missouri Press, 2001.

Smalley, Webster, ed. *Five Plays by Langston Hughes:* Tambourines to Glory, Soul Gone Home, Little Ham, Mulatto, Simply Heavenly. Bloomington: Indiana University Press, 1963.

Tracy, Steven C., ed. *Works for Children and Young Adults: Biographies*. Vol. 12. *The Complete Works of Langston Hughes*. Ed. Arnold Rampersad, Dolan Hubbard, Leslie Sanders, and Steven C. Tracy. Columbia: University of Missouri Press, 2001.

Secondary Works

Abramson, Doris E. *Negro Playwrights in the American Theatre 1925–1959*. New York: Columbia University Press, 1967, 1969.

Alkalimat, Abdul. "Toward a Paradigm of Unity in Black Studies." *The African American Studies Reader*. Ed. Nathaniel Normet, Jr. Durham, N.C.: Carolina Academic Press, 2001. 391–407.

Anderson, Jervis. *This Was Harlem: A Cultural Portrait, 1900–1950*. New York: Farrar, Straus Giroux, 1981.

Baker, Houston A. *Blues, Ideology, and Afro-American Literature.* Chicago: University of Chicago Press, 1984.

———. *Modernism and the Harlem Renaissance.* Chicago: University of Chicago Press, 1987.

Baldwin, James. "Sermons and Blues." *New York Times Book Review,* 29 March 1959: 6.

———. "Here Be Dragons." *The Price of the Ticket: Collected Nonfiction Essays 1948–1985.* New York: St. Martin's/Marek, 1985. 677–90.

Barksdale, Richard K. *Langston Hughes: The Poet and His Critics.* Chicago: American Library, 1977.

———. *Praisesong of Survival: The Collected Essays of Richard K. Barksdale.* Urbana: University of Illinois Press, 1992. viii–xiii.

Beavers, Herman. "Dead Rocks and Sleeping Men: Aurality in the Aesthetic of Langston Hughes." *Langston Hughes Review* 11, no. 1 (spring 1992): 1–5.

Bell, Bernard. *The Afro-American Novel and Its Tradition.* Amherst: University of Massachusetts Press, 1987.

Berry, Faith. "The Universality of Langston Hughes." *Langston Hughes Review* 1, no. 2 (fall 1982): 1–10.

———. *Langston Hughes: Before and beyond Harlem.* Westport, Conn.: Lawrence Hill, 1983.

Berry, S. L. *Langston Hughes.* Chicago: Creative Education, 1994.

Bertschman, Don. "Jesse B. Simple and the Racial Mountain: A Bibliographic Essay. *Langston Hughes Review* 13, no. 2 (winter–summer 1995): 29–44.

Bethune, Brian D. "Langston Hughes's Lost Translation of Federico García Lorca's *Blood Wedding. Langston Hughes Review* 15, no. 1 (spring 1997): 24–36.

Bloom, Harold, ed. *Langston Hughes.* New York: Chelsea House, 1989.

Bogle, Donald. *Toms, Coons, Mulattoes, Mammies, and Bucks: An Interpretive History of Blacks in American Films.* New York: Viking, 1973.

Bone, Robert. *The Negro Novel in America.* 1958. Rev. New Haven, Conn.: Yale University Press, 1965.

———. *Down Home: Origins of the Afro-American Short Story.* 1975. Rev. New York: Columbia University Press, 1988.

Bontemps, Arna, ed. *The Harlem Renaissance Remembered: Essays.* New York: Dodd, 1972.

Brown, Sterling A. *Negro Poetry and Drama and the Negro in American Fiction.* 1937. Rpt. New York: Atheneum, 1969.

Brown, Sterling A., Arthur P. Davis, and Ulysses P. Lee, eds. *The Negro Caravan.* New York: Citadel, 1941.

Butcher, Margaret Just. *The Negro in American Culture.* New York: Knopf, 1956.

Chabot, C. Barry. *Writers for the Nation: American Literary Modernism.* Tuscaloosa: University of Alabama Press, 1997.

Chandler, G. Lewis. "Selfsameness and a Promise." *Phylon* 10 (summer 1949): 189–91.

Chapman, Abraham. "The Harlem Renaissance in Literary History." *College Language Association Journal* 11 (1967): 38–58.

Clarke, John Henrik. "Langston Hughes and Jesse B. Simple." *Freedomways* 8 (spring 1968): 167–69.

Cobb, Martha. *Harlem, Haiti, and Havana: A Comparative Critical Study of Langston Hughes, Jacques Roumain, and Nicolás Guillén.* Washington, D.C.: Three Continents Press, 1979.

Coleman, Gregory D. *We're Heaven Bound: Portrait of Black Sacred Drama.* Athens: University of Georgia Press, 1992.

Cooke, Michael G. *Afro-American Literature in the Twentieth Century: The Achievement of Intimacy.* New Haven, Conn.: Yale University Press, 1984.

Cooper, Floyd. *Coming Home: From the Life of Langston Hughes.* New York: Philomel, 1994.

Craig, E. Quita. *Black Drama of the Federal Theatre Era: Beyond the Formal Horizon.* Amherst: University of Massachusetts Press, 1980.

Cullen, Countee. "Poet on Poet: Review of *The Weary Blues. The Opportunity Reader: Stories, Poetry, and Essays from the Urban League's Opportunity Magazine.* Ed. Sondra Kathryn Wilson. New York: Modern Library, 1999. 314–16.

Dace, Tish, ed. *Langston Hughes: The Contemporary Reviews.* New York: Cambridge University Press, 1997.

Dahl, Linda. *Stormy Weather: The Music and Lives of a Century of Jazz Women.* New York: Pantheon, 1984.

Dandridge, Rita B. "The Black Woman as a Freedom Fighter in

Langston Hughes' *Simple's Uncle Sam.*" *CLA Journal* 18 (December 1974): 273–83.

Davis, Arthur P. "The Harlem of Langston Hughes's Poetry." *Phylon* 13 (4th quarter 1952): 276–83.

———. "Jesse B. Semple: Negro American." *Phylon* 15 (spring 1954): 21–28.

——— *From the Dark Tower: Afro-American Writers, 1900 to 1960.* Washington, D.C.: Howard University Press, 1974.

———. "[James] Langston Hughes." *Dictionary of American Negro Biography.* Ed. Rayford W. Logan and Michael R. Winston. New York: Norton, 1982. 331–34.

Davis, Thadious. "Reading the Woman's Face in Langston Hughes's and Roy De Carva's *Sweet Flypaper of Life. Langston Hughes Review* 12, no. 1 (spring 1993): 22–28.

Deck, Alice A. "The Langston Hughes Society: Its Inaugural Year." *Langston Hughes Review* 1, no. 2 (fall 1982): 27–28.

De Jongh, James. *Vicious Modernism: Black Harlem and the Literary Imagination.* Cambridge: Cambridge University Press, 1990.

Diawara, Manthia. "The Absent One: The Avant-Garde and the Black Imaginary in *Looking for Langston.*" *Representing Black Men.* Ed. Marcellus Blount and George P. Cunningham. New York: Routledge, 1996. 205–24.

Dickinson, Donald C. *A Bio-Bibliography of Langston Hughes, 1902–1967.* Hamden, Conn.: Shoe String [Archeon], 1964, 1967, 1972.

Dickson-Carr, Darryl. *African American Satire: The Sacredly Profane Novel.* Columbia: University of Missouri Press, 2001.

Dixon, Melvin. *Ride Out the Wilderness: Geography and Identity in Afro-American Literature.* Urbana: University of Illinois Press, 1987.

Dodat, François. *Langston Hughes.* Paris: Seghers, 1964.

Du Bois, W. E. B. *The Souls of Black Folk.* 1903. New York: Penguin, 1989.

DuCille, Ann. *The Coupling Convention: Sex, Text, and Tradition in Black Women's Fiction.* New York: Oxford University Press, 1993.

Dunham, Montrew. *Langston Hughes: Young Black Poet.* New York: Atheneum, 1973.

Early, Gerald. "Pulp and Circumstance: The Story of Jazz in High Places." *The Jazz Cadence of American Culture.* Ed. Robert

G. O'Meally. New York: Columbia University Press, 1998. 393–430.

Emanuel, James A. "The Short Stories of Langston Hughes." Ph.D. diss., Columbia University, 1962 [DA 27 July 1966: 474–75A].

———. *Langston Hughes*. New York: Twayne, 1967.

———. "The Literary Experiments of Langston Hughes." *Langston Hughes: Black Genius*. Ed. Therman B. O'Daniel. New York: William Morrow, 1971. 171–81.

———. "The Short Fiction of Langston Hughes." *Langston Hughes: Black Genius*. Ed. Therman B. O'Daniel. New York: William Morrow, 1971. 145–56.

Emanuel, James A., and Theodore L. Gross, eds. *Dark Symphony: Negro Literature in America*. New York: Free Press, 1968. 191–221.

Etheridge, Sharynn O. "Langston Hughes: An Annotated Bibliography (1977–1986)." *Langston Hughes Review* 11, no. 1 (spring 1992): 41–57.

Fabre, Michel. "Hughes's Literary Reputation in France." *Langston Hughes Review* 6, no. 1 (spring 1987): 20–27.

———. *Black American Writers in France, 1840–1980: From Harlem to Paris*. Urbana: University of Illinois Press, 1991.

Farrison, William Edward. "*Not Without Laughter* but Without Tears." *Langston Hughes: Black Genius*. Ed. Therman B. O'Daniel. New York: William Morrow, 1971. 96–109.

Filatova, Lydia. "Langston Hughes: American Writer." *International Literature* 1 (January 1933): 99–107.

Fisher, Dexter, and Robert B. Stepto, eds. *The Reconstruction of Instruction*. New York: Modern Language Association of America, 1979.

Ford, Nick Aaron. *The Contemporary Negro Novel*. Boston: Meador, 1936 [or New York: Macmillan, 1936].

———. "I Teach Negro Literature." *College English* 2 (March 1941): 530–41.

Fraden, Rena. *Blueprints for a Black Federal Theatre, 1935–1939*. Cambridge: Cambridge University Press, 1994.

Gates, Henry Louis. Introduction. *Mule Bone: A Comedy of Negro Life*. 1931. By Langston Hughes and Zora Neale Hurston. Ed. George H. Bass and Henry Louis Gates. New York: Harper Collins, 1991.

————. "Why the Debate over *Mule Bone* Persists." *New York Times Book Review*, 10 February 1991: 5, 8.

Gates, Henry Louis, and K. A. Appiah, eds. *Langston Hughes*. New York: Amistad, 1993.

Gayle, Addison. *The Black Aesthetic*. New York: Doubleday, 1971.

Gelfant, Blanche. *The Columbia Companion to the Twentieth Century American Short Story*. New York: Columbia University Press, 2001.

Gibson, Donald B. "The Good Black Poet and the Good Gray Poet: The Poetry of Hughes and Whitman." *Langston Hughes: Black Genius*. Ed. Therman B. O'Daniel. New York: William Morrow, 1971. 65–80.

Giles, Freda Scott, guest ed. Special Issue on Langston Hughes's Contribution to World Theatre. *Langston Hughes Review* 15, no 1 (spring 1997).

Gloster, Hugh M. *Negro Voices in American Fiction*. New York: Russell and Russell, 1948.

Govan, Sandra Y. "Black Women as Cultural Conservators: Biographers and Builders of Our Cultural Heritage." *Langston Hughes Review* 7, no. 2 (fall 1988): 1–14.

Gresson, Aaron D. "Beyond Selves Deferred: Langston Hughes's Style and the Psychology of Black Selfhood." *Langston Hughes Review* 4, no. 1 (spring 1985): 47–54.

Griffin, Farah Jasmine. *"Who Set You Flowin'?": The African-American Migration Narrative*. New York: Oxford University Press, 1995.

Griffin, Farah J., and Cheryl J. Fish, eds. *A Stranger in the Village: Two Centuries of African-American Travel Writing*. Boston: Beacon, 1998.

Guillaume, Bernice. "The Female as Harlem Sage: The 'Aunt Viney's Sketches.'" *Langston Hughes Review* 6, no. 2 (fall 1987): 1–10.

Harper, Donna Akiba Sullivan. "Langston Hughes as Cultural Conservator: Women in the Life of a 'Negro Everyman.'" *Langston Hughes Review* 7, no. 2 (fall 1988): 15–21.

————. *Not So Simple: The 'Simple' Stories by Langston Hughes*. Columbia: University of Missouri Press, 1995.

Harris, Violet J. "African American Children's Literature: The First One Hundred Years." *Journal of Negro Education*. 59, no. 4 (autumn 1990): 540–55.

————. "Contemporary Griots: African American Writers of Children's Literature." *Teaching Multicultural Literature*. Ed. Violet J. Harris. Norwood, Mass.: Christopher-Gordon, 1990: 538–39.

Hatch, James V. *Black Theater, U.S.A.: Forty-Five Plays by Black Americans, 1847–1974*. New York: Free Press, 1974.

————. *Sorrow Is the Only Faithful One: The Life of Owen Dodson*. Urbana: University of Illinois Press, 1993.

Hawthorne, Lucia Shelia. "A Rhetoric of Human Rights as Expressed in the 'Simple Columns' by Langston Hughes." Ph.D. diss., Pennsylvania State University, 1971.

Helbling, Mark. *The Harlem Renaissance: The One and the Many*. Westport, Conn.: Greenwood Press, 2001.

Hemenway, Robert E. *Zora Neale Hurston: A Literary Biography*. Urbana: University of Illinois Press, 1977.

Henderson, Stephen. *Understanding the New Black Poetry: Black Speech and Black Music as Poetic References*. New York: William Morrow, 1973.

Hernton, Calvin C. "The Poetic Consciousness of Langston Hughes: From Affirmation to Revolution." *Langston Hughes Review* 12, no. 1 (spring 1993): 2–9.

Hicks, Granville, et al. *Proletarian Literature in the United States: An Anthology*. New York: International Publishers, 1935.

Hill, Christine M. *Langston Hughes: Poet of the Harlem Renaissance*. Berkeley Heights, N.J.: Enslow, 1997.

Hill, Errol, ed. *Theater of Black Americans*. Englewood Cliffs, N.J.: Prentice Hall, 1980.

Hubbard, Dolan. "Call and Response: Intertextuality in the Poetry of Langston Hughes and Margaret Walker." *Langston Hughes Review* 7, no. 1 (spring 1988): 22–30.

————. "Langston Hughes." *Dictionary of Missouri Biography*. Ed. Lawrence O. Christensen et al. Columbia: University of Missouri Press, 1999. 409–11.

————. "Langston Hughes Society." *Organizing Black America: An Encyclopedia of African American Associations*. Ed. Nina Mjagkij. New York: Garland, 2001. 299–300.

————. "Society and Self in Alice Walker's *In Love and Trouble*." *Obsidian II* 6, no. 2 (summer 1991): 50–75.

————. "Symbolizing America in Langston Hughes's 'Father

and Son.'" *Langston Hughes Review* II, no. I (spring 1992): 14–20.

Hubbard, Dolan, and James J. Davis. "College Language Association." *Organizing Black America: An Encyclopedia of African American Associations.* Ed. Nina Mjagkij. New York: Garland, 2001. 159–62.

Hudson, Theodore R. "The Duke and the Laureate: Loose Connections." *Langston Hughes Review* II, no. I (spring 1992): 28–35.

Huggins, Nathan Irvin. *Harlem Renaissance.* New York: Oxford University Press, 1971.

Huggins, Nathan Irvin, ed. *Voices from the Harlem Renaissance.* New York: Oxford University Press, 1976.

Hughes, Carl Milton. *The Negro Novelist.* New York: Citadel, 1953.

Hull, Gloria T. *Color, Sex, and Poetry: Three Women Writers of the Harlem Renaissance.* Bloomington: Indiana University Press, 1987.

Hutchinson, Earl Ofari. *Blacks and Reds: Race and Class in Conflct 1919–1990.* East Lansing: Michigan State University Press, 1995.

Hutchinson, George. *The Harlem Renaissance.* Bloomington: Indiana University Press, 1987.

Inge, M. Thomas, Maurice Duke, and Jackson R. Bryer, eds. *Black American Writers: Bibliographic Essays.* 2 vols. New York: St. Martin's, 1978.

Ignatow, David. "Memories of Langston Hughes." *Langston Hughes* 13, no. 2 (winter–summer 1995): 5–11.

Ikonne, Chidi. *From Du Bois to Van Vechten: The Early New Negro Literature, 1903–26.* Westport, Conn.: Greenwood Press, 1981.

Jackson, Blyden. "A Golden Mean for the Negro Novel." *College Language Association Journal* 3 (December 1959): 81–87.

———. "A Word about Simple." *Langston Hughes: Black Genius.* Ed. Therman B. O'Daniel. New York: William Morrow, 1971. 110–19.

———. "From One 'New Negro' to Another, 1923–1972." *Black Poetry in America: Two Essays in Historical Interpretation.* Ed. Blyden Jackson and Louis D. Rubin, Jr. Baton Rouge: Louisiana State University Press, 1974.

———. "Langston Hughes." *Black American Writers: Bibliographic*

Essays. Ed. M. Thomas Inge, Maurice Duke, and Jackson R. Bryer. Vol. 1. New York: Saint Martin's, 1978. 187–206.

———. *A History of Afro-American Literature, Volume I: The Long Beginning, 1746–1895.* Baton Rouge: Louisiana State University Press, 1989.

Jemie, Onwuchekwa. *Langston Hughes: An Introduction to the Poetry.* New York: Columbia University Press, 1976.

Johnson, Abby Arthur, and Ronald Maberry Johnson. *Propaganda and Aesthetics: The Literary Politics Of Afro-American Magazines in the Twentieth Century.* Amherst: University of Massachusetts Press, 1979.

Johnson, James Weldon. *Black Manhattan.* New York: Knopf, 1930.

Johnson, Lemuel. *The Devil, the Gargoyle, and the Buffoon: The Negro as Metaphor in Western Literature.* Port Washington, N.Y.: Kennikat Press, 1971.

Jones, Harry. "Rhetorical Embellishments in Hughes's Simple Stories." *Langston Hughes: Black Genius.* Ed. Therman B. O'Daniel. New York: William Morrow, 1971. 132–44.

Jones, Harry L. "Simple Speaks Danish." *Langston Hughes Review* 4, no. 2 (fall 1985): 24–26.

Julien, Isaac. *Looking for Langston.* Sankofa: London, 1989. Film.

Kellner, Bruce. *The Harlem Renaissance: A Historical Dictionary of the Era.* Westport, Conn.: Greenwood, 1984.

———. "Langston Hughes's *Nigger Heaven Blues.*" *Langston Hughes Review* 11, no. 1 (spring 1992): 21–27.

Kent, George E. "Langston Hughes and Afro-American Folk and Cultural Tradition." *Langston Hughes: Black Genius.* Ed. Therman B. O'Daniel. New York: William Morrow, 1971. 183–210.

LeSeur, Geta. *Ten Is the Age of Darkness: The Black Bildungsroman.* Columbia: University of Missouri Press, 1995.

Lewis, David Levering. *When Harlem Was in Vogue.* New York: Knopf, 1981.

Littlejohn, David. *Black on White: A Critical Survey of Writings by American Negroes.* New York: Grossman, 1966.

Locke, Alain, ed. *The New Negro.* 1925. New York: Atheneum, 1968.

Loggins, Vernon. *The Negro Author: His Development in America.* New York: Columbia University Press, 1931.

Lowe, John. *Jump at the Sun: Zora Neale Hurston's Cosmic Comedy.* Urbana: University of Illinois Press, 1994.

Mandelik, Peter, and Stanley Schatt. *Concordance to Langston Hughes.* Detroit: Gale Research, 1975.

Martin-Ogunsola, Dellita. "The 'Madam Poems' as Dramatic Monologue." *Black American Literature Forum* 15, no. 3 (1981): 97–99.

———. "Ambivalence as Allegory in Langston Hughes's 'Simple' Stories." *Langston Hughes Review* 7, no. 1 (spring 1988): 1–8.

Matheus, John F. "Langston Hughes as Translator." *Langston Hughes: Black Genius.* Ed. Therman B. O'Daniel. New York: William Morrow, 1971. 157–70.

Mayberry, Susan Neale. "Ask Your Mama: Women in Langston Hughes' *The Ways of White Folk.*" *Langston Hughes Review* 13, no. 2 (winter–summer 1995): 12–25.

McKissack, Pat, and Frederick McKissack. *Langston Hughes: Great American Poet.* Berkeley Heights, N.J.: Enslow, 1992.

McLaren, Joseph. "From Protest to Soul Fest: Langston Hughes' Gospel Plays." *Langston Hughes Review* 15, no.1 (spring 1997): 49–61.

———. *Langston Hughes: Folk Dramatist in the Protest Tradition, 1921–1943.* New York: Greenwood, 1997.

Meltzer, Milton. *Langston Hughes: A Biography.* New York: Thomas Y. Crowell, 1968.

Meltzer, Milton, and Stephen Alcorn. *Langston Hughes: An Illustrated Edition.* Brookfield, Conn.: Millbrook Press, 1997.

Mikolyzk, Thomas A. *Langston Hughes: A Bio-Bibliography.* Westport, Conn.: Greenwood, 1990.

Miller, R. Baxter. "'No Crystal Stair': Unity, Archetype, and Symbol in Langston Hughes's Poems on Women." *Negro American Literature* Forum 9, no. 4 (winter 1975): 109–14.

———. "Langston Hughes." *Dictionary of Literary Biography.* Vol. 51: *Afro-American Writers from the Harlem Renaissance to 1940.* Ed. Trudier Harris and Thadious M. Davis. Detroit: Gale, 1987. 112–33.

———. *The Art and Imagination of Langston Hughes.* Lexington: University Press of Kentucky, 1989.

Miller, R. Baxter, ed. *Black Poets between Worlds, 1940–1960.* Knoxville: University of Tennessee Press, 1986.

Miller, R. Baxter, comp. *Langston Hughes and Gwendolyn Brooks: A Reference Guide*. Boston: Hall, 1978.

Mitchell, Loften. *Black Drama: The Story of the American Negro in the Theatre*. New York: Hawthorn, 1967.

Moore, David Chioni. "Local Color, Global Color: Langston Hughes, the Black Atlantic, and Soviet Central Asia: 1932." *Research in African Literatures* 27, no. 4 (winter 1996): 49–70.

Mullen, Edward J. *Langston Hughes in the Hispanic World and Haiti*. Hamden, Conn.: Archon, 1977.

Mullen, Edward J., ed. *Critical Essays on Langston Hughes*. Boston: Hall, 1986.

Murray, Albert. *The Hero and the Blues*. Columbia: University of Missouri Press, 1973.

———. *Stomping the Blues*. New York: McGraw-Hill, 1976.

Myers, Elisabeth P. *Langston Hughes: Poet of His People*. Champaign, Ill.: Garrard, 1970.

Naison, Mark. *Communists in Harlem during the Depression*. Urbana: University of Illinois Press, 1983.

Nelson, Cary. *Anthology of Modern Poetry*. New York: Oxford University Press, 2000.

Nero, Charles. "Re/membering Langston: Homophobic Textuality and Arnold Rampersad's *Life of Langston Hughes*." Ed. Martin Duberman. New York: New York University Press, 1997. 188–96.

Ngandu, Pius. "Le role des noirs américains dans la literature négro-africaine." *Congo-Afrique* 2: 337–44.

Nielsen, Aldon Lynn. *Reading Race: White American Poets and the Radical Discourse in the Twentieth Century*. Athens: University of Georgia Press, 1988.

———. *Writing between the Lines: Race and Intertextuality*. Athens: University of Georgia Press, 1994.

Neilson, Kenneth P. *To Langston Hughes with Love*. Hollis, N.Y.: All Seasons Art, 1996.

Neilson, Kenneth P., comp. *The World of Langston Hughes Music: A Bibliography of Musical Settings of Langston Hughes's Work with Recordings and Other Listings*. Hollis, N.Y.: All Seasons Art, 1982.

Nieman, Donald G. *Promises to Keep: African-Americans and the Consti-*

tutional Order, 1776 to the Present. New York: Oxford University Press, 1991.

Noble, Enrique. "Nicolás Guillén y Langston Hughes." *Nueva Revista Cubana*, La Habana, a. 1961–1962, 41–85.

O'Daniel, Therman B, ed. *Langston Hughes: Black Genius: A Critical Evaluation*. New York: William Morrow, 1971.

O'Daniel, Therman, compiler. "An Updated Bibliography of Langston Hughes." Special issue. *Black American Literature Forum* 15, no. 3 (1981): 104–7.

O'Meally, Robert G., ed. *The Jazz Cadence of American Culture*. New York: Columbia University Press, 1998.

Osofsky, Audrey. *Free to Dream: The Making of a Poet, Langston Hughes*. New York: Lothrop, Lee, and Shepard, 1996.

Osofsky, Gilbert. *Harlem: The Making of a Ghetto*. New York: Harper and Row, 1963.

Ostrom, Hans. *A Langston Hughes Encyclopedia*. Westport, Conn.: Greenwood, 2001.

———. *Langston Hughes: A Study of the Short Fiction*. New York: Twyane, 1993.

Parker, John W. "Literature of the Negro Ghetto." *Phylon* 13 (fall 1952): 257–58.

Peterson, Bernard L., Jr. *Contemporary Black American Playwrights and Their Plays: A Biographical Directory and Dramatic Index*. New York: Greenwood, 1988.

Piccinato, Stefania. *Testo e Contesto Della Poesia di Langston Hughes*. Roma: Bulzoni editore, 1979.

Piquion, René. *Langston Hughes: Un Chant Nouveau*. Introduction par Arna Bontemps. Port-au-Prince, Haiti: Imprimerie de l'Etat, 1940.

Quinot, Raymond. *Langston Hughes ou l'étoile noire*. Bruxelles: Aux Editions du C.E.L.F., 1964.

Rampersad, Arnold. "Langston Hughes and His Critics on the Left." *Langston Hughes Review* 5, no. 2 (fall 1986): 34–40.

———. *The Life of Langston Hughes*. 2 vols. New York: Oxford University Press, 1986–1988.

———. "Biography and Afro-American Culture." *Afro-American Literary Study in the 1990s*. Ed. Houston A. Baker, Jr., and Patricia Redmond. Chicago: University of Chicago Press, 1989. 194–208.

———. "Langston Hughes." *The Oxford Companion to African American Literature*. Ed. William L. Andrews, Frances Smith Foster, and Trudier Harris. New York: Oxford University Press, 1997. 368–70.

Redding, J. Saunders. *To Make a Poet Black*. 1939. Rpt. Ithaca, N.Y.: Cornell University Press, 1988.

———. "Review of *Simple's Uncle* Sam by Langston Hughes." *Afro Magazine*, 12 February 1966. Rpt. *A Scholar's Conscience: Selected Writings*. Ed. Faith Berry. Lexington: University Press of Kentucky, 1992. 172–73.

Reid, Margaret A. "Rhetoric and Protest in Langton Hughes." *Langston Hughes Review* 3, no. 1 (spring 1984): 13–20.

———. *Black Protest Poetry from the Harlem Renaissance and the Sixties*. New York: Lang, 2001.

Rodgers, Lawrence R. *Canaan Bound: The African-American Great Migration Novel*. Urbana: University of Illinois Press, 1997.

Rollins, Charlemae H. *Black Troubadour: Langston Hughes*. Foreword by Gwendolyn Brooks. Chicago: Rand McNally, 1970.

Rose, Tricia. *Black Noise: Rap Music and Black Culture in Contemporary America*. Hanover, N.H.: Wesleyan University Press, 1994.

Sanders, Leslie Catherine. "'Also Own the Theatre': Representations in the Comedies of Langston Hughes." *Langston Hughes Review* 11, no. 1 (spring 1992): 6–13.

———. *The Development of Black Theatre in America*. Baton Rouge: Louisiana State University Press, 1988.

Schatt, Stanley. "Langston Hughes: The Minstrel as Artificer." *Journal of Modern Literature* 4 (1974): 115–20.

Schuyler, George S. "The Negro-Art Hokum." *Voices from the Harlem Renaissance*. Ed. Nathan Irvin Huggins. New York: Oxford University Press, 1976. 309–12.

Sheffey, Ruthe T. "Zora Neale Hurston and Langston Hughes's 'Mule Bone': An Authentic Folk Comedy and the Compromised Tradition." *Trajectory: Fueling the Future and Preserving the African-American Literary Past*. Ed. Sheffey. Baltimore: Morgan State University Press, 1989. 211–31.

Singh, Amritjit. *The Novels of the Harlem Renaissance: Twelve Black Writers, 1923–1933*. University Park: Pennsylvania State University Press, 1976.

Singh, Amrijit, William S. Shriver, and Stanley Brodwin, eds.

The Harlem Reniassance: Revaluations. New York: Garland, 1989.

Smethurst, James Edward. *The New Red Negro: The Literary Left and African American Poetry, 1930–1946*. New York: Oxford University Press, 1999.

Smyth, Mabel M., ed. *Black American Reference Book*. Englewoods Cliffs, N.J.: Prentice Hall, 1976.

Somerville, Siobhan B. *Queering the Color Line: Race and the Invention of Homosexuality in American Culture*. Durham, N.C.: Duke University Press, 2000.

Spencer, Jon Michael. *Blues and Evil*. Knoxville: University of Tennessee Press, 1993.

Spicer, Eloise Y. "The Blues and the Son: Reflections of Black Self Assertion in the Poetry of Langston Hughes and Nicolás Guillén." *Langston Hughes Review* 3, no. 1 (spring 1984): 1–12.

Staton, Sandra L. "Tapping the Laughing Barrel: Ethnic Humor as a Protest Device in the Poetry of Langston Hughes." *Zora Neale Hurston Forum* 12 (spring–fall 1998): 12–21.

Stovall, Tyler. *Paris Noir: African Americans in the City of Light*. Boston: Mariner/Houghton Mifflin, 1996.

Sundquist, Eric J. *To Wake the Nations: Race in the Making of American Literature*. Cambridge, Mass.: Harvard University Press, 1993.

Thurston, Michael. "'Bombed in Spain': Langston Hughes, the Black Press, and the Spanish Civil War." *The Black Press: New Literary and Historical Essays*. Ed. Todd Vogel. New Brunswick, N.J.: Rutgers University Press, 2001. 140–60.

Tolson, Melvin B. *The Harlem Group of Negro Writers*. 1940. Ed. Edward J. Mullen. Westport, Conn.: Greenwood Press, 2001.

Tracy, Steven C. "Simple's Great African American Joke." *CLA Journal* 27, no. 3 (March 1984): 239–53.

———. *Langston Hughes and the Blues*. Urbana: University of Illinois Press, 1988.

———. "'Midnight Ruffles of Cat-Gut Lace': The Boogie Poems of Langston Hughes." *CLA Journal* 32, no. 1 (September 1988): 55–68.

———. "Blues to Live By: Langston Hughes's 'The Blues I'm Playing.'" *Langston Hughes Review* 12, no. 1 (spring 1993): 12–18.

Trotman, C. James, ed. *Langston Hughes: The Man, His Art, and His Continuing Influence*. New York: Garland, 1995.

Turner, Beth. "Simplifyin': Langston Hughes and Alice Childress Re/member Jesse B. Semple." *Langston Hughes Review* 15, no. 1 (spring 1997): 37–48.

Turner, Darwin T. *Afro-American Writers.* New York: Appleton-Century-Crofts, 1970.

———. "Langston Hughes as Playwright." *CLA Journal* 11, no. 4 (June 1968): 297–309. Rpt. in *Langston Hughes: Black Genius.* Ed. Therman B. O'Daniel. New York: William Morrow, 1971. 81–95.

Vaillant, Janet G. *Black, French, and African: A Life of Léopold Sédar Senghor.* Cambridge, Mass.: Harvard University Press, 1990.

Van Vechten, Carl. *"Keep a-Inchin' Along": Selected Writings about Black Arts and Letters.* Ed. Bruce Kellner. Westport: Conn.: Greenwood, 1979

Wagner, Jean. *Les Poètes Nègres des États-Unis.* 1962. Trans. by Kenneth Douglas. Urbana: University of Illinois Press, 1973. *Black Poets of the United States: From Paul Laurence Dunbar to Langston Hughes.*

Walker, Alice. *Langston Hughes: American Poet.* New York: Crowell, 1974.

Ward, Jerry W., Jr. "Langston/Blues Griot." *Langston Hughes Review* 12, no. 2 (fall 1993): 27.

Watkins, Charles A. "Simple: The Alter Ego of Langston Hughes." *Black Scholar* 2 (June 1971): 18–26.

Werner, Craig. *Playing the Changes: From Afro-American Modernism to the Jazz Impulse.* Urbana: University of Illinois Press, 1994.

Williams, Melvin G. "The Gospel According to Simple." *Black American Literature Forum* 11, no. 2 (1977): 46–48.

Wintz, Cary. *Black Culture and the Harlem Renaissance.* Houston: Rice University Press, 1988.

Woll, Allen. *Black Musical Theatre: From Coontown to Dreamgirls.* Baton Rouge: Louisiana State University Press, 1989.

———. *Dictionary of Black Theatre: Broadway, Off-Broadway, and Selected Harlem Theatre.* Westport, Conn.: Greenwood, 1983.

Wolsely, Roland E. *The Black Press, U.S.A.* Ames: Iowa State University Press, 1971.

Woods, Gregory. "Gay Re-Readings of the Harlem Renaissance Poets." *Journal of Homosexuality* 25, nos. 2–3 (August–September 1993): 127–42.

Woodson, Jon. *To Make a New Race: Gurdjieff, Toomer, and the Harlem Renaissance*. Jackson: University Press of Mississippi, 1999.

Wright, Richard. "Blueprint for Negro Writing." *New Challenge: A Literary Quarterly* 1 (fall 1937): 53–65.

———. "Forerunner and Ambassador." *New Republic* (July–December 1940): 600–601.

Young, James O. *Black Writers of the Thirties*. Baton Rouge: Louisiana State University Press, 1973.

Contributors

JAMES DE JONGH, professor of English at the City College and the Graduate School and University Center of the City University of New York (CUNY), is deputy dean and director of the Simon H. Rifkind Center for the Humanities and Arts at City College, as well as director of the CUNY Institute for Research on the African Diaspora in the Americas and the Caribbean (IRADAC). He is the author of *Vicious Modernism: Black Harlem and the Literary Imagination*. He is also a novelist and a playwright; his play *Do Lord Remember Me* was given a successful twentieth-anniversary revival at Hunter College in 1997 and was featured at the National Black Theatre Festival.

DOLAN HUBBARD, professor and chair of the Department of English and Language Arts at Morgan State University, is president of the Langston Hughes Society. A former editor of *The Langston Hughes Review*, he is author of *The Sermon and the African American Literary Imagination*; editor of *Recovered Writers/Recovered Texts: Race, Class, and Gender in Black Women's Literature* and "Critical Essays on W. E. B. Du Bois's *The Souls of Black Folk*"; general co-editor of *The Complete Works of Langston Hughes*; and co-editor of *The Library of Black America Collection of Black Sermons*.

JOYCE A. JOYCE is a professor in the women's studies program and former chairperson and professor of African-American studies at Temple University. A 1995 recipient of the American Book Award for Literary Criticism for her collection of essays *Warriors, Conjurers, and Priests: Defining African-Centered Literary Criticism*, Joyce is also the author of *Richard Wright's Art of Tragedy, Ijala: Sonia-Sanchez and the African Poetic Tradition* and of numerous articles treating African American literature, and the co-editor of *The New Cavalcade: African American Writing from 1760 to the Present*.

R. BAXTER MILLER is a professor of English and director of the African-American Studies Institute at the University of Georgia. He is the author of *Langston Hughes and Gwendolyn Brooks: A Reference Guide, The Art and Imagination of Langston Hughes* (American Book Award, 1991), *Southern Trace in Black Critical Theory: Redemption of Time*, and the forthcoming *New Chicago Renaissance from Wright to Kent*. He has edited and contributed substantial essays to *Black American Literature and Humanism* and *Black American Poets between Worlds, 1940–1960*, along with *The Collected Works of Langston Hughes: The Short Stories*, the fifth volume in the centennial series. He wrote the introduction to the period 1915–1945 and numerous head notes of leading figures for *Call and Response: The Riverside Anthology of African-American Literature*. Miller has written numerous essays, articles, and reviews on African American literature and aesthetics.

JAMES SMETHURST is an assistant professor in the W. E. B. Du Bois Department of Afro-American Studies at the University of Massachusetts–Amherst. He is the author of *The New Red Negro: The Literary Left and African-American Poetry, 1930–1946* (1999). His most recent project is *The Rise of the Black Arts Movement and Literary Nationalism in the 1960s and 1970s* (forthcoming). He is also the co-editor of *Left of the Color Line: Race, Radicalism, and Twentieth-Century Literature of the United States* (2003).

STEVEN C. TRACY is professor of Afro-American studies at the University of Massachusetts–Amherst and a blues singer and harmonica player. He is the author of *Langston Hughes and the Blues*,

Going to Cincinnati: A History of the Blues in the Queen City, and *A Brush with the Blues*; general co-editor of *The Collected Works of Langston Hughes*; and editor of *Write Me a Few of Your Lines: A Blues Reader* and *Work for Children and Young Adults,* vol. 12 in *The Collected Works of Langston Hughes*. Tracy has authored numerous articles, interviews, and reviews dealing with American literature and culture, written liner notes for fifty compact discs, and produced recordings for various blues artists. He has recorded with Steve Tracy and the Crawling Kingsnakes, Big Joe Duskin, Pigmeat Jarrett, Albert Washington, and the Cincinnati Symphony Orchestra.

Index